Types of Ā-Dependencies

Linguistic Inquiry Monographs
Samuel Jay Keyser, general editor

Types of Ā-Dependencies   Guglielmo Cinque

The MIT Press
Cambridge, Massachusetts
London, England

This book was set in Times Roman by Asco Trade Typesetting Ltd., Hong Kong and printed and bound in the United States of America.

Library of Congress Cataloging-in-Publication Data

Cinque, Guglielmo.
    Types of Ā-Dependencies / Guglielmo Cinque.
      p.   cm.—(Linguistic Inquiry Monographs; 17)
    Includes bibliographical references and index.
    ISBN 0-262-03154-X.—ISBN 0-262-53089-9 (pbk.)
    1. Generative grammar.   2. Romance languages—Grammar, Generative.
I. Title. II. Series.
P158.C55   1990   90-37783
415—dc20   CIP

Ad Alfonso e Maria Cinque

Contents

Series Foreword

We are pleased to present this monograph as the seventeenth in the series *Linguistic Inquiry Monographs*. These monographs will present new and original research beyond the scope of the article, and we hope they will benefit our field by bringing to it perspectives that will stimulate further research and insight.

Originally published in limited edition, the *Linguistic Inquiry Monograph* series is now available on a much wider scale. This change is due to the great interest engendered by the series and the needs of a growing readership. The editors wish to thank the readers for their support and welcome suggestions about future directions the series might take.

Samuel Jay Keyser
for the Editorial Board

Acknowledgments

Parts of the material discussed in this book were first presented at the Université de Paris VIII in May 1982 and subsequently elaborated for courses at the Universities of Venice, Vienna, and Geneva.

Chapter 1 draws from an unpublished paper ("Island Effects, Subjacency, ECP/Connectedness, and Reconstruction") circulated in 1983. Chapter 2 is based on another unpublished paper ("Clitic Left Dislocation and the 'Move α' Parameter"), first circulated in 1984. Finally, chapter 3 is the result of an extensive revision of a paper by the same title ("Ā-Bound Pro versus Variable") also presented in 1984 at the VIII Annual GLOW Colloquium in Copenhagen.

I wish to thank the many people who commented on different aspects of this work, in particular Adrian Battye, Adriana Belletti, Paola Benincà, Anna Cardinaletti, Noam Chomsky, Elisabet Engdahl, Giuliana Giusti, Richard Kayne, Jan Koster, Giuseppe Longobardi, Henk van Riemsdijk, and Luigi Rizzi. For detailed comments on earlier versions of these chapters, I am especially indebted to Luigi Rizzi, Richard Kayne, and Giuseppe Longobardi. Part of the research reported here was made possible by grants from the Italian Consiglio Nazionale delle Ricerche and Ministero della Pubblica Istruzione.

Introduction

In recent times the grammar of constituent extraction has attracted considerable attention, particularly in its relation to the theories of binding and government.

Even though a general consensus exists on the basic phenomena and distinctions to be derived (such as that between long and successive cyclic *Wh*-Movement), no complete agreement exists as yet (and perhaps no complete clarity either) about certain fundamental descriptive generalizations: for example, those concerning the classes of elements that are taken to undergo long and successive cyclic movement, respectively, and the nature of the locality conditions holding of each type of movement.

These involve decisions on which phenomena go together and which must be kept distinct, decisions that often require a certain amount of idealization.

The purpose of the chapters that follow is to contribute some new empirical evidence, mainly from Romance, for a particular way of delimiting these descriptive generalizations and the principles from which they derive.

Let me anticipate in rough outline the main conclusions that will be reached in the following chapters.

We will start by distinguishing pretheoretically four major cases of $\bar{A}$-dependencies on the basis of their different behavior with respect to island conditions.

The first is *successive cyclic Wh-Movement*, which is sensitive to both strong and weak islands.

The second is *long Wh-Movement*, which is sensitive just to strong islands.

The third is *apparent Wh-Movement of NPs*, which selectively violates strong islands. For example, it can marginally operate across an adjunct or a complex NP island, (1a–b), but not across a sentential subject or across two consecutive islands, (2a–b):

(1) a. ?L'unica persona che siamo partiti   senza salutare _____
         the only person that we went away without greeting
         è Gianni.
         is Gianni

    b. ?L'unica persona che non conosco nessuno
         the only person that I know of nobody
         in grado di aiutare _____ è proprio lui.
         that can help   is him himself

(2) a. *?L'unica persona che aiutare _____ mi costerebbe   è Giorgio.
         the only person that to help   would cost me a lot is Giorgio

    b. *L'unica persona che ci ho pensato due volte
         the only person that I thought it over
         prima di andarmene senza salutare _____ è Gianni.
         before leaving   without greeting   is Gianni

The fourth type of Ā-dependency is that between a *resumptive pronoun and a sentence-initial phrase* in the left dislocation and relative constructions of various languages, which is totally insensitive to strong (or weak) island conditions. (Of course, not all resumptive pronoun constructions are insensitive to island conditions. See the case of Swedish, briefly discussed in chapter 2; and see Sells 1984 and McCloskey 1989 for a discussion of some of the distinctions that need to be made in this domain.) Here, I will not have much to say about this Ā-dependency except for the few remarks in chapter 2 concerning the English-type left dislocation construction.

The distinction between long and successive cyclic *Wh*-Movement is discussed in some detail in chapter 1. There, I will argue that the class of elements that are able to undergo long *Wh*-Movement is in fact much more restricted than is standardly assumed (as in Chomsky 1986b and related work).

Elaborating on recent work by Rizzi (see Rizzi 1990), I will show that the intrinsic referential character of the moved phrase is a prerequisite for long *Wh*-Movement. Apparently, those phrases that cannot freely "corefer" (hence, I assume, "refer") can indeed be moved only via successive cyclic *Wh*-Movement.

In the same chapter I explore the locality conditions on long and successive cyclic *Wh*-Movement, aiming at a simplification of the system proposed by Chomsky (1986b). If certain asymmetries and redundancies are eliminated, a remarkably simple system appears to emerge, which consists of a single notion of barrier for long *Wh*-Movement and a single notion of barrier for government (in interaction with the Empty Category Principle (ECP) and Rizzi's (1990) Relativized Minimality).

Such a simplification can only be attained, it seems, if the locality conditions on long *Wh*-Movement are kept separate from those on successive cyclic *Wh*-Movement. That a genuine generalization is captured by separating the two is indicated by the properties of a Romance construction, clitic left dislocation, which is discussed in some detail in chapter 2. The construction shows sensitivity to (strong) islands and apparently displays long movement, yet it fails all the more subtle diagnostics for *Wh*-Movement, including successive cyclic *Wh*-Movement. That plausibly means that it is not a *Wh*-Movement construction and that the conditions on long *Wh*-Movement are not conditions on movement per se, but are well-formedness conditions on Ā-chains, whether these are created by movement (as in ordinary *wh*-constructions) or base-generated (as in clitic left dislocation).

The construction will in fact appear to have even more far-reaching consequences for our understanding of *Wh*-Movement. Although it can be characterized as differing from topicalization precisely in lacking null operator movement, the construction nonetheless appears to acquire *Wh*-Movement properties when some nonreferential operator is left-dislocated, which in turn suggests that it is the quantificational nature of the element in Ā-position rather than its derivation "via *Wh*-Movement" that is responsible for its "*Wh*-Movement" properties.

The last Ā-dependency to be discussed is the apparent movement of NPs exemplified in (1) and (2), whose gap will be seen to have important properties in common with parasitic gaps and the gap of *easy-to-please* constructions.

Not that NPs have their own conditions on extraction. We must assume that they can participate in both successive cyclic and long extraction, just like any other category. Rather, NPs—and only NPs—have at their disposal an additional (more liberal) option. This is at the basis of such NP/non-NP contrasts as the following, originally pointed out by Adriana Belletti:

(3) a. ?Mario, che abbiamo discusso la possibilità
       Mario who we have discussed the possibility
       di non invitare _____, ...
       of not inviting

b. *Mario, dal quale abbiamo discusso la possibilità
   Mario by whom we discussed   the possibility
   di non stare _____, ...
   of not staying

(4) a. ?Carlo, che non conosco nessuno
       Carlo who I don't know anybody
       che voglia ancora invitare _____ a casa sua, ...
       who still wants to invite   at his place
    b. *Mario, di cui non conosco nessuno che parli _____, ...
       Mario of whom I know nobody   who speaks

(5) a. Marco, che me ne sono andato
       Marco who I went away
       prima di dover prendere _____ a pugni, ...
       before I had to punch
    b. *Marco, a cui me ne sono andato
       Marco to whom I went away
       prima di dover dare un pugno _____, ...
       before I had to give a punch

In discussing these and other contrasts in chapter 3, I will suggest that
the reason for such a difference between NPs and non-NPs may lie in an
independent property that distinguishes NPs from non-NPs: namely, the
fact that NPs are the only class of elements partitioned by the features
[± pronominal, ± anaphor]. If so, NPs are the only class of elements that
have an *empty* resumptive pronominal at their disposal. In turn, this
suggests the possibility of analyzing such cases as (3a), (4a), and (5a) not
as instances of the movement strategy but as cases of an (empty) resumptive
pronominal strategy that does not involve an $\bar{\text{A}}$-chain (hence the lack of
Reconstruction in such cases).

As is already apparent from (1) and (2), however, the relation between
the empty pronominal and its antecedent is not entirely free. The selective
character of its island condition violations will be argued to be a function
of the movement of the empty pronominal in LF, coupled with the possibility of LF pied piping.

Types of Ā-Dependencies

Chapter 1
Long and Successive Cyclic
Wh-Movement

1.1 Introduction

It is generally agreed that two different types of *Wh*-Movement must be recognized: *long* and *successive cyclic*.[1] Certain elements, prototypically adjuncts, must undergo successive cyclic *Wh*-Movement. Others, prototypically complements of verbs, have an additional option: long *Wh*-Movement.

Pretheoretically, the two types of movement differ in that successive cyclic movement is subject to both *strong* and *weak islands*, whereas long movement is subject only to strong islands. See (1)–(3), which are cases of strong islands, and (4)–(7), which are cases of weak islands (the (a) cases represent long movement; the (b) cases successive cyclic movement):[2]

(1) *Subject island*
    a. *Which books did [talking about *t*] become difficult?
    b. *How would [to behave *t*] be inappropriate?

(2) *Complex NP island*
    a. *To whom have you found someone who would speak *t*?
    b. *How have you found someone who would fix it *t*?

(3) *Adjunct island*
    a. *To whom did you leave without speaking *t*?
    b. *How was he fired after behaving *t*?

(4) Wh-*Island*
    a. ??To whom didn't they know when to give their present *t*?
    b. *How did they ask you who behaved *t*?

(5) *Inner (negative) island*
    a. To whom didn't you speak *t*?
    b. *How didn't you behave *t*?

(6) *Factive island*
    a.   To whom do you regret that you could not speak *t*?
    b.   *How do you regret that you behaved *t*?

(7) *Extraposition island*
    a.   To whom is it time to speak *t*?
    b.   *How is it time to behave *t*?

Beyond the necessity of distinguishing between long and successive cyclic *Wh*-Movement, no general agreement exists in the literature on many fundamental questions concerning this domain, in particular on the questions in (8):

(8) a. What classes of elements undergo long and successive cyclic *Wh*-Movement?
    b. From what principles of the theory does the existence of long and successive cyclic *Wh*-Movement follow?
    c. What is the nature of the locality conditions on long and successive cyclic *Wh*-Movement?

I will begin with questions (8a) and (8b). After examining the answers given by Chomsky (1986b) and Rizzi (1990), who elaborate on much important work of the 1980s, I will discuss some new facts bearing on question (8a), which appear to be more easily integrated into Rizzi's system than into the *Barriers* system, and which appear to suggest a particular refinement of the system proposed by Rizzi whereby the referential status of the trace is a prerequisite for long *Wh*-Movement.

In the second part of the chapter I will reconsider the locality conditions on long and successive cyclic *Wh*-Movement (question (8c). Taking Chomsky's (1986b) proposals as a starting point, I will reformulate them in such a way as to eliminate certain redundancies and capture the relevant generalizations in a maximally simple way.

1.2 Chomsky's (1986b) Analysis of Long and Successive Cyclic *Wh*-Movement

Chomsky (1986b), building on work by Huang (1982) and by Lasnik and Saito (1984), suggests that the answer to (8a) and (8b) is provided by (a particular formulation of) the ECP. Consider (9)–(13):[3]

(9) *Proper government*
    α properly governs β iff α θ-governs or antecedent-governs β. (p. 17)

(10) *γ-marking*
      If β is properly governed, it is assigned [$+\gamma$] indelibly. If β is not
      properly governed, it is assigned [$-\gamma$] indelibly. (pp. 17–18)

(11) Such γ-marking takes place at S-Structure for A-positions, and at
      LF for $\overline{\text{A}}$-positions. (p. 18)

(12) Empty categories (ECs) not required by the Extended Projection
      Principle can delete between S-Structure and LF (possibly after
      having properly governed and γ-marked other ECs). (p. 21)

(13) *γ-checking* (applying at LF)
      *[$-\gamma$]

This formulation of the ECP has, among other consequences, that of
forcing a strict successive cyclic derivation for all categories that (like
adjuncts) are in $\overline{\text{A}}$-positions, and of permitting long *Wh*-Movement of all
categories that are in A-positions (*pace* the Subjacency Condition).[4] Consider briefly how. (14a) is a case of extraction of a θ-governed category;
(14b) a case of a $\overline{\theta}$-governed category in A-position; and (14c–d) cases of
$\overline{\theta}$-governed categories in $\overline{\text{A}}$-position:

(14) a. ?Which particular problem were you wondering how to
            [t′ [phrase t]]?
      b. ?Which student did he wonder whether to [t′ [consider
            [t intelligent]]]?
      c. How have you [t‴ [decided [t″ to [t′ [phrase the problem t]]]]]?
      d. *How are you [t″ wondering [which problem [to [t′ [phrase t]]]]]?

Let us start with (14c). The trace there is not θ-governed. Hence, to be
properly governed (to be assigned [$+\gamma$]), it must be antecedent-governed.
It is if *how* moves successive cyclically, adjoining first to the embedded VP.
Given Chomsky's (1986b) definition of government, *t′* antecedent-governs
t. *t′* cannot delete between S-Structure and LF because, for ECs in $\overline{\text{A}}$-
position like the trace of *how*, γ-marking applies only at LF. If it deleted,
t would not be γ-marked. This also means that the trace left adjoined
to the embedded VP must itself satisfy the ECP (that is, be antecedent-
governed), as must every higher EC needed to antecedent-govern a lower
EC.

Clearly, none of the ECs represented in (14c) can be missing (whence the
strict successive cyclic movement of *how*), nor can any of them delete prior
to LF. The reason why (14d) is ill formed within this system is now
transparent. It violates the ECP. If not *t*, then *t′* fails to be properly
governed (antecedent-governed). As the Spec of the embedded CP is filled

by another *wh*-phrase, the closest antecedent is t''. But this phrase does not antecedent-govern t'. A barrier (by inheritance), CP, intervenes between them.

Consider now (14a) and (14b). In (14b) the trace is not θ-governed. Hence, it must be antecedent-governed. This forces the phrase to adjoin to the higher VP, from which position it can antecedent-govern the original trace and assign it $[+\gamma]$ at S-Structure since the latter is in an A-position. But once it has γ-marked the original trace at S-Structure, the VP-adjoined trace can delete, so that no other intermediate EC will be needed to antecedent-govern it. As a result, the phrase will be free to undergo long *Wh*-Movement from the VP-adjoined position (again, *pace* Subjacency).

Finally, in (14a) the trace is θ-governed by the verb, which thus assigns it $[+\gamma]$ at S-Structure. This marking, carried along to LF, by itself satisfies the ECP. No antecedent government is required and long *Wh*-Movement is again permitted by the ECP.[5]

1.3 Rizzi's (1990) Binding and Government Approach

Despite its remarkable success in deriving many important distinctions, the *Barriers* system raises a number of questions, both conceptual and empirical. Concerning the former, Rizzi (1990) notes the existence of a redundancy between the generalized requirement of head government (see note 4 here) and the θ-government requirement of "proper government." Every phrase that is θ-governed is, a fortiori, head-governed. Thus, both clauses of the conjunctive formulation of the ECP turn out to require some sort of head government. A second conceptual problem inherent in the formulation of proper government is, as often noted, the disjunction between θ-government and antecedent government. To admit a disjunctive statement of this sort amounts to admitting that the nature of the relevant generalization is not understood.[6]

The empirical problems are inherent in the general prediction that phrases in A-positions should be able to undergo long *Wh*-Movement. This does not always seem to be the case.

Consider, for example, measure object NPs and objects of idiomatic VPs. As pointed out by Rizzi (1990) (also see Koopman and Sportiche 1988), these elements fail to undergo long *Wh*-Movement even though they are θ-marked by the verb that selects them. See, for example, (15)–(16), which contain measure phrases, and (17)–(18), which contain the VP idioms *fare giustizia* 'do justice' and *prestare attenzione* 'pay attention':

(15) *Quanti chili   ti ha chiesto   se pesavi?[7]
     how many kilos has he asked you whether you weighed

(16) *Quanti chilometri   non sai
     how many kilometers don't you know
     se Venezia disti da Treviso?
     whether Venice is far from Treviso

(17) *GIUSTIZIA, mi domando quando faranno finalmente!
     justice   I wonder   when they will finally do

(18) *L'attenzione che non ho ancora deciso a chi prestare   è poca.[8]
     the attention that I haven't decided yet to whom to pay is little

These NPs can of course be *Wh*-Moved, apparently at an unbounded distance (via the successive cyclic option). See (19) and (20):

(19) a. Quanti chili   credi   che riuscirà a pesare
        how many kilos do you think that he will be able to weigh
        dopo questa dieta?
        after this diet
     b. Quanti chilometri   credi   che abbia detto
        how many kilometers do you think that he said
        che distava, Venezia?
        that Venice was far

(20) a. GIUSTIZIA, dice   di voler fare!
        justice   he says he wants to do
     b. L'attenzione che ho deciso di prestare a Gianni è poca.
        the attention that I decided to pay Gianni   is little

If we must conclude that long *Wh*-Movement is not simply a prerogative of phrases in A-positions, of which class of elements is it a prerogative?

On the basis of the contrast between ordinary objects, which can be long *Wh*-Moved, and measure or idiomatic NPs, which cannot, Rizzi (1990) suggests that it is the nature of the θ-role involved that matters, over and above the requirement that the target of long *Wh*-Movement be in an A-position. He expresses this condition unitarily by requiring that the target of long *Wh*-Movement be a phrase receiving a θ-role referring to the participants in the event described by the predicate: *agent, theme, goal*, and so on, but not *measure, manner*, or the role assigned to quasi arguments such as idiom chunks. He calls the former *referential*, and the latter *nonreferential*, θ-roles.

Concerning the deeper question of why long *Wh*-Movement should be limited to phrases receiving a referential θ-role, Rizzi proposes a solution in which the classical notion of *referential index* plays a crucial role.

The essence of Rizzi's proposal can be summarized as follows:

(21) a. The use of indices should be restricted, as in the classical theory of Chomsky (1965), to express referential dependencies between different arguments.

   b. Movement does not create indices, but can only carry a (referential) index that is made legitimate by certain referential properties of the elements bearing it" (that is, is assigned to phrases receiving a referential θ-role).

   c. The binding relation (X binds Y iff (i) X c-commands Y and (ii) X and Y have the same index) is defined in terms of the notion of *referential index*.

These assumptions have the effect of restricting binding relations to phrases bearing a referential θ-role.

As Rizzi notes, this restriction subsumes the essential effect of the identification clause of the ECP, capturing the fundamental argument/ adjunct asymmetries. The $\bar{\text{A}}$-dependency between an operator phrase that receives a referential index at D-Structure and its trace can be expressed through binding. But the $\bar{\text{A}}$-dependency between an operator phrase that does not receive a referential index at D-Structure and its trace cannot be so expressed. As the operator phrase must still be somehow connected to its trace, the system must resort to other available means. It is tempting to say that in the modular structure of the theory there are only two ways in which two elements can interconnect: through *binding* or (*antecedent*) *government*. Binding being unavailable except for elements bearing a referential index, only (antecedent) government is left for $\bar{\text{A}}$-dependencies not involving referential indices.

As binding is intrinsically nonlocal (*pace* Subjacency), and (antecedent) government local, the option of long *Wh*-Movement just for phrases bearing a referential θ-role follows, as does the requirement that each link of the successive cyclic derivation obey (antecedent) government.

This is essentially the source for the observed asymmetries. (14c), (19a–b) and (20a–b) are well-formed cases of successive cyclic *Wh*-Movement. The *wh*-phrases involved, not receiving a referential θ-role (hence, index) at D-Structure, cannot connect to the original trace via binding. But they can connect to it via a chain of antecedent government relations since no government barrier intervenes between any of the pairs of positions involved.

(14d), (15)–(16), and (17)–(18) are ill formed since the *wh*-phrase can connect to its original trace neither via binding (it does not receive a referential index at D-Structure) nor via (antecedent) government (a barrier by inheritance, the interrogative CP node, intervenes between the embedded VP-adjoined EC and the matrix VP-adjoined EC).[9]

(14a–b) are well-formed cases of long *Wh*-Movement since here the *wh*-phrase receives a referential θ-role (hence a referential index) at D-Structure and can thus connect to its trace via binding, after movement. The fact that a government barrier (or a potential $\bar{\text{A}}$-antecedent) intervenes between them is thus inconsequential.

The fact that *wh*-phrases not receiving a referential index at D-Structure cannot cross the other weak islands either also follows from the (antecedent) government requirement on each link of the successive cyclic derivation. See, for example, (22)–(24). The (a) cases exemplify the behavior of measure phrases, the (b) cases that of objects of VP idioms:

(22) *Negative island*
    a. *Quanti chili   non pesi?
       how many kilos don't you weigh
    b. *Quanta attenzione   non ti presta mai?
       how much attention doesn't she ever pay you

(23) *Factive island*
    a. *Quanti chili   ti rammarichi che lei pesi?
       how many kilos do you regret that she weighs
    b. *Quanta attenzione   ti rammarichi di non avergli mai prestato?
       how much attention do you regret you never payed him

(24) *Extraposition island*
    a. *Quanti chili   ha certamente contato pesare per lei?
       how many kilos did it certainly matter to weigh for her
    b. *Quanta attenzione   ha certamente contato prestargli?
       how much attention did it certainly matter to pay him

In (23)–(24) a government barrier, the non-L-marked embedded CP, intervenes between two positions of the successive cyclic derivation. In (22) a potential $\bar{\text{A}}$-antecedent (the negation) intervenes (see Rizzi 1990, chap. 1).[10]

If so, the conceptual problems observed above dissolve. The irreducible disjunction between θ-government and antecedent government in the "identification requirement" of the ECP has no primitive theoretical status any more, its effects having been subsumed under two independent principles, binding and government. The ECP can now reduce to the "formal licensing requirement" (a nonpronominal EC must be head-governed), thus eliminating the redundancy observed above and simplifying the overall system.

1.4   The Role of Referentiality

Having reviewed two particular partitionings of the classes of elements undergoing long and successive cyclic *Wh*-Movement, that of Chomsky (1986b) and that of Rizzi (1990), I now turn to some new facts bearing on this question, which appear to suggest the necessity of further restricting the class of elements that undergo long *Wh*-Movement. Since they point to the linguistic relevance of a particular notion of referentiality, they provide confirmation for the general approach of Rizzi (1990), while also suggesting an important refinement of that system.

To anticipate the main conclusions that will be reached, it appears that, of all the phrases that receive a referential θ-role, in Rizzi's sense, only those can be long *Wh*-Moved that are used strictly referentially—in other words, that refer to specific members of a preestablished set. This characterization recalls Pesetsky's (1987) important notion of D(iscourse)-linking, which I will later subsume under the relevant notion of referentiality used here. (For the significance of a somewhat different conception of referentiality in the account of long *Wh*-Movement, see also Aoun 1986 and Aoun et al. 1987).

Within Rizzi's system, this result may be derived if, everything else being held constant, we limit the assignment of referential indices just to (*wh*-)phrases that are used referentially (that are D-linked). Only these will be able to enter binding relations via the referential index mechanism.

Whenever reference to members of a preestablished referential set is inherently impossible for some phrase, or hard to force, then, even if the phrase receives a referential θ-role, it will not be able to enter a binding relation with its trace, so that no long *Wh*-Movement will appear to be open to it.

To check the relevance of referentiality for binding relations, we need some independent way to discriminate between referential and nonreferential phrases. One phenomenon that discriminates between referential and nonreferential phrases is *coreference*. Plainly, only referential phrases can enter coreference relations. So, for example, R-expressions, pronominals, and (lexical) anaphors can corefer, but, as is well known, certain types of quantifiers cannot freely corefer. They can be linked to a pronoun only if they c-command it—in other words, if they "bind" it, in a sense of "binding" that we might try to unify with the sense considered so far, but that I will treat as distinct for the time being. (For a possible unified treatment, see Cinque 1989.) For example, it is possible for the pronoun *lo* 'him' in (25a) to be linked to the R-expression *il museo* 'the museum' even if the latter does not c-command the former. This is because they can freely corefer, both being referential. By contrast, no link between *lo* and the quantified phrases *ogni museo* 'every museum', *nessun museo* 'no museum' is possible in (25b–c); here the quantified phrase neither c-commands the pronoun (at either S-Structure or LF) nor is able to corefer with it, being nonreferential:

(25) a.   [Gli alunni che dovevano visitare *il museo*]
            the pupils who had to visit *the museum*
            lo hanno visitato in fretta.
            visited *it* hurriedly

     b.   *[Gli alunni che dovevano visitare *ogni museo*]
            the pupils who had to visit *every museum*
            hanno finito per visitar*lo* in fretta.
            ended up visiting *it* hurriedly

     c.   *[Gli alunni che non volevano visitare *nessun museo*]
            the pupils who wanted to visit *no museum*
            lo hanno visitato in fretta.
            visited *it* hurriedly

Similarly, *ogni N̄*, *nessun N̄*, unlike ordinary R-expressions, show weak crossover effects:

(26) *Sua* madre ha presentato *Maria* ad un ragazzo.
      her mother introduced *Maria*   to a boy

(27) a.   **Sua* madre ha presentato *ogni ragazza* ad un ragazzo.
            her mother introduced   *every girl*   to a boy

     b.   **Sua* madre non ha presentato *nessuna ragazza* ad un ragazzo.
            her mother introduced   *no girl*   to a boy

Quite independently of the exact account of weak crossover one adopts,[11] the contrast between (26) and (27) appears to be imputable to the same cause: namely, the availability in (26), and the unavailability in (27), of a coreference reading.

    Quite generally, then, we expect that all those NPs that can be linked to a pronoun only if they c-command it (and that show weak crossover effects) will undergo only successive cyclic *Wh*-Movement, not long

Wh-Movement. This is so because they are not referential, hence do not receive a referential index, and hence cannot enter a binding relation.[12] Since only a successive cyclic derivation will be open to them, we expect that no such NPs will extract from weak islands, which block government relations.

1.4.1 Extraction from Weak Islands

As a matter of fact, neither the universal distributive quantifier *ogni $\bar{N}$* nor the negative universal quantifiers *nessun $\bar{N}$, niente* 'nothing', which we saw behave like nonreferential elements in (25b–c) and (27a–b), are extractable from weak islands. ((28) and (29) are examples of topicalization, which in Italian could more appropriately be termed *Focus Movement*.)

(28) a. *OGNI DICHIARAZIONE, mi chiedo perché abbia ritrattato.
　　　　 every statement　　　　　　　 I wonder why he retracted

　　 b. *OGNI MUSEO, non vuole　　　　 visitare.
　　　　 every museum　 he does not want to visit

　　 c. *OGNI DICHIARAZIONE, mi rammarico
　　　　 every statement　　　　　　　 I regret
　　　　 che abbia ritrattato.
　　　　 that he retracted

　　 d. *OGNI MUSEO, è uno scandalo che chiudano.
　　　　 every museum　 it is a scandal　 that they shut

(29) a. *$\left\{\begin{array}{l}\text{NESSUN LIBRO,}\\ \text{NIENTE,}\end{array}\right\}$ mi domando perché abbia comprato![13]

　　　　 $\left\{\begin{array}{l}\text{no book}\\ \text{nothing}\end{array}\right\}$　　　 I wonder　　 why he bought

　　 b. *$\left\{\begin{array}{l}\text{NESSUN LIBRO,}\\ \text{NIENTE,}\end{array}\right\}$ non è vero　 che abbia comprato.

　　　　 $\left\{\begin{array}{l}\text{no book}\\ \text{nothing}\end{array}\right\}$　　　 it is not true that he bought

　　 c. *$\left\{\begin{array}{l}\text{NESSUN LIBRO,}\\ \text{NIENTE,}\end{array}\right\}$ mi rammarico che abbia comprato.

　　　　 $\left\{\begin{array}{l}\text{no book}\\ \text{nothing}\end{array}\right\}$　　　 I regret　　　　 that he bought

　　 d. *$\left\{\begin{array}{l}\text{NESSUN LIBRO,}\\ \text{NIENTE,}\end{array}\right\}$ sarebbe disdicevole

　　　　 $\left\{\begin{array}{l}\text{no book}\\ \text{nothing}\end{array}\right\}$　　　 it would be unbecoming che avesse comprato.

that he bought

Within the present analysis, this implies that the quantifiers do not receive a referential index at D-Structure as a consequence of their nonreferential nature.

Ogni $\bar{N}$ and the similar *qualunque* $\bar{N}$, *qualsiasi* $\bar{N}$ 'whatever $\bar{N}$' and *chiunque* 'whoever' contrast with the nondistributive universal quantifier *tutti NP*, which apparently can undergo long *Wh*-Movement (30) and consistently has an interpretation (the "collective" one) in which it is subject neither to the pronoun binding requirement (31) nor to weak crossover (32). (See also Reinhart 1983 for relevant discussion.)

(30) a. TUTTI I MUSEI, mi chiedo chi possa aver visitato.

  all the museums   I wonder who can have visited

  b. TUTTI I MUSEI, non ha visitato.[14]

  all the museums   he has not visited

  c. TUTTI I MUSEI, mi rammarico che abbiano fatto chiudere.

  all the museums   I regret   that they shut

  d. TUTTI I MUSEI, sarebbe necessario   che chiudessero.

  all the museums   it would be necessary that they shut

(31) [Quelli di loro che hanno visitato *tutti i musei*] *li* hanno trovati

  those of them who visited *all the museums*   found *them*

  uno più interessante dell'altro.

  one more interesting than the other

(32) [Le *loro* affermazioni incaute] hanno finito per rovinare

  their incautious statements   ended up ruining

  tutti i miei amici.

  all my friends

1.4.2 Longobardi's Scope Reconstruction Facts

Longobardi (1987b) makes the important observation that Reconstruction of the scope of an extracted quantifier is blocked not only by strong islands (Longobardi 1986) but also by weak islands. Normally, the scope properties that a quantifier has on the basis of its D-Structure position are preserved when it is moved to an A-position (see Van Riemsdijk and Williams 1981, Cinque 1982, Haïk 1984, and references cited there), though new properties may arise as a consequence of its S-Structure position (see Chomsky 1980b). For example, in (33a), though not in (33b), the quantifier phrase *quanti pazienti* 'how many patients' can be in the scope of the universal distributive quantifier *ognuno dei medici* 'every one of the doctors'. That is, (33a) can be satisfied by a family of answers ("I think that Dr. Rossi can visit 5 in one hour, Dr. Bianchi 7, and so on"), whereas (33b) can be answered by just one number ("Only 7").

(33) a. Quanti pazienti$_i$ pensi   che ognuno dei medici
       how many patients do you think that every one of the doctors
       riesca a visitare t_i in un'ora?
       can visit   in one hour

   b. Quanti pazienti$_i$ pensano che ognuno dei medici
      how many patients think   that every one of the doctors
      riesca a visitarli$_i$ in un'ora?
      can visit them   in one hour

As Longobardi noted, this scope Reconstruction is apparently blocked when the quantifier in question is extracted from a weak island, which otherwise normally allows extraction (and Reconstruction) of complements:

(34) a. ?Quanti pazienti   ti chiedevi
        how many patients did you wonder
        come ognuno dei medici   riuscisse a visitare in un'ora?
        how every one of the doctors could visit   in one hour

   b. ?Quanti pazienti   non pensi
      how many patients don't you think
      che ognuno dei medici   riesca a visitare in un'ora?
      that every one of the doctors can visit   in one hour

   c. ?Quanti pazienti   ti lamenti   che ognuno dei medici
      how many patients do you regret that every one of the doctors
      sia riuscito a visitare in un'ora?
      managed to visit   in one hour

   d. ?Quanti pazienti   sarebbe uno scandalo
      how many patients would it be a scandal
      che ognuno dei medici   visitasse in un'ora?
      that every one of the doctors visited   in one hour

For each question in (34), the family of answers that was possible in (33a) is excluded. (34a–d) are (in fact, only marginally) possible with an interpretation roughly paraphrasable as 'How many patients are such that you wondered how every one of the doctors could visit them in one hour?' (see Longobardi 1987b), in which the quantified phrase acquires a referential reading. (Below we will see independent evidence to this effect.)

   Longobardi (1987b) interprets this fact as suggesting that scope Reconstruction is only possible where the operator can be connected to its variable through a chain of antecedent government relations—hence, not across the boundary of even a weak island. This important insight still raises a question: why should scope Reconstruction require such a chain whereas Reconstruction of other properties does not? See (35a–c) and (36), which exemplify Reconstruction of Principles A, B, and C of the binding theory and pronominal binding, respectively, across a *wh*-island:

(35) a. E' a *se stessa* che non so   se *lei* abbia scritto.
         it's to *herself* that I don't know whether *she* has written
    b. *E' a *lei*   che non so   se Maria abbia scritto.
         it's to *her* that I don't know whether Maria has written
    c. *E' a *Maria* che non so   se *lei* abbia scritto.
         it's to *Mary* that I don't know whether *she* has written

(36)   A chi *lo* ha aiutato,   non so
        to those who helped *him* I don't know
        se *ognuno di loro*   restituirà il favore.
        whether *every one of them* will reciprocate

Given the preceding discussion, it appears that this curious property of scope Reconstruction need not be stipulated. In other words, no special condition need be imposed on this type of Reconstruction. Its properties as exemplified in (34) can rather be seen as simple effects of the nonreferential nature of the extracted quantifier. When it interacts with another quantifier, *quanti* $\bar{N}$ must be interpreted nonreferentially. As a result, the *wh*-phrase is able to connect to its trace only via a chain of antecedent government relations, not via binding (whence the character of (34) noted by Longobardi). On the other hand, when *quanti* $\bar{N}$ does not interact with another quantifier, it (marginally) admits a referential reading—hence the marginal possibility of extracting it from a weak island. Compare (34) with (37):

(37) (?)Quanti pazienti   non ricordi   se lui avesse visitato?
        how many patients don't you remember whether he had visited

It is apparently possible to check the correctness of this analysis by checking the twofold prediction that it makes.

Whenever *quanti* $\bar{N}$ interacts with another quantifier and must therefore be interpreted nonreferentially, no coindexation should be possible between it and a pronoun outside its c-command domain, since both coreference and pronominal binding are unavailable. Conversely, when it does not interact with another quantifier, such coindexation should be marginally possible, since reference (hence, coreference) is marginally available to it, as noted.

This is precisely what we find. Compare (38) with (39):

(38) *[*Quanti pazienti*   ognuno dei medici   potesse visitare]
     how many patients every one of the doctors could visit
     non era chiaro neppure a *loro*.
     was not clear   even to *them*

(39) ?[*Quanti pazienti*   occorressero   non era chiaro neppure a *loro*.
     how many patients were necessary was not clear   even to *them*

Similar considerations apply to such quantifier phrases as *tanti $\bar{N}$...quanti $\bar{N}$* 'as many $\bar{N}$...as', *cosi' tanti $\bar{N}$...che* 'so many $\bar{N}$...that', and the like.

1.4.3 Clitic Left Dislocated Bare Quantifiers

The evidence discussed in this section presupposes an analysis of the Romance construction of *clitic left dislocation* (CLLD) that will be justified extensively in chapter 2. Here I will simply state the relevant conclusions reached there.

CLLD, as opposed to topicalization, does not involve (movement of) an empty operator. This entails, among other consequences, the following contrast:

(40) a. GIANNI   (*lo) ho visto.
         Gianni (focus) (him) I saw
     b. Gianni, *(lo) ho visto.
         Gianni I saw him

A "resumptive" clitic is impossible with a topicalized object but is obligatory with a CLLD object. The contrast follows under Chomsky's (1977) analysis of topicalization and the above assumption concerning CLLD. (40a–b) receive the following analyses:

(41) a. [$_{TOP}$ GIANNI] [$_{CP}$ O_i [$_{IP}$ (*lo) ho visto e_i]]
     b. [$_{TOP}$ Gianni] [$_{CP}$[$_{IP}$ *(lo) ho visto e]]

(41a), with a clitic locally binding the object EC, violates the principle barring vacuous quantification and is thus parallel to (42):

(42) Chi (*lo) hai visto?
      whom have you seen him

(41b), without the clitic, is not a well-formed structure, since the empty object qualifies as none of the various types of empty NPs: it can be neither an anaphor, nor pro, nor PRO, nor a variable, since no empty operator is permitted in CLLD.

Interestingly, if the object phrase in Top (an $\bar{A}$-position) is a bare quantifier ([$_{NP}$ Q]: *qualcosa* 'something', *qualcuno* 'someone', etc.), though not if it is a quantified NP (*qualche $\bar{N}$/alcuni $\bar{N}$* 'some $\bar{N}$', *molti $\bar{N}$* 'many $\bar{N}$', etc.), the resumptive pronoun may be missing:

(43) a. Qualcuno, (lo) troveremo.
          someone   we (him) will find
      b. Qualcosa, di sicuro, io (la) farò.
          something surely   (it) I'll do

(44) a. Qualche errore, Carlo *(lo) ha fatto.
          some error   Carlo (it) has made
      b. Alcuni libri, *(li) ho comperati.
          some books   (them) I bought
      c. Molte lettere, lui *(le) butta via.
          many letters   he (them) throws away

The presence or absence of the resumptive clitic in (43) is not simply optional. It correlates with a difference in the referential properties of the quantifier. If the speaker has something or someone specific in mind (that is, if the bare quantifier is used referentially), the clitic is required. If the interpretation is 'something or other' or 'someone unspecified', the clitic is impossible.

This suggests that bare quantifiers used nonreferentially behave like intrinsic operators, which can identify an EC as a variable at S-Structure, whereas bare quantifiers used referentially and quantified NPs cannot, so that a resumptive clitic is required (see Cinque 1986, Dobrovie-Sorin 1987, 1990).[15]

Being nonreferential when they identify an EC as a variable, left-dislocated bare quantifiers should thus only be able to connect to the associated EC via a chain of antecedent government links and should accordingly be sensitive to weak islands. This is precisely the case:[16]

(45) a. *Qualcuno mi chiedo come troverai.
           someone   I wonder how you'll find
      b. *Qualcosa, mi chiedo chi farà   per noi.
           something I wonder who will do for us

(46) a. *Qualcuno, non credo   che troverà.
           someone   I don't think that he will find
      b. *Qualcosa, di sicuro, non farò.
           something surely   I won't do

(47) a. *Qualcuno, mi pento di aver aiutato.
           someone   I regret   I helped

b. *Qualcosa, mi pento di aver fatto per loro.
   something I regret   I did   for them

(48) a. *Qualcuno, è un vero scandalo che abbia schiaffeggiato.
      someone   it's a true scandal   that he slapped in the face
   b. *Qualcosa, è un vero scandalo che abbia ottenuto.
      something it's a true scandal   that he obtained

1.4.4 Pesetsky's Notion of D-Linking and Referentiality

As mentioned, the notion of "referentiality" (as the ability to refer to specific members of a set in the mind of the speaker or preestablished in discourse) recalls Pesetsky's (1987) important notion of D-linking. I think, in fact, that the two are one and the same notion, or perhaps, more accurately, that the notion of referentiality subsumes that of D-linking.[17]

Pesetsky interprets certain asymmetries existing between two types of wh-phrases in situ as being due to their differing ability to relate to referential sets preestablished in discourse. *Which $\bar{N}$* phrases can (in fact, must) refer to members of a set that both speaker and hearer have in mind (as do the relevant answers).

Bare wh-operators like *who, what* or *how many $\bar{N}$* phrases can do so only quite marginally, and under very special contextual conditions forcing some linking to previous discourse. The simple addition of a phrase like *the hell* or *on earth*, which expresses surprise or ignorance of the possible answers and is thus incompatible with the choice among elements isolated in the previous discourse, suffices to exclude any such discourse linking.

Pesetsky calls the former *D-linked* and the latter *non-D-linked* wh-phrases. By assuming (1) that operators must occupy an $\bar{A}$-position at LF and (2) that only non-D-linked wh-phrases are operators, he is able to account for a number of asymmetries between the two types of wh-in-situ. Only non-D-linked wh-phrases in situ (such as *who, what, how many $\bar{N}$* phrases) are expected to move at LF and should thus show the usual diagnostics of movement (sensitivity to Subjacency, the ECP, and other conditions on movement like the Nested Dependency Constraint). D-linked wh-phrases in situ (such as *which $\bar{N}$*) are instead expected not to move at LF, since they do not qualify as operators. They are rather interpreted in situ via a different mechanism, that of *unselective binding* (see Pesetsky 1987 for more careful discussion).

The relative contrasts between (49) and (50) and between (51) and (52) are thus expected:

(49) a. *Mary asked what who read.

b. *I need to know whom how many people voted for.

(50)   Mary asked what which man read.

(51)   ??Tell me what proves that who is innocent.

(52)   Tell me which piece of evidence proves that which person is innocent.

Pesetsky's conclusions about the behavior of *wh*-phrases at LF are consistent with the conclusions reached in the previous sections about the (movement of) quantifier phrases at S-Structure. Only D-linked (in our terms, referential) phrases can indeed enter a binding relation, whether at S-Structure or at LF. Non-D-linked (nonreferential) phrases are instead forced to enter only chains of antecedent government relations, both at S-Structure and at LF.

It is thus not unexpected that non-D-linked *wh*-phrases do not take scope over a *wh*-island, even in languages (such as French) that allow for extractions out of *wh*-islands, since such LF movement is sensitive to antecedent government relations, just as overt syntactic movement of non-D-linked phrases is (see Huang 1982, Lasnik and Saito 1984):

(53) Qui sait   quand Jean en a acheté   combien?
     who knows when Jean of them has bought how many

We will in fact see in the next section that there is complete parallelism between *wh*-extraction from a *wh*-island at LF and the some extraction in the syntax:

(54) *Combien te rappelles-tu   quand Jean en a acheté?
     how many do you remember when Jean of them has bought

That D-linking, in Pesetsky's sense, implies referentiality is confirmed by the fact that a D-linked *wh*-in-situ (but crucially no non-D linked *wh*-in-situ) can enter *coreference* relations. See the contrast between (55a) and (55b):[18]

(55) a.   Which boy$_i$ started a fight with which girl$_j$ wasn't clear even to them$_{i+j}$.
     b.   *Who$_i$ started a fight with whom$_j$ wasn't clear even to them$_{i+j}$.

1.4.5   (Non-)D-Linked *Wh*-phrases and the *Wh*-Island Constraint

As noted independently by various authors, extraction of interrogative phrases out of indirect questions depends on the character of the extracted *wh*-phrase. Rizzi (1982, chap. 2, fn. 5) and Engdahl (1980a, b) observe that only relatively "heavy" *wh*-phrases can be extracted from *wh*-islands in Italian and Swedish, respectively. But, to judge from the examples, the relevant feature seems once again to be the D-linked versus non-D-linked character of the extracted *wh*-phrase. Only the former can apparently be extracted ((56a) is in fact marginally acceptable if a pause follows *a chi*, and otherwise impossible):

(56) a. ??A chi   ti chiedi   quanti soldi   hai dato?
        to whom do you wonder how much money you gave

   b.   A quale   dei tuoi figli   ti chiedi
        to which one of your children do you wonder
        quanti soldi   hai dato?
        how much money you gave

(57) a. *Vad visste   ingen   vem som skrev?
        what knows no one who wrote

   b.   Sven undrar   vilken bok   alla studenter minns
        Sven wonders which book all students remember
        vilken författare som skrev.
        which author wrote

See Comorovski 1985, 1989, from which (57a–b) are drawn, and Bedzyk 1987 for the explicit claim that only D-linked *wh*-phrases can be extracted from *wh*-islands in Romanian and Bulgarian, respectively. As Comorovski (1989) indeed remarks, "The cross-linguistic generalization that emerges is that only D-linked *wh*-phrases can be questioned out of indirect questions." She proposes a solution for this contrast based on certain presupposition properties of D- and non-D-linked *wh*-phrases in interaction with the semantics of *wh*-islands. Within the present analysis of long *Wh*-Movement, however, nothing at all is needed to account for the asymmetry in question.

Only D-linked (hence, referential) *wh*-phrases can enter a binding relation with their trace, whence their insensitivity to *wh*-islands (weak islands, more generally). Non-D-linked (nonreferential) *wh*-phrases instead can only move successive cyclically, whence their sensitivity to weak islands.

The other often noted asymmetry between questioning (impossible or marginal) and relativization (marginal or perfect) in extraction from *wh*-islands[19] appears to be amenable to the same account. The relative *wh*-phrase can plausibly be referential more easily than the interrogative *wh*-phrase, which behaves more typically like a nonreferential operator.[20]

1.4.6   A-Chains and Government and Binding Chains
The evidence discussed in the previous sections thus points to the existence of a further condition on binding. For a phrase to enter a binding relation

with its trace, it must not only occupy an A-position and receive a referential θ-role. *It must also have intrinsic referential properties*—properties that allow it, for example, to be D-linked, in Pesetsky's (1987) sense, partially a matter of lexical variation (*which N̄* versus *who* (*the hell*), and so on).

We have seen that such a requirement can be built in Rizzi's (1990) system by requiring that the principle licensing referential indices be made sensitive to the intrinsic referential nature of the phrase. This additional condition on binding allows us to reconsider Rizzi's (1990) account for why NP-Movement can only enter a chain of government relations (Chomsky 1986b, sec. 11). Since NPs in NP-Movement processes (Passive, Raising, and so on), as well as in Clitic Movement, are clearly in A-positions receiving a referential θ-role at D-Structure, Rizzi (1990, chap. 3) suggests that their obligatorily entering a government-type rather than a binding-type relation is forced by an independent requirement: namely, that θ-role and Case transmission, crucially involved in such processes, is a property of chains, and that chains can be taken to be defined in terms of antecedent government. As no comparable θ-role and Case transmission are involved in Ā-relations, no requirement of antecedent government is then forced with them.

However, the suggested referentiality requirement for binding opens up a different way of interpreting the necessary antecedent government requirement on A-chains (and clitic chains). It seems plausible to say that traces of NP-Movement and Clitic Movement, unlike variables, are not referentially autonomous, in that they are only subparts of a discontinuous referential element: the A-chain (see Cinque 1989, Browning 1989a). If so, they will not be able to enter a binding relation, provided that we impose on binding the requirement that *the trace* be intrinsically referential (this being, in part, a function of the nature of its antecedent, as noted).

One desirable consequence of this analysis is that we may then keep the notion of chain for both government and binding relations—a move that is in fact necessary if Reconstruction is a property of chains (see Cinque 1982), given that binding as well as government relations display Reconstruction effects. See, for example, (35b), repeated here as (58), in which the pronominal violates Principle B of the binding theory under Reconstruction (however Reconstruction is formally derived; see Cinque 1982, Barss 1986, 1988, and references cited there):

(58) *E' a *lei*   che non so   se *Maria* abbia scritto.
    It's to *her* that I don't know whether *Maria* has written

Chains (and the concomitant property of Reconstruction) seem to find their motivation on other grounds: whenever a phrase in an A- or $\bar{A}$-position is not licensed independently of another A- or $\bar{A}$-position, it must enter a chain with it (again see Cinque 1982, for discussion along these lines). Whether it enters a binding or a government chain (where, in the latter, each link must satisfy antecedent government) will depend on the referential or nonreferential nature of the trace, which depends in turn on the referential or nonreferential nature of the operator, as noted.

Related to this is the question whether referential traces (in the above sense) can enter *both* a binding chain *and* the stricter government chain (in other, more traditional terms, whether elements participating in long *Wh*-Movement can also participate in successive cyclic *Wh*-Movement).

The implicit assumption is that they can. But one may conceive of the possibility that the two modes of connecting a phrase in an $\bar{A}$-position and its trace could be mutually exclusive, so that nonreferential phrases will enter only a government chain and referential elements only a binding chain. This possibility may be desirable on other grounds (such as parsing), as pointed out to me by Maria Teresa Guasti. (The experimental results of De Vincenzi (1989) in fact appear to lend some credence to this idea.)

This points, then, to the possible existence of two operator/variable configurations, differing "semantically" in terms of referentiality, and syntactically in terms of the kind of chain that (as a consequence of their "semantics") they are able to enter: binding chains or government chains.

Let us now consider the locality conditions on long and successive cyclic *Wh*-Movement, now identified with binding chains and (antecedent) government chains, respectively.

1.5   Chomsky's (1986b) Locality Conditions on Long and Successive Cyclic *Wh*-Movement

As noted, long *Wh*-Movement is subject to strong islands, whereas successive cyclic *Wh*-Movement is subject to both strong and weak islands.

Chomsky (1986b) proposes that the sensitivity to strong islands (as well as weak islands) manifested by successive cyclic *Wh*-Movement follows from the requirement that each link of the successive cyclic chain satisfy (antecedent) government. So, for example, in the subject, complex NP, and adjunct island cases seen above, there is a maximal projection (the subject and relative CP in the first two, and the adjunct CP or PP in the latter) that fails to be L-marked, hence functioning as a blocking category and a barrier to (antecedent) government. The sensitivity to strong islands manifested by long *Wh*-Movement follows instead from a separate principle: Subjacency.

There are thus two distinct ways to derive strong island effects, one based on government and the other on Subjacency. This amounts to building a certain redundancy into the system, though perhaps an unavoidable one, if it were the case that Subjacency effects are overridden, for successive cyclic *Wh*-Movement, by the more restrictive condition that also derives weak islands.

Chomsky (1986b) attempts to reduce this redundancy by employing a common notion of *barrier* in the formulation of (antecedent) government and Subjacency:[21]

(59) γ is a barrier for β iff (a) or (b):
   a. γ is a maximal projection which immediately dominates δ, δ a non-L-marked maximal projection dominating β. (definition of barrier "by inheritance")
   b. γ is a non-L-marked maximal projection dominating β, $\gamma \neq$ IP. (definition of "inherent" barrier)

These definitions give some form to the intuitive idea of Cattell (1976) and others that every maximal projection that is not the complement of a lexical category is a barrier (except IP). And they add that even a maximal projection that is a complement of a lexical category becomes a barrier for some element if it immediately dominates another barrier (or IP) dominating that element. We will come back later to the apparent special character of IP in Chomsky's (1986b) definition of barrier.[22]

The definition of barrier (59) takes part in both the definition of (antecedent) government (60) and that of Subjacency (61).

(60) α governs β iff α m-commands β and *there is no γ, γ a barrier for β*, such that γ excludes α. (= (18) of Chomsky 1986b, 9)[23]

(61) β is subjacent to α iff there are fewer than two *barriers for β* that exclude α. (see (59) of Chomsky 1986b, 30 and corresponding text)

By utilizing the same notion of barrier for the theories of government and bounding (Subjacency), Chomsky thus aims at a unified approach to these theories and at the elimination of the redundancy noted above in the derivation of strong islands.

The unification (and the concomitant elimination of the redundancy) is only partial, however. First, because *one* barrier suffices to derive strong islands for government, whereas *two* are needed to derive them for Subjacency—clearly a residue of asymmetry. Second, because two additional notions of barrier are introduced, one holding exclusively of government (the "minimality" barrier), the other exclusively of Subjacency (the weak barrier constituted by the most embedded IP, or CP, designed specially for *wh*-islands)—another instance of asymmetry. Third, because the notion of barrier holding of government and Subjacency can be given a unified definition only at a certain cost. As we will see, the notion of barrier by inheritance can be dispensed with for government but is crucial for Subjacency, so that the retention of a unified notion ultimately entails a redundancy (for government).

It would be desirable to eliminate these asymmetries and redundancies between the theories of government and bounding, or at least to minimize them, if we were to discover an irreducible residue of difference. I attempt this in the next section. After eliminating some such asymmetries and redundancies, I arrive in fact at the conclusion that a residue of difference exists and that it may be convenient to expose it in a perspicuous way. In section 1.7 I formulate this residue of difference in the form of two (minimally) different definitions of barrier: one for government chains and the other for binding chains, in the sense of section 1.4.

1.6   Simplifying Chomsky's (1986b) Locality Conditions

1.6.1   Eliminating the Notion of Minimality Barrier
Let us begin with the notion of minimality barrier, which holds of government alone (Chomsky 1986b, 42). If we could eliminate it entirely, the theories of government and bounding would come one step closer together. This indeed appears feasible.

Chomsky (1986b) defines the notion of minimality barrier as follows (see (92) and corresponding text):

(62)   In the configuration ...α...$[\gamma$...δ...$\beta]$, γ is a barrier for β if γ is the immediate projection of δ, a zero-level category distinct from β.[24]

In addition to its role in barring government by a head into the domain of another head, the minimality barrier has two further consequences in Chomsky's analysis. The first is to block the extraction of an adjunct from a complex NP of the noun complement type, independently of choice of inherent barriers. For example, in (63) $\bar{N}$ qualifies as a minimality barrier, thus blocking antecedent government of t'' by t''', even if CP and NP were not to qualify as barriers:

(63)   *How did John [$_{VP}$ t''' announce [$_{NP}$ a [$_{\bar{N}}$ plan [$_{CP}$ t'' to [$_{VP}$ t' fix the car t]]]]]?

The second consequence of the minimality barrier is that it seems to provide an analysis of *that*-trace effects:

(64) *Who did you believe [$_{CP}$ t' [$_{\bar{C}}$ that [$_{IP}$ t would win]]]?

In (64) $\bar{C}$ qualifies as a minimality barrier (when C is lexical), thus blocking antecedent government of *t* by *t'*.

It appears, however, that the latter two results of the notion of minimality barrier follow from independent principles. Concerning the complex NP case (63), there is evidence that an inherent barrier is indeed present. As Chomsky notes elsewhere (1986b, 36), that the CP complement of N may be a barrier is suggested, if Stowell's (1981) theory is correct, by the fact that the complementizer of CP cannot be missing (*John expressed the feeling *(that) the meeting should not be held*). This conclusion is confirmed by the impossibility of genuine complement extraction from such a CP. Chomsky (1986b, 35) contrasts the ill-formed (63) with the almost unexceptionable (65):

(65) (?)Which book did John announce a plan (for you) to read?

But (65) is not really representative, because it involves an NP gap, which, if we are right, can be related to an antecedent via a different strategy (see chapter 3). Indeed, if we select a PP complement, which has no access to such a strategy, the result is clearly ungrammatical:

(66) *With whom did John announce a plan to go out?

This points to the barrierhood of CP, and that of NP, by inheritance. As to why the complement CP of a noun should count as a barrier, Chomsky (1986b, 36 and sec. 11) suggests that nouns may not be L-markers, and Grimshaw (1990) gives ample evidence that they are defective θ- (hence, L-)markers.

The second alleged consequence of minimality, the derivation of *that*-trace effects, raises certain conceptual problems: Why should an empty C not trigger a minimality violation? Why does *that* not trigger a minimality violation with simple adjunct extractions *How did you say that he fixed the car?*)?

Besides, an independent way exists to derive *that*-trace effects that does not incur these problems: the condition of head government, imposed on the trace over and above antecedent government (see Rizzi 1990, chap. 2, Koopman and Sportiche 1988, Longobardi 1985b, forthcoming).[25]

Thus, adjunct extraction from noun complements and *that*-trace effects do not provide any independent grounds for a notion of minimality barrier.

This leaves us with the original motivation for minimality: the necessity of preventing a head from governing into the domain of another head. But this can be expressed without recourse to a notion of minimality barrier valid for government alone. For example, if Rizzi's (1990) notion of *Relativized Minimality* is adopted, this result follows independently.

(67) *Relativized Minimality*

X α-governs Y only if there is no Z such that

a. Z is a potential α-governor for Y, and

b. Z c-commands Y and does not c-command X

(where α ranges over *heads*, A-specifiers, or Ā-specifiers)

The intuitive idea expressed by (67) is that minimality effects are triggered only in the presence of intervening elements of the same type: heads for head government, and A- and Ā-specifiers for antecedent government in A- and Ā-chains, respectively. So, government by a head X into the c-domain of another head Z is barred even in the absence of a special notion of minimality barrier, which can thus be eliminated altogether (along with the problems outlined in note 25). See Rizzi 1990 for further discussion of these and related issues.

Now, if it were also possible to eliminate the special notion of barrier valid for Subjacency only (the most embedded tensed IP, or CP, barrier), then we would have a truly unified notion of barrier (of the inherent and inheritance varieties) for both government and bounding.

Let us suppose that this is possible (I will come back to this issue in section 1.9, suggesting that it is). An asymmetry persists, however, despite the higher degree of unification attained: the fact that one barrier is sufficient for government but two are needed for bounding.

Is this really so for all cases? A still higher degree of unification could perhaps be reached, if we could show that even for bounding one barrier suffices (at least, for a proper subset of its cases). We will explore the feasibility of this further simplification starting from a particular redundancy hidden in the *Barriers* system: namely, the fact that the notion of barrier by inheritance for government is almost always redundant, and, where prima facie it is not, it can apparently be eliminated.

1.6.2 A Redundancy: The Notion of Barrier by Inheritance for Government (and Bounding)

Let us begin with strong islands. The notion of inherent barrier appears to be sufficient to derive them:

(68) a. *Subject island*

    *Non so   come$_i$ [$_{IP}$[$_{CP}$ poterla riparare t_i] sarebbe utile].

    I don't know how   to be able to fix it   would be useful

  b. *Complex NP island*

    i. *Non so   come$_i$ giustifichino [$_{NP}$ quelli

       I don't know how they justify   those

       [$_{CP}$ che l'hanno riparato t_i]].

       who fixed it

    ii. *Non so   come$_i$ giustifichino [$_{NP}$ i tentativi

       I don't know how they justify   the attempts

       [$_{CP}$ di liberarlo t_i]].

       to free him

  c. *Adjunct island*

    *Non so   come$_i$ [$_{IP}$ fosse entrato   [$_{CP}$ che piangeva t_i]].

    I don't know how   he had gone in   while she cried

In all of (68a–c) (and the same is true of the other strong islands), there is an inherent barrier, the non-L-marked CP, which blocks antecedent government quite independently of the barriers by inheritance IP, NP, NP, and IP, respectively.

The same conclusion holds for some of the weak islands, factive and extraposition CPs. The reason is the same, if—as is generally assumed—the CP is not L-marked (and hence is a barrier). See Kayne 1984 and section 1.7.1.

(69) *Factive island*

    *Non so   come$_i$ si sia pentito [$_{CP}$ di essersi comportato t_i].

    I don't know how he repented   of having behaved

(70) *Extraposition island*

    *Non so   come$_i$ vi potrebbe danneggiare

    I don't know how it could harm you

    [$_{CP}$ che si comportasse t_i].

    that he behaved

True enough, certain cases exist that would seem to require a notion of barrier by inheritance even for government. For each of them, however, there is an independent way to block government that does not involve such a notion.

The first has to do with government across sentential maximal projections. As shown by Kayne (1984), government must be permitted to cross a CP (as in the case of a V head governing a trace in Spec CP), just as it is permitted to cross IP (as in exceptional Case marking, Raising, and other cases). If so, neither CP nor IP must count as an inherent barrier (when the CP is L-marked). Nonetheless, one must ensure that in (71) the verb does not come to govern the Spec IP:

(71) John decided [$_{CP}$ *e* [$_{IP}$ PRO to see the movie]].

So it must be that CP counts as a barrier by inheritance, blocking government.[26] But this conclusion is not necessary. The notion of Relativized Minimality suffices to block government of a head across CP and IP since another head, C (itself inert for government), intervenes.

A second case, discussed by Chomsky (1986b), that would seem to crucially involve the notion of barrier by inheritance for government is provided by adjunct extraction from a *wh*-island:

(72) *How did Bill [$_{VP}$ *t'''* [$_{VP}$ wonder [$_{CP*}$ who [$_{IP}$[$_{VP}$ *t''*
    [$_{VP}$ wanted [$_{CP}$ *t'* [$_{IP}$ to fix the car *t*]]]]]]]]?

Here, no inherent barrier intervenes between any of the pairs of positions $\{t, t'\}$, $\{t', t''\}$, $\{t'', t'''\}$, $\{t''', how\}$. But since extraction is forbidden, there must be a barrier. The barrier by inheritance (from IP), CP*, is apparently the only candidate—whence the conclusion that this notion is crucial for government too. But, once again, that conclusion is not necessary, at least if we adopt Relativized Minimality (which is violated in (72) by the intervention of *who* between *t''* and *t'''*).

It thus seems that there is no real need for a notion of barrier by inheritance in the case of government. It is completely redundant, its effects following either from the notion of inherent barrier or from that of Relativized Minimality.

Suppose that, following the fruitful practice of eliminating redundancies from the system, we discard the notion of barrier by inheritance from the theory of government (adopting Relativized Minimality). By doing so, however, we introduce a new asymmetry between government and bounding (Subjacency). The notion of barrier by inheritance now holds of the latter theory only.

Related to this asymmetry appears to be the other noted by Chomsky (1986b) that one barrier suffices for government, whereas two are apparently needed for Subjacency. The barrier by inheritance provides the extra barrier needed for Subjacency. However, there is evidence, to be reviewed directly, that at least for the derivation of strong islands, *one* barrier (an inherent barrier) is sufficient even for the theory of bounding. This will force us to reconsider the very opportunity of retaining the notion of barrier by inheritance even for bounding.

Three cases falling under Subjacency, where there is but one barrier, are complement extraction from (certain) adjuncts, complement extraction from relative clauses extraposed from an object, and complement extraction from degree clauses (the CP associated with such adjectival modifiers as *too* and *enough*). Let us begin with the first case, exemplified in (73) (recall that, to be sure we are dealing with real movement, we must select a non-NP target):

(73) *To whom$_i$ did [$_{IP}$ they leave [$_{PP}$ before speaking t_i]]?

Chomsky (1986b, 31) suggests that this case of Huang's (1982) Condition on Extraction Domains (CED) follows from (1-) Subjacency in that the adverbial PP qualifies as an (inherent) barrier (it is not L-marked) and transmits barrierhood to IP so that two barriers are crossed simultaneously. But this account crucially presupposes that the adjunct inside IP be excluded by VP, as shown in (74a). If it were adjoined to VP, as in (74b), then *to whom* could itself adjoin to VP, thus voiding the barrierhood of IP and consequently crossing only one barrier (PP).

(74) a. ...[$_{IP}$ they [$_{VP}$ leave] [$_{PP}$ before ... t ...]]
      b. ...[$_{IP}$ they [$_{VP}$ t' [$_{VP}$[$_{VP}$ leave] [$_{PP}$ before ... t ...]]]]

There is in fact evidence from VP-Preposing and *do so* substitution that the adverbial PP in (73) can be adjoined to VP:[27]

(75) a. ... and leave before speaking to John, they certainly did.
      b. They left before speaking to John, and I did so too.

Therefore, it must be concluded that *to whom* has crossed only one (inherent) barrier and that that suffices to trigger a Subjacency violation.[28]

A comparable conclusion can be reached on the basis of complement extraction from a relative clause extraposed from an object, if, as is standardly assumed, the extraposed CP is in this case adjoined to VP.[29] See the ungrammaticality of (76b), derived from (76a) by crossing only one barrier (CP):[30]

(76) a. Avevo [$_{VP}$[$_{VP}$ presentato qualcuno t] a Gianni
         I had introduced   someone   to Gianni
         [$_{CP}$ che voleva parlare   con sua figlia]].
              who wanted to speak with his daughter
      b. *Con chi$_i$ avevi [$_{VP}$[$_{VP}$ presentato [$_{NP}$ qualcuno t] a Gianni]
         with whom had you introduced   someone   to Gianni
         [$_{CP}$ che voleva parlare t_i]]?
              who wanted to speak

Degree clauses also qualify as strong islands, as shown by (77a–b), in spite of the fact that they contain only one (inherent) barrier, the extraposed CP complement of *too* and *enough* (see Chomsky 1986b, 33ff.):[31]

(77) a. *To whom were they [AP too angry [CP PRO to talk *t*]]?

   b. *To whom were they [AP angry enough [CP PRO not to talk *t*]]?

The existence of cases such as these, where only one (inherent) barrier suffices to trigger a Subjacency violation, raises the question whether we really need two barriers in the remaining cases falling under Subjacency. In the other strong islands (CP and NP subjects, complex NPs, and so on) an inherent barrier also exists, the non-L-marked CP* and NP* of (78)–(79), which could well suffice to trigger a Subjecency violation, by analogy with the case just considered of adjunct, extraposed relative, and degree clauses:

(78) a. *?A chi*i*   credi   che [IP [CP* parlare *t*i] sarebbe vitale]?
         to whom do you think that   to speak   would be vital
   b.   *Whom*i* did [IP[NP* your interest in *t*i] disturb John]?

(79) a. *A chi*i*   hai conosciuto [NP qualcuno
         to whom have you met   someone
         [CP* che volesse parlare *t*i]]?
               who wanted to speak
   b.   *Con chi*i*   avete discusso   [NP la possibilità
         with whom have you discussed   the possibility
         [CP* di uscire *t*i]]?
               of going out

The logic of the matter is clear. Since there are at least three strong islands for which one inherent barrier must suffice to trigger a bounding violation, and since all other strong islands also contain an inherent barrier (in addition to a barrier by inheritance: IP and NP in (78) and (79), respectively), barriers by inheritance come to be entirely redundant for bounding as well, with respect to the class of strong islands.

   The second conclusion is that, for strong islands, Subjacency must apparently qualify as 0- rather than 1-Subjacency, in Chomsky's (1986b) terms.

   Let us summarize the discussion so far.

   In attempting to attain a higher degree of unification of the theories of government and bounding, we have seen that it is possible to dispose of the government notion of minimality barrier, adopting Relativized Minimality. We have also seen that the notion of barrier by inheritance (and the concomitant redundancy) can be eliminated from the theory of government, and even from the theory of bounding, at least for the class of strong islands.

It would thus appear possible to attain an extreme degree of unification and simplification of the notion of barrier valid for the two theories (any non-L-marked XP). But there is a residue, the weak islands, which constitute a barrier for government, though not for bounding. See the contrasts in (4)–(7), repeated here:

(4) Wh-*island*
   a. ??To whom didn't they know when to give their present *t*?
   b. *How did they ask you who behaved *t*?
(5) *Inner (negative) island*
   a. To whom didn't you speak *t*?
   b. *How didn't you behave *t*?
(6) *Factive island*
   a. To whom do you regret that you could not speak *t*?
   b. *How do you regret that you behaved *t*?
(7) *Extraposition island*
   a. To whom is it time to speak *t*?
   b. *How is it time to behave *t*?

If the contrasts in (4) and (5) can be attributed to the independent application of Relativized Minimality and are thus compatible with the unified notion of inherent barrier, those in (6) and (7) cannot. The (inherent) barrier that suffices to block government must not suffice to block binding. The latter class of weak islands thus appears to constitute the ineliminable residue of difference between government and binding/bounding.

The *Barriers* approach, though keeping a (largely) unified notion of (inherent and inheritance) barrier, expresses this residue of difference in the *number* of barriers relevant for government (one) and for bounding (two). We have seen, however, that quite apart from the cost inherent in this (in terms of redundancies), the choice of expressing the difference between the two theories in terms of the number of barriers crossed fails in at least some cases, where one barrier must suffice even for bounding.[32]

This suggests, then, the opportunity of exploring the other logical possibility for expressing the above residue of difference. Instead of taking the notion of barrier to be the same and only the number of barriers to be different for the two theories, one can envisage the possibility that the notion of barrier itself is (partially) different for the two theories, while the number of barriers involved remains constant (one). This is the line that I will pursue in the next section (see Manzini 1988 for a proposal in the same spirit).

1.7 Locality Conditions on Binding and Government Chains

1.7.1 The Definition of Barrier for Binding (the Theory of Bounding)

What appears to distinguish strong from weak islands is the fact that (with the exception of preverbal sentential subjects in Romance, English, and the like) strong islands are all cases of maximal projections that are neither L-marked nor θ-marked (by a $[+V]$ element),[33] whereas weak islands are all θ-marked maximal projections. This is clearly the case for *wh*-islands, which are even L-marked by a $[+V]$ element (when complements of a V or A), but it is also the case for such other weak islands as the sentential complements of factive and manner-of-speaking verbs, and the extraposed subject clauses of transitive, unergative, and psych-movement verbs. Let us briefly consider each case in turn.

The CP complements of factive and manner-of-speaking verbs are presumably θ-marked by these verbs as internal arguments, under VP. Some evidence for this is provided by the fact that their infinitival complements in Italian are (obligatorily) introduced by the complementizer *di* '(lit.) of' (*Deploro/rimpiango/etc.* [di *non averlo potuto leggere*] 'I deplore/regret/etc. not to have been able to read it'): a clear diagnostic, in this language, of internal argumenthood (see Cinque 1990a).

Their weak islandhood suggests that they are not L-marked by the V. If L-marking is defined (as in Chomsky 1986b, 14) *as direct θ-marking by a lexical head* (*where α directly θ-marks β if α and β are sisters, that is, are dominated by the same lexical projections*), then factive and manner-of-speaking complements must not be dominated by $\bar{V}$, as ordinary direct objects are. In fact, Kayne (1981b, fn. 23) provides evidence that manner-of-speaking verbs must be higher than direct objects, in fact even higher than indirect objects.[34]

The same is presumably true of factive complements. (See Cardinaletti's (1989a, chap. 3) argument based on German that they are higher than $\bar{V}$ and not dominated by NP, contra Kiparsky and Kiparsky 1970). See also Koster 1989 for the conclusion that the preverbal position of factive CPs in Dutch is derived (hence different from that of NPs). The extraposed sentential subject of transitive and unergative verbs is an external argument in VP-adjoined position, an A-position, as argued in much recent work (see, among others, Koopman and Sportiche 1988, Belletti 1988). In other words, it is *indirectly* θ-marked by the verb, but not L-marked, as required.

Finally, the extraposed sentential subject of unergative psych-verbs of the *worry, frighten* class is also in VP-adjoined (hence, non-L-marked) position at S-Structure, though it is clearly θ-marked by the verb (in fact, as an internal argument, at D-Structure, if Belletti and Rizzi (1988) are right).[35]

One could thus conceive of retaining the notion of (inherent) barrier based on L-marking for government relations, and of introducing a new notion of (inherent) barrier for binding relations (long movement), based on the somewhat looser condition of θ-marking (direct or indirect).

This is the alternative way, mentioned above, of expressing the ineliminable difference between government and binding/bounding. Strong islands are barriers for both government and binding, because they are neither L-marked nor θ-marked maximal projections. Weak islands are barriers to government but not binding, because they are not L-marked, but are θ-marked maximal projections.

The apparently exceptional behavior of preverbal sentential subjects, which, though (indirectly) θ-marked, nonetheless qualify as barriers for binding relations (that is, as strong rather than weak islands), can be brought under the aegis of "normality," if we introduce into the definition of barrier for binding the notion of *canonical direction* proposed by Kayne (1983) and others:[36]

(80) *Definition of barrier for binding* (first approximation)
   Every maximal projection that is not θ-marked in the canonical direction is a barrier for binding.

Some evidence that the requirement of canonical direction is a weaker condition additional to, and distinct from, the fundamental requirement of θ-marking is apparently provided by the fact that complement extraction from preverbal sentential subjects gives rise to an ungrammaticality milder than that produced by extracting a complement from the other strong islands (which violate the stricter θ-marking requirement). See the contrast between (81) and (82a–e):[37]

(81) ??Una persona a cui$_i$ credo   [$_{CP}$ che
   a person   to whom I think   that
   [$_{IP}$[$_{CP}$ riuscire a parlare t_i oggi] sarà impossibile]]...
   to be able to speak today will be impossible

(82) a. *Una persona a cui$_i$ sono uscito
   a person   to whom I went out
   [$_{PP}$ senza riuscire a parlare t_i]...
   without being able to talk

b. *Una persona a cui$_i$ ho incontrato
   a person   to whom I met
   [$_{NP}$[$_{CP}$ chi è riuscito a parlare t_i]]...
            who managed to speak

c. *Una person a cui$_i$ sono troppo arrabbiato
   a person   to whom I am too angry
   [$_{PP}$ per parlare t_i]...
        to talk

d. *Una persona a cui$_i$ io ho tanti soldi
   a person   to whom I have as much money
   [$_{CP}$ quanti Carlo ne ha regalati t_i in un giorno]...
        as Carlo gave in one day

e. *Una persona a cui$_i$ erano così arrabbiati
   a person   to whom they were so angry
   [$_{CP}$ che non hanno voluto parlare t_i]...
        that they didn't want to speak

The contrast can be explained as a consequence of the fact that the stricter θ-marking requirement is violated in (82a–e), but not in (81), which merely violates the canonical direction requirement.[38] In the present analysis, the special status of preverbal sentential subjects is thus expected to be a feature of binding alone (being due to an at least partial satisfaction of binding requirements). It is not expected to extend to government. And, indeed, no contrast is found between sentential subjects and the other strong islands in adjunct extraction (that is, with government relations). For example:

(83) *Il modo in cui$_i$ [$_{IP}$[$_{CP}$ formulare la richiesta t_i]
     the way in which   to phrase the demand
     sarebbe un errore]...
     would be a mistake

(84) a. *Il modo in cui$_i$ sono uscito [$_{PP}$ senza formulare
        the way in which I went out   without phrasing
        la richiesta t_i]...
        the demand

     b. *Il modo in cui$_i$ conosco [$_{NP}$[$_{CP}$ chi ha formulato
        the way in which I know   who phrased
        la richiesta t_i]]...
        the demand

   c. *Il modo in cui$_i$ sono troppo arrabbiato [$_{PP}$ per formulare
      the way in which I am too angry   to phrase
      la richiesta t_i]...
      the demand

This is not surprising, since sentential subjects fail to be L-marked, just like any other strong island.

   Let us return to the notion of barrier for binding chains, which needs to be further qualified. Though θ-marked in the canonical direction, complements of nouns and prepositions (that is, [−V] categories) still appear to qualify as strong islands for binding. This suggests the need to introduce in the definition of barrier for binding the specification that only [+V] categories are capable of lifting the barrierhood of a maximal projection:

(85) *Definition of barrier for binding* (revised)
     Every maximal projection that is not θ-marked *by a* [+V] *category* in the canonical direction is a barrier for binding.

   Let us consider the relevant evidence, beginning with Ns. As (86a–b) show, extraction (of non-NPs, for the noted reasons) from a maximal projection θ-marked in the canonical direction by a [−V, +N] category is impossible (the asterisk in (86) suggests, incidentally, that antecedent government, to which we will return, is also impossible in the same context):[39]

(86) a. *Gianni, da cui$_i$ disapprovo i tentativi
        Gianni by whom I disapprove the attempts
        [$_{CP}$ di andare a stare t_i],...
              to stay
     b. *Maria, alla quale$_i$ hanno respinto l'insinuazione
        Maria to whom   they rejected the insinuation
        [$_{CP}$ di aver raccontato tutto t_i],...
        of having told   everything

Of course, the possibility of (limited) cases of reanalysis should be pointed out. With such expressions as *avere l'impressione* 'have the impression', *avere speranza* 'have hopes', *make the claim, express a desire*, and the like, even extraction of non-NPs is possible:[40]

(87) a. Gianni, al quale$_i$ ho l'impressione   che non vogliano
        Gianni to whom I have the impression that they don't want
        parlare t_i,...
        to speak
     b. John, to whom$_i$ I made the claim you would never talk t_i,...

The peculiar behavior of such complex NPs was noted by Ross (1967, 139ff.), who observed one fact that can be taken as evidence that they indeed involve "reanalysis" of some sort. The complementizer *that* in English can be omitted in the complement of Vs but not in that of Ns:[41]

(88) a. Kleene proved (that) this set is recursive.
     b. The proof *(that) this set is recursive is difficult.

The *that* following the N of such "modal" expressions as *have hopes* and *make the claim* can, on the other hand, be omitted:[42]

(89) a. ?I'm making the claim the company squandered the money.
     b. I have a feeling the company will squander the money.

The paradigm can be regularized if the sentence is taken to be a complement of a reanalyzed (V + N) V rather than of an N.[43] In most cases a single V exists that corresponds to the V + N complex: *have hopes – hope*, *make the claim – claim*, and so on.

Let us now turn to extractions from the sentential complement of a preposition, beginning with Italian.

At first sight, the well-formedness of the following examples would seem to provide evidence against (85):

(90) a. Un argomento di cui$_i$ non sono disposto a parlare t_i...
        a topic   about which I am not willing   to speak
     b. Una persona a cui$_i$ mi pento di non aver parlato t_i...
        a person   to whom I regret   not to have spoken

(90a–b) contain predicates that subcategorize for a PP headed by *a* and *di*, respectively. This can be seen from the ability of the Ps to be followed, with the same predicates, by a lexical NP instead of the infinitive:

(91) a. Sono disposto al ritiro.
        I am ready for the withdrawal
     b. Mi pento del mio gesto.
        I regret my gesture

It would thus seem plausible to analyze (90a–b) as instantiating the structure in (92),

(92) ...[$_{PP}$[$_P$ *a/di*] [$_{CP}$[$_{IP}$ PRO V$_{Infinitive}$...]]]...

parallel to the structure [$_{PP}$[$_P$ *a/di*] [$_{NP}$...]] exemplified by (91).

These cases are generally taken to contrast with such cases as (93),

(93) a. Lui ha continuato a parlare.
        he went on talking

b. Lui cercava di parlare.

  he was trying to talk

for which the absence of corresponding *a NP, di NP* sequences (**Ho continuato alla lettura* 'he continued to the reading'; **Lui cercava del colloquio* 'he tried of the talk') renders it plausible to analyze *a* and *di* not as prepositions taking sentential objects but as infinitival complementizers followed by IP (for discussion along these general lines. See Kayne 1984, chap. 5, Rizzi 1982, chap. 3, and Manzini 1980).

If this standard analysis of (90)–(93) were correct, the conclusion that XP complements of $[-V]$ categories are barriers for binding would indeed be falsified by the well-formedness of (90).

Before concluding from this that reference to $[+V]$ categories in (85) is to be abandoned, we must be sure that the standard analysis is indeed correct. A deeper scrutiny, however, suggests that it is not.

One relevant observation is that, quite generally, the preposition of subcategorized PPs in Italian cannot take a sentential object.[44] This is illustrated in (94)–(96), where the (a) cases show the P followed by a nominal object, the (b) cases a P followed by a tensed sentential object, and the (c) cases a P followed by an infinitival sentential object. The latter two cases are systematically excluded:[45]

(94) a. Contavo   [sul [$_{NP}$ la sua onestà]].

    I was counting on   his honesty

  b. *Contavo   [su [$_{CP}$ che Gianni fosse onesto]].

    I was counting on   that Gianni was honest

  c. *Contavo   [su [$_{CP}$ PRO essere onesto]].

    I was counting on   to be honest

(95) a. L'ho dedotto [da   [$_{NP}$ l loro silenzio]].

    I deduced it   from   their silence

  b. *L'ho dedotto [da   [$_{CP}$ che non sono stato accettato]].

    I deduced it   from   that I was not accepted

  c. *L'ho dedotto [da   [$_{CP}$ PRO non essere stato accettato]].

    I deduced it   from   not to have been accepted

(96) a. La sua fortuna consiste [in [$_{NP}$ questo]].

    his luck consists   in   this

  b. *La sua fortuna consiste [in [$_{CP}$ che ha molti amici]].

    his luck consists   in   that he has many friends

  c. *La sua fortuna consiste [in [$_{CP}$ PRO avere molti amici]].

    his luck consists   in   to have many friends

The generalization that subcategorized Ps in Italian cannot take a sentential object has apparently only two (partial) exceptions: the prepositions *a* and *di*. *A* 'to/at', when subcategorized, can be followed by a sentential object.[46] For example:

(97) a.   Sono contrario al [la tua partenza].
           I am against   to your departure
     b.   %Sono contrario a [che tu parta subito].
           I am against   to that you leave immediately
     c.   Sono contrario a [partire subito].
           I am against   to leaving immediately

("%" indicates that (97b) belongs to a more formal style than either (97a) or (97c).)

The preposition *di* can apparently also be followed by a sentential object, but only when it is infinitival. For example:

(98) a.   Sono contento del [la tua partenza].
           I am glad   of   your departure
     b.   *Sono contento di [che tu parta subito].[47]
           I am glad   of that you leave immediately
     c.   Sono contento di [partire subito].
           I am glad   of to leave immediately

Note that if we abstract from the well-formedness of (97b), which belongs, in any event, to a different stylistic level, the behavior of the two prepositions becomes entirely parallel. The only normal type of sentential object they accept is the *infinitival* sentence.

This exception to the generalization that ("subcategorized") Ps in Italian do not take sentential objects is very curious. For it is a striking coincidence that the only Ps *partially* contradicting that generalization (in that they may be followed by infinitival, though not tensed, sentences) are *a* and *di*, which we know independently have a usage as infinitival complementizers too.

The partial exception disappears if, instead, we take all instances of *a* and *di* followed by an infinitival sentence to be instances of their use as infinitival complementizers, even when they follow predicates that otherwise subcategorize for a PP headed by the preposition *a* or *di* (followed by an NP).

If we assume that, then the generalization turns out to hold virtually absolutely,[48] and the strange limitation of *a* and *di* to infinitival complements is explained.

If so, the cases in (90) cease to be evidence that extraction from the complement of a P in Italian (perhaps, more generally, in Romance)[49] is admitted. *A* and *di* are in the C of a subcategorized CP, which is quite compatible with the idea that CP complements of Ps are islands.

There is comfirming evidence that such an extraction is indeed impossible. Recall that, in a more formal style of Italian, the P *a* must indeed be assumed to "subcategorize" for a CP, which can be either tensed or infinitival (the only marked real exception to the noted generalization; see (97)). If so, we do have a genuine case of the configuration (99), in Italian, in which to test the above prediction.

(99) ...$[_V[_{PP} P[_{CP}[_{IP}...t...]]]]$

The prediction is borne out, since extraction of a non-NP from a tensed complement of *a* appears to be impossible:

(100) a. *Carlo, [con il quale]$_i$
           Carlo   with whom
           sono favorevole $[_{PP}$ a [che parlino t_i]],...[50]
           I am in favor   that they speak

      b. *Questo affare, [di cui]$_i$ sono contrario $[_{PP}$ a $[_{CP}$ che trattiate t_i
           this business   of which I am against   that you deal
           con loro]],...
           with them

These cases contrast with the following cases of "apparent NP extraction," which are uniformly judged to be (relatively) acceptable:

(101) a. ?Questa disputa, che$_i$ sono favorevole
           this controversy which I am in favor
           $[_{PP}$ a $[_{CP}$ che voi dirimiate t_i al più presto]],...
              of   that you settle   as soon as possible

      b. Questo affare, che$_i$ sono contrario $[_{PP}$ a
           this business   which I am against   to
           $[_{CP}$ che trattiate t_i con loro]],...
           that you deal with them

This is not surprising given the possibility (to be justified in chapter 3) of analyzing these structures in terms of $\bar{A}$-bound pros rather than in terms of genuine extraction with $\bar{A}$-chain formation.[51] On the basis of these facts, we thus conclude that the notion of barrier for binding (85) should indeed make reference to a [+ V] category. If "preposition stranding" as found in English, though not in Romance, implies that the preposition is nondistinct from a verb (see below for discussion), then a specific prediction follows:

that extraction from a CP governed by a ("subcategorized") P should be possible in English but not in Romance, since the CP is a maximal projection θ-marked in the canonical direction by a [+V] category.

The prediction does not seem to be testable, however, given that CPs governed by a subcategorized P are disallowed in English as they are in Italian. One construction instantiating structure (99) would seem to be the NP-*ing* construction exemplified by such cases as *I was counting on [him giving a present to Mary]*. But Reuland (1983) provides evidence that the appropriate analysis construes the preposition in the C of the gerundive clause, so that the well-formedness of (102) is not informative:[52]

(102) a. The girl to whom$_i$ he was counting [$_{CP}$ on [them giving a present t_i]]...

   b. The man from whom$_i$ we were looking forward [$_{CP}$ to [PRO receiving a letter t_i]]...

   c. The man to whom$_i$ they insisted [$_{CP}$ on [PRO sending an invitation t_i]]...

To summarize, we have seen that for binding to be possible, three requirements must be met simultaneously: that every maximal projection dominating the trace and not dominating the antecedent be (1) θ-marked (either directly or indirectly) (2) by a [+V] category, (3) in the canonical direction. If any one of these requirements is violated, the maximal projection counts as a barrier for binding and binding is impossible (even if the other requirements are satisfied).

The relevant examples showing a selective violation of each of these requirements are reproduced here for convenience:

(103) *Requirement of θ-marking*
   *Gianni, a cui$_i$ me ne sono andato [$_{PP}$ senza parlare t_i],...
   Gianni to whom I went away   without speaking

(104) *Requirement of θ-marking by a [+V] category*
   *Gianni, da cui$_i$ disapprovo [$_{NP}$ i tentativi
   Gianni by whom I disapprove   the attempts
   [$_{CP}$ di andare a stare t_i]],...
       to stay

(105) *Requirement of canonical direction*
   ??Gianni, a cui   non so   se [parlare t oggi]
   Gianni to whom I don't know if   to speak today
   sarà possibile,...
   will be possible

We will return to the status of VP and IP with respect to the notion of barrier for binding after considering the notion of barrier for (antecedent) government. VP and IP will be shown not to constitute a barrier for either binding or (antecedent) government.

1.7.2 The Definition of Barrier for Government

Let us consider more closely the notion of barrier for government assumed so far (in essence, Chomsky's (1986b) notion of inherent barrier, that is, any non-L-marked maximal projection).

Chomsky's (1986b) notion of L-marking as direct θ-marking by a lexical head appears to make the right prediction for a class of cases not yet considered: indirect CP complements. If "direct θ-marking" implies that the θ-marker and the θ-markee are sisters, then it follows (if Kayne's (1984) binary branching hypothesis is correct) that indirect CP complements will not be L-marked, hence will be barriers to antecedent government relations. This appears to be correct, to judge from the following cases, where an adjunct is extracted from an indirect CP complement in Italian:[53]

(106) a. *La ragione per la quale$_k$ [$_{VP}$[$_{\overline{V}}$ lo informò]
      the reason for which   he informed him
      [$_{CP}$ di essersene andato t_k]]...
      to have left

   b. *Il modo in cui$_k$ [$_{VP}$[$_{\overline{V}}$ l'ho minacciato]
      the way in which   I menaced him
      [$_{CP}$ di comportarmi in pubblico t_k]]...
      to behave in public

(107) a. *E' [per aiutarlo]$_k$ che [$_{VP}$[$_{\overline{V}}$ mi ha convinto]
      it is to help him   that   he convinced me
      [$_{CP}$ che avrei dovuto andarmene t_k]].
      that I should have left

   b. *Il modo in cui$_k$ [$_{VP}$[$_{\overline{V}}$ mi ha costretto]
      the way in which   he forced me
      [$_{CP}$ a comportarmi t_k]]...
      to behave

If the NP-*ing* constructions of (102) are CPs, and if they are outside $\overline{V}$ (being indirect complements of the V), then the impossibility of adjunct extraction from them lends further support to the idea that L-marking involves direct θ-marking as Chomsky (1986b) proposes:

(108) a. *How were you counting on him behaving in public?
   b. *How strong do you look forward to drinking your coffee?

As with the notion of θ-marking entering into the notion of barrier for binding, the *Barriers* notion of L-marking must, however, be restricted to [+ V] lexical heads. This is because neither nouns nor prepositions are apparently capable of L-marking their CP complements. For nouns, this was already pointed out in connection with such cases as (63), repeated here without structure as (109):

(109) *How did John announce a plan to fix the car?

Cases such as (110) show that the same holds for prepositions:

(110) In che modo$_k$ eravate contrari [$_{PP}$ a
       in which way were you against   to
       [$_{CP}$ che lo trattassimo t_k]]?
         that we treated him

The need to refer to [+ V] categories in the definitions of barrier for both binding and government thus renders the two notions interestingly symmetrical (at least in part):

(111) a. *Definition of barrier for binding*
          Every maximal projection that is not θ-marked by a [+ V]
          category in the canonical direction is a barrier for binding.
       b. *Definition of barrier for government*
          Every maximal projection that is not L-marked by a [+ V]
          category is a barrier for government.

In the next section we will consider further amending both definitions by referring to the more general notion of *selection*.

1.7.3 A Refinement: The Role of Selection

Consider the status of VP and IP with respect to the definition of barrier for government. These maximal projections are not L-marked because I and C are not lexical categories (and presumably because they also fail to θ-mark VP and IP, respectively; on I, see further below). Hence, they qualify as barriers for government both in Chomsky's (1986b) original definition and in the modified version suggested here. They must not count as barriers, however. Chomsky voids their barrierhood in two distinct ways: by admitting adjunction to VP, in one case, and by stipulating that IP is not an inherent barrier, in the other (since adjunction to IP is not allowed).

   Chomsky adduces essentially two reasons for not admitting adjunction to IP. One is to prevent extraction of an adjunct from a *wh*-island (**How$_i$ did you wonder* [$_{CP}$ *who* [$_{IP}$ t_i [$_{IP}$ [$_{VP}$ *fixed the car*] t_i]]]?). If *how* could adjoin to IP, CP would no longer inherit barrierhood, in Chomsky's system. This reason loses its force, however, if one adopts Relativized Minimality. Extraction of *how* is blocked independently by the intervening *who*, even if adjunction to IP is permitted.

The second reason involves the reduction of strong islands to Subjacency. If adjunction to IP were allowed (in a system where Subjacency is triggered by the crossing of two barriers), no such reduction would be possible, as is apparent from (112a–b):

(112)   a.   *The book O_i that $[_{IP}$ t_i $[_{IP}[_{CP}$ reading $t_i]$ would be fun]]...

       b.   *To whom$_i$ did $[_{IP}$ $t_i[_{IP}$ they $[_{VP}$ leave] $[_{PP}$ before speaking $t_i]]]$?

Only one barrier would be crossed in (112a–b): CP and PP, respectively. In other systems of assumptions, however, such as the present one or Manzini's (1988), where a bounding violation is triggered by the crossing of only one barrier, adjunction to IP could well be admitted. This would still be beside the point, however. To admit free adjunction to VP and IP is tantamount to saying that these maximal projections are never (inherent) barriers: a statement nondistinct from the mere stipulation that they are not barriers.

A more interesting tack would be to find a principled reason why they behave like maximal projections L-marked by a [+V] category, although they are not. Perhaps L-marking is but a special case of a more general property that includes, as a distinct case, the relation between the non-lexical categories C and I and their complements IP and VP.

XPs directly θ-marked by some head are c-selected (ultimately, s-selected) by it, together with indirectly θ-marked XPs (see Chomsky 1986a). VP and IP are also c-selected, it seems, by I and C, respectively, even if not s-selected by them: I cannot take any complement other than VP and C cannot take any complement other than IP.[54]

This suggests, then, the possibility of utilizing the notion of c-selection in the definition of barrier for government or, to generalize, *direct selection*: a notion that, for lexical categories, will ultimately mean direct s-selection and, for nonlexical categories, direct c-selection (the notion of selection also plays a crucial role in Longobardi's (1985c, 1988) theory of bounding).

Finally, concerning the [+V] requirement, it can be noted that I and C, if not intrinsically [+V] categories, are at least compatible with [+V] elements (witness their ability to host verbs in some languages). Thus, they can be taken to be (at least) nondistinct from [+V] categories.

The definition of barrier for government can therefore be reformulated as follows:[55]

(113) *Definition of barrier for government* (final)
Every maximal projection that fails to be *directly selected* by a
category nondistinct from [+ V] is a barrier for government.

The definition of barrier for binding can likewise be reformulated in terms
of the more general notion of selection (subsuming direct and indirect
θ-marking):

(114) *Definition of barrier for binding* (final)
Every maximal projection that fails to be *(directly or indirectly)*
selected in the canonical direction by a category nondistinct from
[+ V] is a barrier for binding.

The ineliminable difference between the two notions of barrier is thus
constituted by (1) *direct selection* for government versus *direct or indirect*
selection for binding, and (2) the *canonical direction* requirement, holding
of binding alone.

We have already discussed (1) at length. As for (2), we have not yet asked
whether it can be generalized to government as well. Apparently, though,
it cannot.

If the necessary successive cyclic extraction from Verb-second complements in German (see note 38) is precisely a consequence of the fact that
an intermediate CP (the Verb-second complement) is on the noncanonical
side of the V, thus barring the binding option, then we have evidence that
government is not sensitive to issues of canonical direction (also see Koster
1987, 194). This is because in (115) t^* is appropriately head- and antecedent-governed. Thus, CP cannot count as a government barrier, despite
being selected on the noncanonical side of the verb:[56]

(115) Wen$_i$ hast du [$_{VP}$ gesagt [$_{CP}$ t^* [$_{\bar{C}}$ wird
who have you said will
[$_{IP}$ er t_i sehen]]]]?
he see

This difference between government and binding has perhaps the more
general consequence that as a rule, in languages with mixed branching,
successive cyclic *Wh*-Movement but not long *Wh*-Movement will be
possible.

The reformulation of government and binding barriers in terms of the
notion of selection allows us to do away with adjunction to VP (and IP),
something that appears desirable for various general reasons.

First, it makes it possible to envisage the complete elimination of
(*Wh*-)Movement via adjunction—a welcome result, inasmuch as it renders
the theory of grammar more restrictive.[57]

Second, it permits the elimination of certain technical problems arising from the decision to admit (*Wh*-)Movement via adjunction to maximal projections. One was the stipulation that no intermediate adjunction must be allowed to maximal projections that are arguments, the rationale for which is not entirely clear (see Chomsky 1986b). Another is the fact that (*Wh*-)Movement via adjunction to maximal projections that are *not* arguments must also be severely limited. For example, one must prevent adjunction to adverbial PPs (see Chomsky's (1986b, 66) stipulation that only NPs can adjoint to such PPs, and the discussion in chapter 3), to extraposed relatives or comparative CPs, and to predicative NPs (see Longobardi 1987b, fn. 43). Otherwise, no barrier would be there to block extraction from them.

Third, as the case of clitic left dislocation discussed in chapter 2 shows, the transparency of VP and IP for binding cannot be obtained by resorting to adjunction, since clitic left dislocation does not involve (*Wh*-)Movement, though it enters ("base-generated") binding relations.

Finally, expressing the transparency of VP and IP for government independently of adjunction permits an optimally simple account of Head Movement and NP-Movement, which cannot resort to adjunction. We briefly discuss this in the next section.[58]

1.7.4   Head Movement and A-Chains

In Chomsky 1986b, sec. 11, the fact that Head Movement and NP-Movement only apply in a strict successive cyclic fashion (that is, only enter chains of antecedent government relations) follows essentially from abandoning the θ-government half of proper government for Vs (or, rather, from subsuming it under the antecedent government half). That is, θ-government by V is no longer sufficient to satisfy the ECP. This has practically no consequences for Ā-movement, for which adjunction to VP always yields proper government via antecedent government, and for which the γ-marking procedure at S-Structure for A-positions ultimately permits long *Wh*-Movement. It has the desired consequences for Head Movement and NP-Movement, since these can never adjoin to VP (without producing "improper movement"; see Chomsky 1986b, 73).

If, however, long *Wh*-Movement is nothing other than a binding relation, and if a binding relation requires a referential trace, then the strict successive cyclic derivation of Head Movement and NP-Movement may be taken to follow plainly from the nonreferential character of head traces and NP-traces, as noted earlier.

The point at issue is a different one, however. As noted, the definition of barrier for government assumed here, which considers VP and IP intrinsically transparent for government (that is, noninherent barriers) appears to yield a surprisingly simple account of Head Movement and NP-Movement (in interaction with Relativized Minimality).

Concerning V-Movement, for example, it is no longer necessary to hold the questionable (Chomsky 1986b, 71) assumption that I θ-marks VP in order to render L-marking of VP possible after V-Raising to I (in languages that allow it) to void the barrierhood of VP.[59] Concerning NP-Movement, no extensions of the notion of chain (and antecedent government) of the type suggested by Chomsky (1986b, sec. 11) are needed anymore. If VP counts as an inherent barrier, a simple case of passive like (116)

(116) $[_{IP}$ John$_i$ $[_{I'}$ I $[_{VP}$ was $[_{VP}$ invited t_i]]]].

requires an extended chain (*John$_i$, I$_i$, was$_i$, invited$_i$, t$_i$*) with chain coindexing via Spec-Head and Head-Head agreement, and the convention that there be no "accidental coindexing,' to exclude superraising cases (see Chomsky 1986b, 75ff.). If VP is not a barrier, NP-Movement will apply undisturbed.

A question arises in connection with superraising and superpassive cases:

(117) a. *John$_i[_{VP}$ seems $[_{CP}$ that $[_{IP}$ it $[_{VP}$ appears $[_{IP}$ t$_i$ to be intelligent]]]]].

   b. *John$_i[_{VP}$ seems $[_{CP}$ that $[_{IP}$ it $[_{VP}$ was $[_{VP}$ told t$_i$ that he should leave]]]]].

Here it would seem that NP-Movement is allowed to apply in too unrestricted a manner, for in (117a–b) none of the intervening maximal projections qualifies as a barrier for government under the definition suggested above, since each of them is directly selected by a head nondistinct from a $[+V]$ category.

The derivations shown in (117a–b) are nonetheless blocked by Relativized Minimality. An A-position (the [NP, IP]-position filled by *it*) intervenes between *John* and its trace. (For the same conclusion, see Rizzi 1990, chap. 1).

1.8 The Conditions on the Trace: The (Residue of the) ECP

The notions of barrier for binding and for government can be viewed, in a certain sense, as conditions on extraction domains (for binding and government, respectively). They impose certain requirements on the domains (the XPs) that intervene between the trace and the c-commanding antecedent. What remains to be discussed is the nature of the conditions on the trace of a binding or government relation.

A condition on traces already exists: the ECP, now reduced, following Rizzi (1990) and Koopman and Sportiche (1988), to the "formal licensing" requirement of the conjunctive definition (the "identification" requirement, θ-government or antecedent government, having been subsumed under the two relations of binding and government). The formal licensing requirement, given earlier as (ia) in note 4, is repeated here as (118):

(118) *Definition of the ECP*
A nonpronominal EC must be properly head-governed.[60]

The question is, Does this condition suffice, or are there further conditions, possibly distinct for traces of binding and government?

In this section I will argue that the conditions on the traces of binding and government are indeed the same and that they reduce to the ECP, provided that we slightly modify it by introducing into its definition reference to a *head nondistinct from* $[+V]$, as turned out to be necessary for the definitions of binding and government barrier.

Consider (119a–c). As their ungrammaticality indicates, neither binding nor government is possible in such contexts:

(119) a. *Il presidente, al quale$_i$ ho sentito
        the president to whom I heard
        [$_{NP}$ un appello t_i] alla radio, . . .
        a petition   on the radio
   b. *Gianni, il quale$_i$ ho parlato
        Gianni whom   I spoke
        [$_{PP}$ con t_i], . . .[61]
        with
   c. *Gianni, da cui$_i$ ci comportiamo
        Gianni from whom we behave
        [$_{AdvP}$ diversamente t_i], . . .
            differently
        (Compare *Ci comportiamo diversamente da Gianni.*)

First, let us approach the question from the point of view of binding (which is potentially available since the trace appears to satisfy the conditions on binding discussed above: being in an A-position; having a referential θ-role; and being compatible with a referential use). The forms in (119) are not excluded by the theory of bounding developed above (since no barrier for binding intervenes between the trace and its antecedent); nor are they excluded, for that matter, by Subjacency (as formulated in Chomsky

1986b). NP and PP in (119a–b) are both L-marked (by a verb); hence, they are neither blocking categories nor barriers. Movement of *al quale/il quale* to Spec CP conforms to Subjacency, in fact to 0-Subjacency, if intermediate adjunction to VP is allowed:[62]

(120) a. [al quale$_i$[$_{\overline{C}}$ C [$_{IP}$[$_{VP}$ *t* [$_{VP}$ ho sentito [$_{NP}$ un
            [$_{\overline{N}}$ appello *t$_i$*]]]]]]]
      b. [il quale$_i$[$_{\overline{C}}$ C [$_{IP}$[$_{VP}$ *t* [$_{VP}$ ho parlato [$_{PP}$ con *t$_i$*]]]]]]

Even assuming that the verb does not L-mark the AdvP (but note that it presumably θ-marks it, since the Adv is selected by the verb), movement of *da cui* in (119c) still satisfies 1-Subjacency. Only one barrier is crossed in its movement to Spec CP (namely, AdvP):

(121) [da cui$_i$[$_{\overline{C}}$ C [$_{IP}$[$_{VP}$ *t* [$_{VP}$ ci comportiamo [$_{AdvP}$ diversamente *t$_i$*]]]]]]

All of (119a–c) are instead excluded, if we add the further condition to the trace of a binding relation that it be governed by a [+V] head (thus ruling out nouns, prepositions, and adverbs as local governors of this trace).

This means that certain cases of apparently well formed long extraction from NP must not be genuine. Chomsky (1977, 112ff.), for example, discusses two, concluding in fact that they are only apparent. The first is exemplified by (122):

(122) About whom did John write a book?

Following Bach and Horn (1976) and Cattell (1976), Chomsky assigns to (122) the structure (123), which involves no genuine extraction from NP:

(123) [$_{PP}$ About whom] did [$_{IP}$ John write [$_{NP}$ a book] [$_{PP}$]]?

Part of the evidence for this rests on the fact that the sequence *a book* in (122) *can* be separately *Wh*-Moved (*What did John write about Nixon?*) and "pronominalized" (*John wrote it about Nixon*), thus behaving like an autonomous constituent already at D-Structure.

Somewhat different are cases like (124),

(124) [$_{PP}$ Of whom] did he see a picture [$_{PP}$]?

for which no comparable evidence exists of a [V NP PP] configuration at D-Structure (compare *What did he see of John?*, *He saw it of John*). But in these cases, as Chomsky notes, no genuine extraction from NP may be involved either. As such cases of "extraction" are lexically conditioned (possible with *see* or *find*, but not with verbs like *destroy*), it is plausible to posit a lexically governed extraposition or "restructuring" process, which separates the PP from the NP before *Wh*-Movement, along the lines of (125) (see Chomsky 1977, 114ff.):

(125) a. He saw [a picture [of whom]]?   (D-Structure)
     b. He saw [a picture [*t*]] [of whom]?   (intermediate structure)
     c. Of whom did he see [a picture [*t*]] [*t*]?   (S-Structure)

Chomsky (1986b, 45), however, reports examples like the Spanish (126a) and English (126b) (= his (97c–c′) as real cases of long extraction of the θ-marked object of a noun:

(126) a. [De cual de estas ediciones] no sabes si hay traducción francesa *t*?
     b. Of which of these editions don't you know whether there is a French translation?

He contrasts them with extractions of the subject of a NP, which (for ECP reasons) have access only to a successive cyclic derivation (blocked by an intervening *wh*-island). See (127a–b) (= Chomsky's (97b–b′)), which are judged deviant:

(127) a. [De qué pintor] me preguntaste si van a exponer varios dibujos *t*?
     b. By which painter did you ask me whether they are going to exhibit several drawings?

That (126a–b) involve a genuine case of long extraction from NP is dubious, however. (Long or successive cyclic) extraction of nongenitive complements of Ns is normally excluded, as shown for example by (119a) and by (128):

(128) *The country on which we remember [an attack *t*] is Poland.

It would thus be surprising if only genitive complements of Ns were to be "long extractable."

    Suppose that they are not, just like any other complement. The well-formedness of (126a) must then be explained differently. Genitive PPs also appear to participate in a construction in which the PP is base-generated in initial position, yielding either a "whole/part" or a special "aboutness" interpretation. Base generation is, for example, inescapable in such cases as (129) (see Barbaud 1976, Koster 1984, 65):

(129) a. Dei tuoi parenti, mi chiedo se anche Gianni
         of your relatives I wonder if Gianni too
         sarebbe disposto a farlo.
         would be willing to do it
     b. Di quale libro non ricordi   più ora
         of which book don't you remember any longer
         se trattasse di questi argomenti?
         if it dealt with these topics

    c. Di quale libro non ricordi   se la (sua) traduzione
       of which book don't you remember if (its) translation
       fosse ben fatta?
       was well done

Be that as it may, (the Italian translation of) (126a) seems, in fact, to be good with the special interpretation of (129c). By the same token, it seems to me that the Italian translation of (127) too is possible with the same "aboutness" interpretation (especially if *sapere* 'know' is used instead of *domandarsi* 'wonder'). Support for this conjecture comes from the following observation.

There is another context that (like *wh*-islands) appears to exclude successive cyclic extraction but (unlike *wh*-islands) is for some reason incompatible (or quite marginal) with a base-generated genitive PP: the extraposed sentential subject of an unergative V. For example:

(130) a. ??Di quale libro conta   che la traduzione
       of which book does it matter that the translation
       sia ben fatta?
       is well done
    b. *Dei tuoi parenti, importa   che Gianni venga.
       of your relatives it does matter that Gianni comes

Interestingly, in this context, long extraction of the genitive object of an NP is correspondingly marginal (in Italian):

(131) *Di quale di queste edizioni conta   che vi sia
      of which of these editions   does it matter that there be
      una traduzione francese?
      a French translation

A different case is provided by the extraction of the subject of NP in Romance, to which I return below.

Following standard assumptions, I also interpret the grammaticality of the English translation of (119b) (*Gianni, whom I spoke with,...*) and similar cases of preposition stranding as due to the possibility, available in English but not in Romance, of "reanalyzing" P as a category nondistinct from [+V]. More precisely, adapting (and somewhat modifying) an idea of Pollock's (1988), we may express the standard notion of reanalysis as the property (of English prepositions) of being underspecified with respect to V (and N) features ([UV, UN])—a possibility contingent upon their nondistinctness from Vs in terms of Case assignment and possibly other properties (see Kayne 1981c, Rizzi 1990, chap. 3, app.).[63]

If we had reasons to postulate the same condition for the trace of government, then we would have an indication that one and the same condition does hold for both kinds of traces—a condition that looks too close to the ECP to be a different principle:[64]

(132) Binding and government traces must be governed by a head non-distinct from [+ V].

Let us turn, then, to government relations for evidence to this effect. The ill-formedness of (119a–c), as instances of successive cyclic *Wh*-Movement, follows in the *Barriers* system from the presence of a minimality barrier ($\bar{\text{N}}$, $\bar{\text{P}}$ and $\overline{\text{Adv}}$, respectively).[65] In the present system, which adopts Relativized Minimality, no such explanation is available. A head cannot count as a potential antecedent for a trace of $\bar{\text{A}}$-movement. The successive cyclic derivation of (119) is, however, excluded if traces of government too must be governed by a head nondistinct from [+ V]. As noted, it is plausible to assume that this condition on binding and government traces is nothing other than the ECP.

(133) (*Revised*) *definition of the ECP*
       A nonpronominal EC must be properly head-governed by a head nondistinct from [+ V].[66]

A number of problems for this reformulation of the ECP must now be considered and explained away.

A first problem concerns the alleged capacity of nouns to head-govern the trace of internal NP-Movement in passive cases like *the city$_i$'s destruction t_i*.

A second, related problem is the N's apparent capacity to head-govern the trace of a postnominal subject extracted from NP via Spec, in Romance (see Longobardi 1987b). Given the arguments discussed by Giorgi and Longobardi (1990, chap. 3) that subjects of NPs (perhaps, more generally, XPs) are generated to the right of the head in Romance (and in Spec, in Germanic), the trace of the extracted subject must find an appropriate head governor.[67]

Since Kayne's important work of the early 1980s (see, in particular, Kayne 1981b, 1983), it is generally admitted that nouns, unlike verbs, are not "structural governors" (that is, they cannot govern positions that they do not subcategorize)—whence the ill-formedness of (134a–c) and the like:

(134) a. *Mary$_i$'s likelihood [t_i to leave]
            (Compare *Mary is likely to leave.*)
       b. *Mary$_i$'s appearance [t_i nice]
            (Compare *Mary appears nice.*)

c. *this theorem$_i$'s demonstration [t_i to be false]
   (Compare *This theorem was demonstrated to be false.*)

Were it not for the passive case, and the case of subject extraction from NP in Romance, one could simply say that nouns are not governors at all, thus accounting for (134) and simultaneously for the impossibility of extracting noun complements via long or successive cyclic *Wh*-Movement.

Following Longobardi (1987b) and Rizzi (1990, chap. 3, app.) (also see Kayne 1984, 63), one could assume that movement to the Spec NP and only that movement has the special property of turning (via Spec-Head agreement) a noun into a proper head governor just for the trace of the NP agreeing with the head, even though this may somewhat weaken the generalization that only [+V] categories are proper governors.

Since both NP-Movement and subject extraction from NP in Romance, and only these, place the moved constituent in the Spec NP (see Longobardi 1987b for detailed justification), only their traces will be able to be properly head-governed.[68]

Let us turn to prepositions.

(133) makes the right prediction for (119b). As for English, we have already noted that preposition stranding in this language is compatible with (133), under the plausible assumption that Ps can be nondistinct from [+V].[69]

A seemingly serious problem is the apparent possibility of extracting the PP complement of certain prepositions in Italian. See, for example, (136), derived from (135):

(135) Maria è caduta [$_{PP}$[$_P$ addosso/vicino/etc.] [$_{PP}$ a NP]].
       Maria has fallen   on   NP

(136) a. Gianni, a cui$_i$ Maria è caduta
           Gianni on whom Maria has fallen
           [$_{PP}$[$_P$ addosso/vicino/etc.] [$_{PP}$ t_i]], . . .
       b. Maria gli$_i$ è caduta [$_{PP}$[$_P$ addosso/vicino/etc.] [$_{PP}$ t_i]].
           Maria on him has fallen

That the structure is as indicated (implying genuine extraction) and not
. . .V[$_{PP}$[$_P$ *addosso/vicino/etc.*]] (. . .) [$_{PP}$ *a NP*] . . . is shown by the impossibility of moving the first P(P) alone. See (137):[70]

(137) *Addosso/vicino/etc. non è caduta   a lui, ma a suo fratello.
         on   she has not fallen him   but his brother

I would like to propose that (136) is rendered possible in Italian by the same underspecification mechanism at work in English. This suggestion is

compatible with the fact that Italian disallows simple preposition stranding
(recall (119b)), if we think that a P may be underspecified for $[\pm V]$ only
if it is nondistinct from V. Prepositions followed by an NP are distinct
from V in Italian in terms of Case assignment, as originally proposed by
Kayne (1981b), but they are nondistinct from V, even in Italian, whenever
they do not assign Case, as when they take a PP complement.

There is supporting evidence for this conjecture. Extraction of the
preposition's PP complement in Italian obeys the same conditions that
hold for simple preposition stranding in English: the PP from which
extraction takes place must be subcategorized (governed) by a predicate
(see the contrast between (138a) and (138b), noted in Rizzi 1988, 526):

(138) a. La ragazza alla quale$_i$ Gianni si era messo accanto t_i...
        the girl   to whom Gianni sat   near

     b. *La ragazza alla quale$_i$ Gianni era felice   accanto t_i...
        the girl   to whom Gianni was happy near

The fact that when the relevant requirements are satisfied long extraction
(binding) is possible (see (139a–b), which contain extractions from two
weak islands) suggests that movement does not necessarily proceed via
Spec PP (unlike, perhaps, what happens in Germanic, for which see Van
Riemsdijk 1978 and Longobardi 1987b, 43):[71]

(139) a. Gianni, al quale$_i$ *mi chiedo quando* siano andati
        Gianni to whom I wonder when   they have gone
        [$_{PP}$ incontro t_i],...
            toward

     b. Gianni, al quale$_i$ *non* era caduta   [$_{PP}$ addosso t_i],...
        Gianni (to) whom she had not fallen   on

I thus tentatively conclude that the condition on traces (ECP) should refer
to nondistinctness from $[+V]$ heads in the general case, as do the conditions "on extraction domains" (the definitions of barrier for binding and
government). This parallelism thus confirms the insight that underlies
various analyses of bounding theory, from Kayne's (1981b) extended
notion of the ECP, to Huang's (1982) CED, to Longobardi's (1985b, 1988)
symmetry principles, that the conditions on extraction domains are largely
similar to the conditions on the trace.

1.9 Some Remarks on *Wh*-Islands and Subjacency

As we have seen, the islandhood of *wh*-islands for antecedent government
relations (as in adjunct extraction) follows from Relativized Minimality.

Traditionally, *wh*-islands are also taken to be "mild" islands for long *Wh*-Movement (binding), falling under Subjacency, perhaps differently parametrized from language to language. See Rizzi 1982, chap. 2 and Chomsky 1981 for the original suggestion that the nodes counting for Subjacency are S (now IP), in English, and $\bar{\text{S}}$ (now CP), in Italian, giving different effects for the two languages.

Chomsky (1986b, 36–39) reinterprets the standard account along the following lines. Consider (140a–c):

(140) a.   [To whom]$_i$ did you wonder [$_{CP}$ what$_j$[$_{IP}$ to give $t_j t_i$]]?

b.   *?[To whom]$_i$ did you wonder [$_{CP}$ what$_j$[$_{IP}$ they gave $t_j t_i$]]?

c.   (?)[A chi]$_i$ ti chiedevi [$_{CP}$ che cosa$_j$[$_{IP}$ avessero dato $t_j t_i$]]?

In such cases as (140a) movement of *to whom* to the matrix clause VP, and ultimately Spec CP, crosses one barrier (by inheritance), CP. If the most embedded tensed IP, in English, and CP, in Italian, is taken as an extra barrier, then two barriers are crossed in (140b), IP and CP, though still only one is crossed in (140c) (CP, which is a barrier both inherently and by inheritance). This roughly produces the reported judgments on (140). The lessened acceptability of (141)–(142) is taken by Chomsky (1986b, 38) to "suggest [...] that the violations are cumulative":

(141) a.   What did you wonder [$_{CP'}$ who [$_{VP'}$ knew [$_{CP}$ who [$_{VP}$ saw t]]]]?
(= Chomsky's (80))

b.   What did you wonder [$_{CP'}$ who [$_{VP'}$ said [$_{CP}$ that Bill [$_{VP}$ saw t]]]]?
(= Chomsky's 82a))

(142) a.   Che cosa ti domandavi [$_{CP'}$ chi [$_{VP'}$ sapesse [$_{CP}$ chi [$_{VP}$ aveva visto t]]]]?

b.   Che cosa ti domandavi [$_{CP'}$ chi [$_{VP'}$ avesse detto [$_{CP}$ che Bill [$_{VP}$ aveva visto t]]]]?

In the system developed so far, essentially the same results could be obtained if we were to consider a tensed interrogative *wh*-clause as a special binding barrier (stronger in English-type languages than in Italian-type languages), with cumulative effects.[72]

However, this general approach raises some conceptual and empirical questions, the latter due in part to the often unclear status of the data. To begin with, English and Italian might be (and indeed have been claimed to be) much closer to each other than originally assumed, even though it is always delicate to compare judgments cross-linguistically. For one thing, many English speakers appear to accord fairly closely with the Italian judgments (see Grimshaw 1986, Chomsky 1986b, 37); moreover, extraction of interrogative *wh*-phrases from *wh*-islands in Italian gives rise to relatively degraded sentences, perhaps similar to the corresponding English cases considered originally (see Rizzi 1982, chap. 2, fn. 5, and related text). I suggested earlier that in selecting a *wh*-phrase to be extracted from a *wh*-island, care should be taken to choose one that allows a referential reading (and can thus enter into binding). Otherwise, binding will be unavailable and only the successive cyclic option will be left, which is filtered out by Relativized Minimality. Bare interrogative *wh*-phrases (*who, what, chi, che cosa,* and so on) appear to allow such a referential reading only marginally (as opposed to *which*-phrases, relatives, topicalized phrases, and the like) a property that is perhaps at the root both of the intermediate status of many of the examples discussed in the literature and of the "mild" islandhood itself for long *Wh*-Movement attributed to *wh*-islands.

When a suitable phrase and context are chosen, even "double *wh*-island violations" in fact appear to be possible, both in Italian and in English:[73]

(143) a.   Carlo è una persona a cui$_i$ non so
           Carlo is a person   to whom I don't know
           chi potrebbe chiedersi se affidare i propri figli t_i.
           who could wonder   whether to entrust his own children

      b. ?Maria, a cui$_i$ mi hanno chiesto se sapessi
          Maria to whom they asked me   if I knew
          chi aveva scritto t_i, . . .
          who had written

(144) a.   A car that$_i$ I wouldn't know who to ask how to fix t_i . . .[74]

      b. ?These are the only vegetables which$_i$ I don't know where to
          find out how to plant t_i.

The optimal case both for the *Barriers* system of assumptions and for the one developed here would be for long *Wh*-Movement to be essentially free out of *wh*-islands.[75]

The facts appear to be almost so, but not quite. Certain residues remain. One is the tensed/untensed contrast, which is also found in other constructions (parasitic gap, *easy-to-please,* and related null object constructions, which will be discussed in chapter 3). A second is related to the availability of preposition stranding in English (but not in Italian), which gives rise to certain language-internal contrasts that are not entirely understood. Chomsky (1986b, 39) discusses the marginality of (145b), more severe than that of (145a):

(145) a.   To whom did you wonder what John gave?

      b.   Who did you wonder what John gave to?

A third residual problem is the fact that long *Wh*-Movement (binding) across one (or more) *wh*-island(s) degrades more rapidly, as structure is added, than that of ordinary complement CPs, although it never appears to give rise to discrete and dramatic changes, as does successive cyclic movement (government) out of a *wh*-island.

Pending better insights into these residual issues, I will conclude my discussion here and turn to the more general question of Subjacency as a separate condition on long *Wh*-Movement (binding).

On the basis of the empirical phenomena considered thus far, it seems that the notion of (1-)Subjacency is both too strong and too weak. It is too strong in that it rules out long *Wh*-Movement from two *wh*-islands (under the cumulative interpretation), whereas some such extractions must be admitted as in (143)–(144).[76] It is too weak in that it fails to rule out long *Wh*-Movement from (certain) adjuncts, from relative clauses extraposed from an object or from degree clauses, all of which involve but one barrier (see section 1.6.2).[77]

A question that arises is whether (abstracting from the important methodological role that the notion has played) (1-)Subjacency is but an artifact of two particular generalizations that may turn out not to be genuine. One is the decision to group together structures, such as the *wh*-island, the complex NP island, the adjunct island, and the subject island, that do not form a homogeneous class (one weak island and three strong islands). We have seen that, leaving aside *wh*-islands as the odd member, Subjacency could be interpreted as 0-Subjacency, with the notion of barrier for Subjacency (binding/bounding) defined as in (114), "every maximal projection that fails to be selected in the canonical direction by a category nondistinct from [+V]." The other is the decision to employ the same notion of barrier for binding/bounding that holds for government. This decision also imposes 1-Subjacency, rather than 0-Subjacency, since the barrier that suffices for government (say, a non-L-marked factive complement CP) must not suffice for Subjacency. This in turn forces the introduction of a notion of barrier "by inheritance," which is entirely dispensable for government and can be dispensed with for Subjacency too, if we give two (partially) different definitions of barrier for the two theories, as suggested.

1.10 Summary

We began the chapter by posing three questions, (8a–c). Concerning the first (What classes of elements undergo long and successive cyclic *Wh*-

Movement?), we found evidence that long *Wh*-Movement is limited to phrases that not only are in A-positions (Chomsky 1986b) and receive a referential θ-role (Rizzi 1990), but also are intrinsically referential (D-linked, in Pesetsky's (1987) terms). All phrases not satisfying these conditions have access only to successive cyclic *Wh*-Movement. This motivates recognizing two different types of operator/variable configurations, depending on the referential/nonreferential nature of the trace (and the relative operator).

Concerning the second question (From what principles of the theory does the existence of long and successive cyclic *Wh*-Movement follow?), we have essentially adopted Rizzi's (1990) theory, which recognizes only two ways in which the content of a trace can be identified: binding and (antecedent) government, which subsume long and successive cyclic movement, respectively. We have only slightly departed from Rizzi's system in admitting binding chains in addition to government chains.

Concerning the third question (What is the nature of the locality conditions on long and successive cyclic *Wh*-Movement?), we have tried to eliminate certain asymmetries and redundancies from the *Barriers* system of assumptions, eventually arriving at an interestingly simple set of locality conditions,

1. A (single) definition of barrier for binding/bounding

(114) Every maximal projection that fails to be (*directly or indirectly*) *selected in the canonical direction* by a category nondistinct from [+V] is a barrier for binding.

2. A (single) definition of barrier for government

(113) Every maximal projection that fails to be *directly selected* by a category nondistinct from [+V] is a barrier for government.

3. A condition of head government on traces (the ECP)

(133) A nonpronominal EC must be properly head-governed by a head nondistinct from [+V].

in combination with Rizzi's (1990) notion of Relativized Minimality. All three conditions make crucial reference to a head nondistinct from [+V], and the first two crucially refer to the notion of selection, whose introduction has also permitted other simplifications, from disposing of movement via adjunction to maximal projections, to eliminating the *Barriers* special notion of extended chain for NP-Movement.

Chapter 2

An Apparent
Wh-Construction: Clitic Left
Dislocation in Romance

2.1 Introduction

In this chapter I will consider in detail certain aspects of a construction peculiar to Romance that bears in interesting ways on the analysis developed in chapter 1. I will refer to it as *clitic left dislocation* (CLLD) (see Van Haaften, Smits, and Vat 1983), since the generally optional pronoun matching the left-peripheral phrase can only be a *clitic*, not a tonic, pronoun.

The properties of this construction will turn out to have nontrivial implications for a number of central theoretical issues. For one thing, it will appear that, even though the construction exhibits two properties that are normally considered diagnostic of a (*Wh*-)Movement construction (namely, sensitivity to strong islands and Connectivity), it cannot be so analyzed within the current theory. See section 2.3 for a detailed justification of this claim, which will be supported and highlighted by a systematic comparison with topicalization, a construction that differs minimally from CLLD (in fact forming a syntactic minimal pair with it). A significant number of differences between the two will be reviewed, and seen to reduce to the single fact that topicalization, though not CLLD, involves *Wh*-Movement.

If the evidence is correctly interpreted, then, sensitivity to strong islands and Connectivity will have to be dissociated from *Wh*-Movement and be made dependent on some more abstract property that both *Wh*-Movement constructions and CLLD share. I will suggest that this property is the possibility of entering binding chains (in the sense of chapter 1), which must be able to arise in either of two ways: via movement or base generation.

If binding chains are sensitive to strong islands, irrespective of their origin, the principle of bounding theory that derives strong islands must be a *condition on representation* rather than one on movement. Thus, CLLD turns out to provide some genuine empirical evidence to determine an issue that has primarily been discussed from a conceptual point of view (Chomsky 1980b).

Given that (antecedent) government chains are also characterized by (1) sensitivity to strong islands and (2) Connectivity, why do we say that CLLD enters only into binding chains? As we will see in section 2.3.4, the answer is that, under ordinary conditions, CLLD shows only properties of long *Wh*-Movement, and none of successive cyclic *Wh*-Movement. In other words, phrases that can enter only into a successive cyclic derivation will appear not to be able to be dislocated in CLLD—whence the conclusion that the construction enters only into binding chains.

The observation that unbounded ("base-generated") dependencies that correspond to long *Wh*-Movement can be found separated from successive cyclic *Wh*-Movement, as in CLLD, thus constitutes an interesting argument for the dissociation of binding, and its locality conditions, from (antecedent) government, and its locality conditions. CLLD is, in a certain sense, a pure representation of binding.

Its properties are interestingly more complex, however, and in fact point to a rather far-reaching conclusion: that the *Wh*-Movement/non-*Wh*-Movement dichotomy is reducible to another dichotomy: presence or absence of (nonreferential) operators. We will return to this issue in section 2.6.

Before turning to the arguments for the non-*Wh*-Movement nature of CLLD, within the current theory, we must carefully distinguish CLLD from the construction discussed by Ross (1967), Chomsky (1977), and others under the name of *left dislocation* (LD), whose analogue is also present in Romance.[1]

2.2   LD and CLLD

That LD and CLLD are two distinct constructions becomes apparent if we compare some of their most obvious properties.

The "left-dislocated" phrase of CLLD can be any maximal phrase:

(1) a. [$_{PP}$ Al mare],   ci siamo già stati.
        to the seaside there-(we)-have already been

    [_AP_ Bella],   non lo è mai stata.
       beautiful not-it-(she) ever was

    [_VP_ Messo da parte],   non lo è mai stato.
       got out of the way not-it-(he) ever was

    [_QP_ Tutti], non li ho visti ancora.
       all   not-them-(I) have seen yet

    [_CP_ Che bevi],   lo dicono tutti.
       That (you) drink it says   everybody

This contrasts with LD, which essentially allows for "left-dislocated" *NPs* only (compare, for example, *To John, I have already spoken to him*).

The "left-dislocated" phrase of CLLD can occur at the front of virtually any subordinate clause type:

(1) b. L'unica persona che a Gianni,   non gli ha mai fatto
      the only person which to Gianni not-to-him-has ever done
      un favore, . . .
      a favor

      Non so proprio chi, questo libro, potrebbe recensirlo
      I don't know   who this book   could review it
      per domani.
      for tomorrow

      Da quando, al mercato,   ci va lui,
      since when   to the market he goes there
      non mangiano più bene.
      they don't eat well anymore

Here again CLLD contrasts with LD, which typically occurs in root contexts and (to different degrees of marginality) in the complement of only a few classes of propositional attitude verbs (see, among others, Ross 1967, 424, Emonds 1970, 19–20, Postal 1971, 136, fn. 18, Gundel 1975, Baltin 1982).

In CLLD there is no (theoretical) limit to the number of "left-dislocated" phrases. See, for example, (1c):

(1) c. Di vestiti, a me, Gianni, in quel negozio,
      clothes   to me Gianni in that shop
      non mi ce ne   ha mai comprati.
      (he) not-to-me-there-of-them ever bought

On the contrary, LD allows no more than one "left-dislocated" phrase (see Postal 1971, 136, fn. 17, where the impossibility of such sentences as *Mary, John, she likes him* is noted).

In CLLD the IP-internal resumptive element, if present, can be a *clitic* pronoun only:

(1) d.   In quella città, non *ci* sono mai stato.
          in that town   not-there-(I)-have ever been
          *In quella città, non sono mai stato   là.
          in that town   not (I) have ever been there

No such requirement holds of LD (*Quella città, non sono mai stato là* 'That town, I've never been there').

In CLLD there is obligatory Connectivity between the "left-dislocated" phrase and the IP-internal position (whether or not the latter is bound by a clitic). One case is Connectivity with respect to the binding theory:

(1) e.   A lei/*se stessa, Maria dice che non ci pensiamo   mai.
          of her/herself   Maria says that (we) not-there-think ever
          A *?lei/se stessa, Maria non ci pensa.
          of her/herself   Maria not-there-thinks

See Cinque 1977, 1983c, and Van Haaften, Smits, and Vat 1983 for more detailed discussion of this and other types of Connectivity in CLLD.

As is well known, LD shows no kind of Connectivity between the "left-dislocated" phrase and the IP-internal resumptive pronoun (for evidence to this effect, see the works just cited).

The relation between the "left-dislocated" phrase and the resumptive element in CLLD is sensitive to island constraints:

(1) f.   *[$_{PP}$ *A Carlo*], ti parlerò   solo del
              to Carlo I will talk to you only about
          [$_{NP}$ le persone [$_{CP}$ che *gli* piacciono]].
              the people   that *to him* appeal
          *Se [$_{AP}$ *ricco*], credi   che [$_{IP}$[$_{CP}$ esser*lo* stato]
           if   *rich*   you think that   to have been *it*
           non gli giovi],   ti sbagli.
           does not help him you are wrong
          *[$_{PP}$ *A voi*], Mario corre più di [$_{CP}$ quanto non *vi* sembri].
              to you Mario runs more than   it *to you* seems
          *[$_{PP}$ *A casa*], lo abbiamo incontrato [$_{PP}$ prima che
              home   we met him   before that
           ci andasse].
           he *there* went

The first example contains a complex NP, the second a sentential subject, the third a comparative clause not reducible to a complex NP (see Bracco 1980), the fourth an adverbial clause.

As is well known, LD shows no such property (Chomsky 1977).

2.3 CLLD: Arguments for Its Non-*Wh*-Movement Nature

2.3.1 The Resumptive Clitic and the Licensing of Parasitic Gaps

The properties of CLLD, and especially properties (1e–f) (Connectivity and sensitivity to islands), seem to invite the conclusion that this construction differs from LD precisely in involving *Wh*-Movement. Matters are not that simple, however.

One important question that a *Wh*-Movement analysis of CLLD must address is the cooccurrence of *Wh*-Movement with a clitic pronoun that matches in features the putatively moved phrase. Essentially two possibilities suggest themselves, both of which have in fact been proposed in the recent literature. The first consists in regarding the construction as an instantiation of the clitic-doubling phenomenon familiar from other languages, the second in regarding the clitic pronoun as an overt spelling out of the pronominal features left on the (*wh*-)trace. Neither proposal is without problems, however. I will examine each one briefly, concluding that neither is a viable account of the phenomenon.

Various considerations render a clitic-doubling analysis of CLLD unlikely (at least for Italian).[2] In clitic-doubling languages it is ordinarily the case that whenever a clitic may "double" a moved phrase in some *Wh*-Movement construction, it may do so in all other constructions displaying the properties of *Wh*-Movement, and it may also double a corresponding unmoved phrase (see Steriade 1980, Jaeggli 1982, Borer 1984a, and Dobrovie-Sorin 1987, 1990). Neither of these properties, however, is found in Italian. Clitics cannot "double" a moved phrase in ordinary *wh*-constructions, nor can they "double" a corresponding unmoved phrase:[3]

(2) a. *(A) chi lo conoscete?
       who   him-(do-you-)know
  b. *Lo conosciamo (a) Gianni.
       him-(we-)know Gianni

This simply amounts to the conclusion that Italian is apparently not a clitic-doubling language.[4] It could still be claimed that, for some reason, clitic doubling is limited in Italian to just CLLD structures, as in (3):

(3) a. Gianni, lo conosciamo.
       Gianni we know him
    b. Di questa faccenda, non ne voglio   parlare.
       of this matter   not-(I)-of-it want to talk

But even this weaker (and unenlightening) conclusion meets with problems. CLLD, for example, does not conform to what is sometimes referred
to as "Kayne's generalization" (see Chomsky 1981, 227, and the references
cited above concerning the clitic-doubling phenomenon). Kayne observed
that it is systematically the case that a clitic-doubled direct object in
clitic-doubling languages cannot be "bare." It must be introduced by a
preposition. But this is clearly not the case in CLLD:[5]

(4) Non so   se il vino, lo volete   adesso o dopo.
    I don't know if wine   you want it now or later

The prospects of assimilating the clitic in CLLD to the independent phenomenon of clitic doubling thus look unrewarding, to say the least.[6]

The alternative of regarding the clitic as the overt "spelling out" of a
wh-trace (and CLLD as a "Move α" construction) does not look promising
either. One piece of evidence against this analysis may be provided by the
inability of the clitic to license a parasitic gap. Chomsky (1982) discusses
the apparent inability of clitics to license parasitic gaps in (Spanish) relative
clauses employing the resumptive pronoun strategy. He suggests that a
principled account can be given if, in essence, the relevant Ā-binder (either
an abstract operator base-generated in Spec CP or the head of the relative
clause) can be coindexed with the parasitic gap (and the "resumptive"
pronoun) at LF only. This will entail a violation at S-Structure, where the
parasitic gap fails to qualify as any one of the possible types of empty
categories (Chomsky 1982, 58ff.). It cannot be a well formed PRO, because
it is governed; it cannot be a well-formed pro, because it is not identified;
it cannot be a well-formed NP-trace, because it is free in its governing
category. Finally, it is not a well-formed variable, because it is not Ā-bound
at S-Structure. Under these assumptions, it thus follows that (ordinary)
resumptive (clitic) pronouns will never be able to license a parasitic gap.
The ungrammaticality of (5a) thus contrasts with the grammaticality of
(5b), where syntactic movement creates an operator in Spec CP coindexed
with the parasitic gap at S-Structure, thus authorizing it as a variable:[7]

(5) a. *El reloj   de que me hablaste,   que lo han conseguido arreglar
        the clock you spoke to me about which they got to fix (it)
        sin mover e,   ha quedado muy bien.
        without moving now works very well

b.   El reloj de que me hablaste, el cual han conseguido arreglar *t* sin mover *e*, ha quedado muy bien.

Now, it is clear that this account of (5a) cannot carry over to the inability of the clitic in CLLD to license a parasitic gap, under the analysis in which the former is the spelling out of a *wh*-trace. In such a case, there *is* a syntactically moved operator in Spec CP coindexed with the clitic and the parasitic gap at S-Structure, just as in (5b) (alternatively, there is a real gap chain with which the parasitic gap chain can form a composed chain). If anything, the licensing of a parasitic gap here would be expected.[8]

If we assume that the (clitic) resumptive pronoun of CLLD is not the spelling out of a *wh*-trace (because CLLD does not involve *Wh*-Movement), the impossibility of parasitic gaps with CLLD follows directly:

(6)   *Gianni, l'ho cercato   per mesi,   senza trovare *e*.
      Gianni I have looked for for months without finding

This, of course, is not to say that pronouns may never be the (S-Structure) spelling out of (*wh*-)traces. Apparently that possibility is realized in some languages. Swedish, for instance, systematically allows resumptive pronouns in *wh*-constructions just where a corresponding gap would violate the ECP (typically, the subject position of tensed clauses introduced by a filled Comp; see the discussion in Engdahl 1985, sec. 2, which is the source of (7) and (8), and Sells 1984):[9]

(7)   Vilket ord   visste ingen   hur [$_{IP}$ dct/*t stavas]?
      which word knew no one how   it is spelled

As Engdahl suggests, a case can be made that such resumptive pronouns in Swedish are the spelling out of a *wh*-trace, for they act like $\bar{\text{A}}$-bound variables in the relevant respects (p. 14). Not only can they occur in *all* *wh*-constructions and behave like gaps in across-the-board contexts, they are also found to license parasitic gaps, as illustrated in (8):

(8)   Vilken fange   var det lakarna   inte kunde avgora om
      which prisoner was it   the-doctors not could decide if
      han verklingen var sjuk   utan   att tale med ____ personligen?
      he really   was ill-SG without to talk with   in person
      'Which prisoner was it the doctors couldn't determine if really was ill without talking to in person?'

The resumptive clitic in Italian CLLD shares none of these properties. It cannot occur in ordinary *wh*-constructions. It does not behave like a gap in across-the-board contexts. And, what is perhaps more telling, it does not license parasitic gaps. The systematic contrast with the Swedish case makes it plausible not to regard the resumptive pronoun in Italian CLLD as the spelling out of a *wh*-trace.

In turn, the implausibility of analyzing the CLLD resumptive pronoun as either an instance of clitic doubling or the spelling out of a *wh*-trace is itself indirect evidence that CLLD does not involve *Wh*-Movement. That rule is, in fact, ordinarily incompatible (in Italian) with the presence of a clitic locally binding the *wh*-trace (see (2a)).[10] Interestingly, topicalization, which is a regular (nonovert) *wh*-construction, consistently excludes resumptive pronouns:[11]

(9) *GIANNI, l'ho cercato, non Piero.
    Gianni (focus) I looked for not Piero

Note that except for the obligatory absence of resumptive clitics and the impossibility of topicalizing more than one constituent (properties to which we will return), topicalization is identical to CLLD with respect to the properties of (1). Virtually all of the differences to be observed below between the two constructions will be seen to reduce to a single difference: presence, in topicalization, versus absence, in CLLD, of *Wh*-Movement.

2.3.2 CLLD and Subjacency

If *Wh*-Movement is constrained by Subjacency as (re)formulated by Chomsky (1986b), then we have a separate reason not to take CLLD to involve *Wh*-Movement. There appear to be perfectly grammatical CLLD structures that Subjacency would exclude if they were derived by *Wh*-Movement.

Consider, for example, a case such as (10),

(10) Loro, il libro, credo che a Carlo sia sicuro
     them the book I think that to Carlo it is certain
     che non glielo daranno mai.
     that they will never give it to him

where three different constituents are separately left-dislocated from the most deeply embedded clause. Whatever derivation is chosen, a violation of Subjacency as interpreted by Chomsky (1986b) (or of the strict cycle) will ensue. In that system, whenever Spec CP is filled, extraction of a constituent out of that CP will cross a barrier, CP itself, which inherits barrierhood from IP (no matter whether CP is L-marked or not). So, for example, in the Italian sentence (11)

(11) Anna, a cui$_i$ non ricordo   [$_{CP}$ quando
        Anna to whom I don't remember   when
        [$_{IP}$ hanno dato il premio t_i]], . . .
             they gave the prize

the *wh*-phrase *a cui* will cross a single barrier, CP (given that tensed IP is not a barrier in this language).

If the crossing of two consecutive *wh*-islands, as in (12), yields a more degraded sentence in Italian than the crossing of a single *wh*-island,

(12) *?Gianni, a cui$_i$ non so   [$_{CP}$ quando si saprà
        Gianni to whom I don't know   when   one will know
        [$_{IP}$ cosa daranno t_i]], . . .
             what they will give

then the two separate crossings of a single barrier (CP) shown in (12) must cumulate to yield a full Subjacency violation. Otherwise, a well-formed derivation would be associated with (12), which would be expected to be on a par with (11), contrary to fact (see Chomsky 1986b, 31–42, and, for a somewhat different approach, section 1.9 above).

However, if repeated crossings of a single barrier by the same constituent cumulate, counting as a Subjacency violation, then a *Wh*-Movement derivation of such multiple CLLD structures as (10) should be expected to yield a Subjacency violation. Consider, for example, the (simplified) derivation shown in Figure 2.1.[12] Here, at least one constituent crosses a single barrier of type CP twice, violating Subjacency. So the derivation in figure 2.1 should be as ill formed as (12), which it is not.

Topicalization, on the other hand, allows only one topicalized constituent per sentence (for independent reasons),[13] thus behaving like ordinary *wh*-constructions.

2.3.3 Successive Cyclicity and Aux-to-Comp

Another property suggesting that CLLD does not involve *Wh*-Movement is that, unlike ordinary *wh*-constructions, it apparently cannot avail itself of successive cyclic derivations. If we consider adjuncts, which can only move successive cyclically, we detect a clear contrast between ordinary *Wh*-Movement constructions and CLLD. For example:

(13) a. PER QUESTA RAGIONE$_i$, ha detto che se ne andrà t_i.
           for this reason (focus)   he said   that he will leave
       b. Per quale ragione$_i$ ha detto   che se ne andrà t_i?
           for what reason   did he say that he will leave

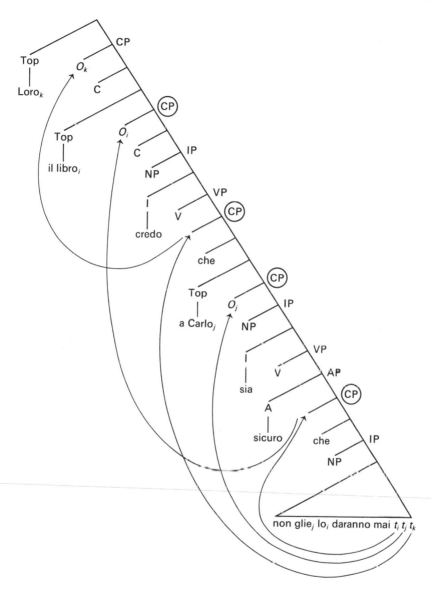

Figure 2.1

c. La ragione per la quale$_i$ ha detto che se ne andrà t_i...
   the reason why   he said   that he will leave

(14) *Per questa ragione$_i$, ha detto che se ne andrà t_i.
     for this reason   he said   that he will leave

(15) a. IN MODO DEFINITIVO$_i$, ha detto che l'aggiusterà t_i.
        in a definitive way (focus)   he said   that he will fix it
     b. In che modo$_i$ ha detto   che l'aggiusterà t_i?
        which way   did he say that he will fix it
     c. Il modo in cui$_i$ ha detto che l'aggiusterà t_i...
        the way in which he said   that he will fix it

(16) *In modo definitivo$_i$, ha detto che l'aggiusterà t_i, prima o poi.
      in a definitive way   he said   that he will fix it   sooner or later

Why is the construal of the "fronted" adjunct possible in (13a–c) and (15a–c) but not in the corresponding CLLD cases (14) and (16)? (Note again the minimal contrast between CLLD and topicalization: (13a) versus (14) and (15a) versus (16).)

If CLLD does not involve any form of movement (hence does not involve any successive cyclic movement), the contrast follows directly. t is antecedent-governed in (13) and (15), due to the presence of a trace of successive cyclic movement in the VP-adjoined position (or the specifier position of the embedded CP), but it is not in (14) and (16), for lack of such an intermediate trace:

(17) a. $[_{Top}$ Per questa ragione$_i$] $[_{CP}$ ha detto $[_{CP}$ che $[$se ne andrà $t_i]]]$?
     b. $[_{Top}$ PER QUESTA RAGIONE$_i$] $[_{CP}$ $O_i[$...$[_{CP}$ t_i che $[_{IP}[_{VP}$ t_i $[_{VP}$ se ne andrà $t_i]]]]]$.

In fact, the contrast is detectable in "short" movement cases as well. (18a) differs in interpretation from (18b):

(18) a. Per questa ragione,   hanno arrestato Mario.
        because of this reason they have arrested Mario
     b. Hanno arrestato Mario   per questa ragione.
        they have arrested Mario for this reason

The fact that (18a) does not share the meaning of (18b) suggests that *per questa ragione* cannot be reconstructed into the IP-internal position that it occupies in (18b). This is what we expect, in fact, if CLLD does not involve *Wh*-Movement. The IP-internal empty category will thus fail to be antecedent-governed, since its antecedent is too far away. A barrier, CP, intervenes between them:

(19) $[_{Top}$ Per questa ragione$_i$] $[_{CP}[_{IP}$ NP VP $t_i]]$

As expected, the corresponding topicalization case (20) differs from CLLD in displaying only the interpretation of (18b), which suggests that reconstruction into (hence movement from) the IP-internal adjunct position is required in this case (see below for discussion):

(20) PER QUESTA RAGIONE, hanno arrestato Mario.[14]

Successive cyclic movement also appears to be necessary to account for the contrast between (21) on one hand and (22) on the other, in which the subject of the infinitive has been *Wh*-Moved under relativization and question formation:

(21)   *Riteniamo Gianni essere intelligente.
        we consider Gianni to be intelligent

(22) a. Gianni, che riteniamo   essere intelligente, ...
        Gianni who we consider to be intelligent
     b. Chi ritenevate   essere intelligente?
        who did you consider to be intelligent

Discussions by Rizzi (1982, chap. 3, 1990, chap. 1)—and, for the parallel French facts, by Kayne (1980), Chomsky (1980a, 32), and Pollock (1986)—imply the derivation shown in (24):

(23)   *Riteniamo $[_{CP}[_{IP}$ Gianni essere intelligente]].

(24) a. Gianni, O_i che $[_{IP}$ riteniamo $[_{CP} t_i[_{IP} t_i$ essere intelligente]]], ...
     b. Chi$_i$ ritenevate $[_{CP} t_i[_{IP} t_i$ essere intelligente]]?

If CLLD involved *Wh*-Movement, we might expect it to be possible to dislocate the subject of an infinitival sentence in the same successive cyclic fashion. Apparently, however, it is not possible. See (25a), with the putative derivation (25b):

(25) a. (Consideriamo Anna stupida.) *?Gianni, invece,
        (We consider Anna stupid.)   Gianni on the contrary
        riteniamo essere intelligente.
        we consider to be intelligent
     b. ...Gianni $O_i(...)$ riteniamo $[_{CP} t_i[_{IP} t_i$ essere intelligente]].

The ill-formedness of (25a) contrasts again rather clearly with the essential well-formedness of the corresponding topicalization case (at the appropriate stylistic level):

(26) GIANNI$_i$,   riteniamo $[_{CP} t_i[_{IP} t_i$ essere intelligente]],
     Gianni (focus) we consider   to be intelligent
     non Carlo.
     not Carlo

Alongside the successive cyclic derivation, another *Wh*-Movement derivation is potentially open to (22) and (25a)—one dependent on the previous application of the Aux-to-Comp rule (Rizzi 1981, 1982, chap. 3) in the infinitival clause, as shown in (27)–(28):

(27) a. Gianni, O_i che riteniamo [$_{CP}$ essere$_k$[$_{IP}$ $t_i t_k$ intelligente t_i]], . . .

    b. Chi$_i$ ritenevate [$_{CP}$ essere$_k$[$_{IP}$ $t_i t_k$ intelligente t_i]]?

(28)   Gianni, O_i invece riteniamo [$_{CP}$ essere$_k$[$_{IP}$ $t_i t_k$ intelligente t_i]], . . .

In the present case a successive cyclic movement of the subject of the infinitive is no longer needed. The preverbal subject position of the infinitive receives (nominative) Case in situ as a function of the Aux-to-Comp rule (again see Rizzi 1982, chap. 3).

At any rate, the ill-formedness of (25a) indicates that even this movement derivation is unavailable (due, I suggest, to the non-*Wh*-Movement nature of CLLD).[15]

Note that the EC in (25a) is not locally bound by a clitic. One might suggest that this, rather than lack of *Wh*-Movement, is the cause of its ungrammaticality. However, a clitic "resuming" the left-dislocated constituent is normally optional, except for object clitics (to which we will return). In particular, where no clitic form exists that corresponds to a certain (left-dislocated) constituent, none is required (*Da Gianni, non è stato salutato* 'By Gianni, he was not greeted'; *Per Mario, non ho mai lavorato* 'For Mario, I never worked').

Although personal Agr(eement) might rightly be taken to function as a kind of clitic in tensed clauses, no clitic or Agr appears to be available to the subject of infinitival clauses. So none should be required.

In any event, what is relevant is that, under a *Wh*-Movement analysis of CLLD, there would be no obvious reason why a clitic should be obligatorily present (thus explaining on independent grounds the ill-formedness of (25a)). As we will see, quite the opposite situation obtains under a non-*Wh*-Movement analysis of CLLD.

2.3.4 The *Ne*-Cliticization Test

Additional evidence that CLLD should not be analyzed as involving movement is provided by its behavior with respect to a more subtle diagnostic criterion for *Wh*-Movement in Italian. This is based on a peculiarity of the pronominalization of the $\bar{N}$ associated with an indefinite quantifier as analyzed by Belletti and Rizzi (1981) and by Rizzi (1982, chap. 4). Such an $\bar{N}$ is obligatorily pronominalized with the clitic *ne* (lit. 'of-it/them') whenever the quantifier NP is in the object position of the VP, a properly governed position (that is, whenever it is the direct object or the inverted subject of a passive or ergative verb). It is obligatorily a zero pronominal (PRO, Belletti and Rizzi suggest, following Kayne (1979, app.)) whenever the quantified NP is in (preverbal) subject or left-dislocated position (both, arguably, ungoverned positions).[16] The relevant paradigm is given in (29)–(30):

(29) a. *(Ne$_i$)   ho smarrite [$_{NP}$ quattro t_i] (di quelle lettere).
      of-them (I) lost   four   (of those letters)

  b. *(Ne$_i$)   sono andate smarrite [$_{NP}$ quattro t_i].
      of-them have gone lost   four

(30) a. [$_{NP}$ Quattro t_i] (*ne$_i$)   sono andate smarrite (non distrutte).
      four   of-them have gone lost   (not destroyed)

  b. [$_{NP}$ Quattro t_i], credo   che (*ne$_i$)   siano andate smarrite
      four   I think that   of-them have gone lost
      (non distrutte).
      (not destroyed)

(For more careful discussion, see Pollock 1986 and the references cited in note 16.)

What is relevant to present concerns is that the obligatoriness of *ne* is preserved under *Wh*-Movement, as shown by the following paradigm, discussed by Rizzi (1982, 150):

(31) a. Quante pietre   hai preso?
      how many stones have you taken

  b. *Quante   hai preso?
      how many have you taken
      (Compare *Ho preso tre* 'I have taken three.')

  c. Quante   ne hai prese?
      how many of-them have you taken
      (Compare *Ne ho prese tre* 'I have taken three of-them.')

Given that *Wh*-Movement can only take place from properly governed positions (because of the ECP), we expect that extraction of the subject of a tensed IP introduced by a complementizer will take place from the postverbal position, which is the only properly governed one of the preverbal and postverbal subject positions. This in turn predicts that extraction of a pronominalized quantified subject of a passive or ergative V necessarily involves the *ne* option, since this is obligatory when the NP is in the (properly) governed object position. That is indeed the case, as Rizzi notes:[17]

(32) a. Quante pietre   hai detto   che sono cadute?
        how many stones did you say that fell down
     b. Quante   hai detto   che *(ne) sono cadute?[18]
        how many did you say that of-them-fell down

The "fronting" of a subject quantifier of an ergative V (whose $\bar{N}$ is pronominalized) would thus seem to constitute a test to establish whether a certain left-peripheral construction involves *Wh*-Movement or not. In this context, the contrast between the CLLD case (30b) and the corresponding topicalization case (33) is instructive:

(30) b. [$_{NP}$ Quattro t_i] credo   che (*ne$_i$) siano andate smarrite
        four   I think that of-them have gone lost
        (non distrutte).
        not destroyed

(33) Speaker A: Sono arrivate dieci lettere.
                have arrived   ten letters
                'Ten letters have arrived.'
     Speaker B: No, QUATTRO pare   che *(ne) siano arrivate,
                no   four   it appears that of-them have arrived
                NON DIECI.
                not ten

Topicalization, but not CLLD, behaves like a *Wh*-Movement construction. (30b) in fact raises two separate questions: (1) Why is *ne* not obligatory (as in regular *Wh*-Movement constructions)? (2) Why is it actually impossible?

   The answer to the first question is that the EC in (30b), unlike that in (33), need not be in the (properly) head-governed object position. It can instead be in the preverbal subject position locally bound by Agr, which acts in this case like a subject resumptive clitic (see (34)) parallel to the object case in (35):[19]

(34) [$_{NP}$ Quattro PRO]$_i$ credo   che [$_{IP}$ e_i Agr$_i$ siano andate smarrite].
        four   I think that   have gone lost

(35) [$_{NP}$ Quattro PRO]$_i$ credo   che [$_{IP}$ le$_i$ abbiano smarrite e_i].
        four   I think that   they have lost them

As for why *ne* is actually impossible in (30b), suggesting that the postverbal properly head-governed subject position is unavailable to CLLD, we may note that independent principles rule out all possible derivations from such a position. Consider (36):

(36) a. [$_{NP}$ Quattro t_k]$_i$ . . . Agr ne$_k$ siano andate [$_{VP}$ smarrite t_i]

    b. [$_{NP}$ Quattro PRO]$_i$ . . . Agr ne$_k$ siano andate [$_{VP}$ smarrite t_i]

    c. [$_{QP}$ Quattro]$_i$ . . . Agr ne$_k$ siano andate [$_{VP}$ smarrite $t_i t_k$]

(36c) is ruled out because the phrase in Top, not being referential, cannot enter into a binding chain with its trace; nor can it enter into a government chain, since the construction does not involve movement of a null operator (see the next section for more evidence to this effect). (36b) is excluded because *ne* has no source (or EC to be construed with under Reconstruction). Finally, (36a) is excluded (in addition perhaps to the reasons that exclude (36c) by the fact that t_i cannot qualify as any of the possible empty NP types. It cannot be PRO or NP-trace; it cannot be a variable (because there is no operator to bind it); and it cannot be pro, because Agr fails to identify it in [NP, VP], for minimality reasons.

2.3.5 The Complex Distribution of the Resumptive Clitic

Yet another argument for the non-*Wh*-Movement status of CLLD comes from a basic property of the construction: the fact that resumptive clitics in CLLD are all optional except for object clitics (*lo, la, li, le,* and so on):

(37) a. A casa, non (ci) sono stato   ancora.

      home   not (there) have (I) been yet

    b. Di questa faccenda, non (ne) voglio   più parlare.

      of this matter   not (of-it) (I) want to speak anymore

    c. Bella,   pare   che non (lo) sia mai stata.

      beautiful it seems that not (it) (she) ever was

    d. Influenzato dalla pittura fiamminga, non (lo) è stato.

      influenced by Flemish painting   not (it) he was

    e. Gianni, *(lo) vedrò   domani.

      Gianni   (him) (I) will see tomorrow

Why should the object be singled out as obligatorily requiring a clitic to bind it? Interestingly enough, such incoherence in the paradigm can be made to follow from independent principles of the theory if we again assume that CLLD does not involve *Wh*-Movement. One obvious difference between (37e) and all the other cases for which the clitic appears optional is that the EC is an NP in the former case and some category distinct from NP in the latter cases: a PP in (37a–b), an AP in (37c), and a VP in (37d).

Let us consider the consequences of taking this to be the relevant factor in the asymmetry shown in (37). NPs seem to have a special status among the various categories. They are the only category that is systematically partitioned, in both the overt and empty variants, into the four distinct classes [−pronominal, +anaphor], [+pronominal, +anaphor], [+pronominal, −anaphor], [−pronominal, −anaphor] (see Chomsky 1982), and consequently the only natural class of elements subject to the binding theory.

Granting the essential correctness of this characterization, let us go back to paradigm (37) and consider the structure of (37e) as opposed to the structure of (37a), which we may regard as representative of all the non-NP cases:

(38) [[$_{PP}$ A casa] [$_{CP}$ C[$_{IP}$ NP non (ci) sono stato]]].

(39) [[$_{NP}$ Gianni] [$_{CP}$ C[$_{IP}$ NP (lo) vedrò domani]]].

We will further assume that the presence of the resumptive clitic is entirely optional throughout the construction, as indicated by the large majority of the cases (the null hypothesis, in any event). How are we to account, then, for the apparent obligatoriness of the resumptive clitic in (37e), the NP case? The logic of the answer will be as follows: whereas nothing excludes either option (presence or absence of the clitic) when the EC is a non-NP, a number of general principles converge, when the EC is an NP, to exclude the option with no clitic.

To see this, we may consider whether the theory associates any well-formed derivation to the variant of (37e) without the clitic. I adopt here the intrinsic definition of ECs discussed by Chomsky (1982), though a comparable result could be obtained under the contextual definition (for arguments that the former definition should be preferred to the latter, see Chomsky 1982, 1986a, Safir 1982, and Brody 1984).

Let us consider the various possibilities in turn. If the EC is assigned the combination of features [+pronominal, +anaphor] (= PRO), the structure is excluded by the binding theory in the familiar manner. If the EC is [−pronominal, +anaphor] (= NP-trace), the structure is again excluded by Principle A of the binding theory since the anaphor is A-free in its governing category. If it is [+pronominal, −anaphor] (= pro), the structure is similarly excluded because pro is not properly identified (see Chomsky 1982 and chapter 3).

This leaves us with one last possibility: that the EC is [−pronominal, −anaphor], that is, a variable. A general, and minimal, requirement on variables is that they be locally $\bar{\text{A}}$-bound (and operator-bound). This requirement may in fact be enforced by a general (contextual) definition of variable such as that in (40):[20]

(40) Variable $=_{def}$ [$_{NP}$ e] in A-position locally $\bar{A}$-bound and operator-bound.

If, following Chomsky (1981, 102), we further assume (41) as a tentative definition of "operator,"

(41) Operator $=_{def}$ bare quantifiers, *wh*-phrases, and null NPs in Spec CP.

then the NP *Gianni* in (37e) will not qualify as an operator (it is neither a quantifier nor a *wh*-phrase, nor is it in Spec CP—if nonnull NPs are impossible there; see Kayne 1984, chap. 10) and thus cannot identify an EC in IP as a variable.[21] So, if we assume that CLLD does *not* involve *Wh*-Movement, which would create an empty NP in Spec CP (an operator) binding the EC in IP, even the last possibility left for the variant of (37e) without the clitic is excluded on general grounds, by the principle barring free variables.[22]

In sum, it appears that no well-formed derivation can be associated with the cliticless variant of (37e)—a desirable result, since it directly explains why resumptive clitics happen to be obligatory in the object case. (If a clitic is present, no problems arise, the resulting configuration being a normal clitic-"trace" configuration, subject to antecedent government; recall chapter 1).[23]

If non-NP ECs are not required to qualify as either PRO, pro, NP-trace, or variable (because they are not partitioned by the features [±pronominal, ±anaphor], then no comparable restriction is placed on such cases—whence the optionality of the resumptive clitic. The PP EC of (37a), for example, falls neither under the binding theory nor under the requirement, holding of variables only, that an operator $\bar{A}$-bind the EC.

Thus, a simple and independently motivated account of the curious asymmetry found in paradigm (37) is possible if we assume crucially that CLLD does not involve *Wh*-Movement.[24]

Topicalization, which does involve *Wh*-Movement as standardly assumed, again differs minimally from CLLD in the expected way, since no clitic is required (or is in fact possible) in a structure corresponding to (37e). Following Chomsky (1977), the EC there is $\bar{A}$-bound by a null NP in Spec CP:

(42) [GIANNI$_i$[$_{CP}$ NP$_i$[$_{IP}$ vedrò e_i domani]]].

(41), the notion of operator assumed in the account of the obligatoriness of the clitic in the object case, in interaction with the nonmovement hypothesis for CLLD suggested here, makes one straightforward prediction. Should there be an object bare quantifier in place of a name in the left-dislocated position, a resumptive clitic would no longer be required, since the object EC would come to be $\bar{\text{A}}$-bound by a proper operator (a bare quantifier in an $\bar{\text{A}}$-position external to IP). This expectation is fulfilled, as shown by the following examples, originally pointed out to me by Paola Benincà as exceptions to the otherwise obligatory presence of object clitics in CLLD:[25]

(43) a. Qualcosa,   farò   (non preoccuparti).
        something (or other) I will do (don't worry)

    b. Qualcuno,   troverò   di sicuro per questo compito.
        someone (or other) I will find surely   for this task

The grammaticality of (43a–b) contrasts with the ungrammaticality of the cliticless variants of (44a–d), which contain quantified NPs instead of (bare) quantifiers in the left-dislocated position:

(44) a. Qualche sbaglio, ogni tanto, $\left\{\begin{array}{l} *\text{fa anche Gianni} \\ \textit{lo}\ \text{fa anche Gianni} \end{array}\right\}$.

        some mistake   every now and then   makes (*it*) even Gianni

    b. Tutti i tuoi errori, prima o poi, $\left\{\begin{array}{l} *\text{pagherai} \\ \textit{li}\ \text{pagherai} \end{array}\right\}$.

        all your errors   sooner or later   you will pay (*them*)

    c. Alcune cartoline, $\left\{\begin{array}{l} *\text{ho ricevuto anch'io} \\ \textit{le}\ \text{ho ricevute anch'io} \end{array}\right\}$.

        some postcards   have received (*them*) even I

    d. Molte lettere $\left\{\begin{array}{l} *\text{mi hanno spedito in ufficio} \\ \text{me}\ \textit{le}\ \text{hanno spedite in ufficio} \end{array}\right\}$.

        many letters   to-me-(*them*) have sent to my office

I take this contrast to support Chomsky's notion of operator, (41), figuring in the definition of variable given in (40). The reason why the clitic appears obligatory again in (44) is that the NP in left-dislocated position fails to qualify as an operator and is thus unable to identify the IP-internal EC as a variable.

As far as the linguistic concept of "operator" at issue here is concerned, it seems that quantified NPs behave more like names than quantifiers.

Such a difference between bare quantifiers and quantified NPs may in fact correlate with a structural difference, if bare quantifiers are instantiations of the maximal N projection ($\bar{\bar{\text{N}}}$) rather than of the specifier node, as indicated in (45):[26]

(45) a. Bare quantifiers: $[_{\text{NP}}[_{\text{QP}}\ \text{Q}]]$
    b. Quantified NPs: $[_{\text{NP}}[_{\text{QP}}\ \text{Q}]\ [_{\bar{\text{N}}}\ \text{N}]]$

Going back to (43), we may ask whether a resumptive clitic, though not required, is at all possible in these contexts. As (46)–(47) show, a resumptive clitic is apparently optional in such cases:

(46) Qualcosa, (la) vedo anch'io.
     something (it) I see as well

(47) Qualcuno, (l') ho trovato,   non preoccuparti.
     someone   (him) I've found don't worry

However, it turns out that this optionality is indeed only apparent, arising from the fact that left-dislocated bare quantifiers are systematically ambiguous between one use as (bare) quantifiers (in which the clitic is impossible) and one use as quantified NPs (in which the clitic is as obligatory as in (44)).

One relevant observation is that the presence versus absence of the clitic in (46)–(47) correlates systematically with a property of the interpretation of the NP: whether it is referential (specific) or nonreferential, respectively. When a specific referential interpretation is clearly forced by the context, the clitic appears to become obligatory again:

(48) Speaker A: Li conosci, quelli?
                 'Do you know them, those people?'
     Speaker B: Sì, qualcuno, *(l') ho già conosciuto.
                 yes someone   (him) I already know

(49) Qualcosa, su cui   avevo fatto incidere le sue iniziali,
     something on which I had his initials engraved
     $\begin{cases} \text{glicl'ho appena data} \\ \text{*gli ho appena dato/a} \end{cases}$.
     I just gave (*it*) to him

This may suggest that the "pure" quantifier use of an NP is incompatible with a specific referential interpretation of the NP. When the referential reading is forced, only the namelike quantified-NP use is possible (which requires the presence of a resumptive clitic).

A particularly clear indication that the optionality of the clitic is only apparent in (46)–(47) is provided by a peculiarity of *qualcosa*. For many speakers *qualcosa* changes gender according to whether it is used as a (bare) quantifier or a quantified NP, being masculine (the unmarked gender, in Italian) when used as a (bare) quantifier, but feminine when used as a quantified NP (similarly to *qualche cosa*).

This can be seen by selecting two different contexts, one forcing the nonreferential use of *qualcosa* (which correlates with the (bare) quantifier use), the other the referential use (which correlates with the quantified-NP use):

(50) a. E' successo qualcosa,   mentre ero via?
         did something happen (+masc) while I was away
     b. *E' successa qualcosa,   mentre ero via?
         did something happen (+fem) while I was away

(51) a. Qualcosa   mi era caduta in testa
         something (+fem) fell on my head
         ma non ho fatto in tempo a vederla.
         but I had no time   to see it (+fem)
     b. *?Qualcosa   mi era caduto in testa
         something (+masc) fell on my head
         ma non ho fatto in tempo a vederlo.
         but I had no time   to see it (+masc)

The contrast in (50) shows that *qualcosa*, as a quantifier, has only masculine gender. The contrast in (51) indicates that *qualcosa*, as a quantified NP, is (preferably) feminine.

Now consider the contrast in the following CLLD context:

(52) a. Qualcosa, prima o poi   *la*   farò.
         something sooner or later it (+fem) I will do
     b. *Qualcosa, prima o poi   *lo*   farò.
         something sooner or later it (+masc) I will do
         (Compare *Qualcosa, prima o poi farò.*)

The clitic can only be feminine. This shows that *qualcosa* as a quantifier is incompatible with a clitic.

These observations about left-dislocated quantifiers thus indicate that bare quantifiers (used nonreferentially), but not quantified NPs, can act as operators. They also suggest that, in general, (nonderivative) variables cannot be $\bar{\text{A}}$-bound both by an operator and by a clitic (something that appears to be true for the clear cases of *Wh*-Movement constructions). Finally, they constitute indirect confirmation for the non-*Wh*-Movement nature of CLLD. The complex pattern of obligatory, optional, and impossible resumptive clitics, though entirely natural under a non-*Wh*-Movement analysis of CLLD in interaction with Chomsky's notion of operator, would hardly be comprehensible under the opposite analysis.

The account proposed for paradigm (37) draws the crucial distinction not between object ECs and all other ECs (which would be a curious bifurcation, in any event) but between NP ECs and non-NP ECs. In other words, it does not single out object ECs as something special. Rather, it predicts that subject ECs should behave alike, being excluded in the variant without a resumptive clitic.

At first sight, that prediction would seem to be unverifiable, given the pro-drop nature of Italian. In such sentences as (53)

(53) Gianni, credo che ——— sia già arrivato.
     Gianni I believe that   (he) has already arrived

it is impossible to distinguish the derivation in which the subject EC is not locally bound (which is predicted to be ill formed just like the corresponding object case) from the derivation, always available in a pro-drop language, in which the subject EC is locally bound by Agr (which would act, in this respect, very much like a resumptive clitic). Given that at least one well-formed derivation can always be associated with any sentence like (53), there would seem to be no way to test the empirical prediction of the analysis for the ordinary case.

One case in which the prediction could be checked in a standard pro-drop language would be one in which the subject NP position receives Case but no pronominal Agr is available that could locally bind the NP position. Exactly one such case appears to exist in Italian: in the Aux-to-Comp constructions discussed by Rizzi (1981, and 1982, chaps. 3 and 4). Limiting ourselves for convenience to one of these constructions, we may characterize the features relevant to our discussion in the following way: In the infinitival complement to a restricted class of verbs (largely verbs of opinion) lexical subjects are permitted (at a more marked stylistic level) when the auxiliary is preposed to Comp, but not when it follows the subject:

(54) a.   Ritenevano non esser io disposto ad aiutarli.
       they believed not-to-be I willing   to help them
    b. *Ritenevano io non esser disposto ad aiutarli.

The contrast can be interpreted as an effect of the creation in (54a) of a special context of (structural) nominative Case assignment dependent on the preposing of the auxiliary to C.

The construction differs from tensed structures (the ordinary context of nominative Case assignment), however, in that the pro-drop properties of the former are only a subset of those available to the latter. In essence, a pronominal subject can be dropped in the Aux-to-Comp construction only if its interpretation is that of a pleonastic pronoun, not that of a personal pronoun:

(55) a. *Maria li ha aiutati benché ritenessimo
          Maria helped them though we believed
          non essere *e* disposta a farlo.
          she was not willing to
          Compare:
          Ritenevamo non esser lei disposta a farlo.
          we believed not-to-be she willing to
      b. Ritenevamo non essere *e* necessario partire immediatamente.
          we believed not-to-be necessary   to leave immediately
          Compare:
          e   è necessario partire immediatamente.
          pro (pleon.) is necessary to leave immediately

This contrast can be straightforwardly accounted for if it is assumed that
the Aux-to-Comp construction (unlike the ordinary tensed sentence case)
contains no Agr with nominal features of number, person (or gender)
capable of rendering the personal interpretation possible (see Rizzi 1982,
chaps. 3 and 4). This conclusion is supported by the fact that no such
feature is realized on the overt inflection of the verb (which is an infinitival
form).

The construction thus appears to provide the abstract context suggested
above in which the prediction made by the proposed analysis can be
checked. Indeed, if the subject NP of the Aux-to-Comp construction is a
(nominative) Case marked position that is not locally bound by a nominal
cliticlike Agr, we expect no CLLD of that subject NP to be possible, for
exactly the same reasons that ruled out CLLD of the object NP in the
cliticless variant of (37e). This expectation appears to be fulfilled:

(56) (Consideriamo Ava stupida.)*? Gianni, al contrario,
      we consider   Ava stupid   Gianni on the contrary
      riteniamo   essere intelligente.
      we consider to be intelligent

Topicalization again turns out to contrast minimally with CLLD in that
it is apparently possible (at the appropriate stylistic level) to topicalize the
subject NP in the Aux-to-Comp construction. Compare (56) with (57):

(57) Solo LEI, ritenevamo essere adatta a quel compito.
      only her   we believed to be suitable for that task

The (relative) contrast can once again be explained if topicalization, unlike
CLLD, does involve *Wh*-Movement. (57) is thus entirely parallel to (58),
in which the subject has been extracted through an overt instance of
Wh-Movement:

(58) Quante persone   ritenevate   essere adatte a quel compito?
how many people did you believe to be suitable for that task

2.4   A Surprising Behavior under Negation

The conclusion that successive cyclic movement is not available to CLLD is apparently contradicted by a well-defined class of cases.

The ungrammatical examples (59a–d) all become grammatical if a negation precedes the EC with which the CLLD phrase is construed, as in (60a–d):

(59) a. *Per questa ragione$_i$, ha detto che se ne andrà e_i. (= (14))
        for this reason   he said   that he will leave
     b. *In modo definitivo$_i$,   ha detto che l'aggiusterà e_i,
        in a definitive manner he said   that he will fix it
        prima o poi. (= (16))
        sooner or later
     c. *Per un'altra ragione$_i$, Carlo è morto e_i.
        for another reason   Carlo died
     d. *In modo scortese$_i$, Carlo di solito si comporta e_i.
        In a rude manner   Carlo usually behaves

(60) a. Per questa ragione$_i$, ha detto che non se ne andrà e_i.
        for this reason   he said   that he will not leave
     b. In modo definitivo$_i$,   ha detto che non l'aggiusterà e_i.
        in a definitive manner he said   that he will not fix it
     c. Per un'altra ragione$_i$, Carlo non è morto e_i.
        for another reason   Carlo did not die
     d. In modo scortese$_i$, Carlo di solito non si comporta e_i.
        in a rude manner   Carlo usually does not behave

This state of affairs is doubly puzzling. First, it is not immediately obvious why the presence of a negation should affect the construction's normal incompatibility with successive cyclic movement, apparently turning a non-*Wh*-Movement into a *Wh*-Movement construction (at least, in this particular circumstance). Second, the grammaticality of (60a–d) raises another, more serious puzzle. Adverbials, which (unlike complements) can only move via successive cyclic movement, are known not to be extractable from a negation island (see Ross's (1984) original discussion of "inner islands" and Rizzi's (1990, chap. 1) reduction of negation islands to Relativized Minimality). This is illustrated by the systematic contrast between (61a–c), all containing phrases that can undergo long *Wh*-Movement, and the ungrammatical (62a–c), which contain phrases that can only be moved successive cyclically:

(61) a.   Bill is here, *which* they do*n't* know.

    b.   It is *this car$_i$* that I think that John did*n't* fix e_i in that way.

    c.   *Which book* did you *not* receive?

(62) a.   *Bill is here, *as* they do*n't* know.

    b.   *It is *in this way* that I think that John did*n't* fix his car.

    c.   **How angry* was*n't* he?

If anything, one should expect the presence of the negation to block, not to "unblock," the CLLD of adverbials in (60a–d).

However, there is an interpretation of this apparent anomaly that is compatible with, and in fact supports, the conclusion that CLLD does not involve movement of an empty operator, explaining both puzzles simultaneously.

In the preceding sections we have seen that many systematic contrasts between topicalization and CLLD can be explained by analyzing the former, but not the latter, as a *Wh*-Movement construction. Given the formal near-identity of the two constructions, in particular the fact that the "fronted" constituent appears to be operatorlike in neither, we have assumed that the difference lies in the fact that topicalization, but not CLLD, involves the movement of an empty operator to the Spec CP adjacent to the constituent in Top.

Suppose, now, that this is not an accidental difference between the two constructions, and that the presence of an empty operator in topicalization is tied to the quantificational force of the construction, which involves the "fronting" of a *focused* element, in Italian. Put differently, it is the presence of quantificational force in topicalization, and its absence in CLLD, that renders the employment of an empty operator possible in the former and impossible in the latter.[27] In fact, we have already seen that where such a quantificational force becomes available to CLLD (in the case of (certain) left-dislocated bare quantifiers) this construction too acquires *Wh*-Movement properties (no obligatoriness of a clitic for objects, licensing of parasitic gaps, and so on).

Suppose, now, that another option exists for contributing quantificational force to a phrase (hence, for "licensing" an empty operator moving to Spec CP): *amalgamation* with a negation, whose quantificational character is hardly disputable.

This notion of amalgamation needs to be made more precise. It is well known that a quantifier in the scope of a negation can amalgamate with it. See, for example, (63), where the quantifier *molti* 'many' is in the scope of the sentential negation *non* 'not', and the amalgamated reading 'not + many' = 'few' is accordingly possible (see Klima 1964):

(63) Franco non ha visto molti film di Forman.
     Franco has not seen many films by Forman

For a quantifier to be in the scope of the negation, it is necessary (though not sufficient) that the quantifier be c-commanded by the negation in the same simple clause at S-Structure. Notoriously, if the c-command requirement fails at S-Structure, as in the passive counterpart of (60) (*Molti film di Forman non sono stati visti da Franco* 'Many films by Forman have not been seen by Franco'), the quantifier cannot be interpreted in the scope of (hence cannot amalgamate with) the negation, and the only available reading is 'For many x, $x = \ldots$, not $(\ldots x \ldots)$. That being c-commanded by a negation in the same simple clause is not sufficient for being in its scope is shown by such cases as (64), where the explicit contrast apparently forces another c-commanded constituent to be in the scope of the negation:

(64) Franco non ha visto molti film di Forman con Maria,
     Franco has not seen many films by Forman with Maria
     ma con Carla.
     but with Carla

Here, *molti* is not in the scope of *non* and consequently cannot amalgamate with it to yield the reading 'not + many' = 'few'. Apparently, no more than one constituent may be in the scope of negation.

We can express the scope of negation explicitly via the following scope convention:

(65) In the structure $[\ldots neg \ldots X(P) \ldots]$, where *neg* is a clausal negation c-commanding $X(P)$ in the same simple clause at S-Structure, coindex *neg* and $X(P)$ (with superscripts).

We will further assume that the convention cannot apply more than once. (65) will then yield representations such as (66) and (67) from (63) and (64), respectively:

(66) Franco *non*^{i} ha visto $[_Q \text{molti}]^i$ film di Forman.

(67) Franco *non*^{i} ha visto molti film di Forman $[_{PP} \text{con Maria}]^i$, ma con Carla.

On the basis of (65), we may then define the following amalgamation convention (see Rizzi 1982, 123):

(68) In the structure $[\ldots neg^i \ldots Q^i \ldots]$, where Q is a quantifier belonging to a certain class,[28] Q^i amalgamates with neg^i at LF.

In a Quantifier Raising (QR) framework, this would assign (66) the LF representation (69):

(69) Not + many (= few) x, x = films by Forman, Franco saw x

In the same framework, the other reading of (63) follows from a different application of the scope convention, whereby the verb, rather than *molti*, is coindexed with the negation (*Franco non^i ha visto^i molti film di Forman*). If so, the amalgamation convention cannot affect *neg* and *molti*, since only phrases coindexed with the negation (that is, in its scope) can amalgamate with it.

Let us now return to the suggestion that "amalgamation" with a negation (now interpreted as a function of superscript coindexing) is a way of acquiring quantificational force, hence of licensing an empty operator where one is not otherwise licensed, as in CLLD.

If we adopt this hypothesis, which is based on the independent notion of scope (of clausal negation), both puzzles noted above dissolve at the same time.

Recall that (14) is ungrammatical because no null operator is available in CLLD (so that e_i ultimately fails to be related to its antecedent via a chain of antecedent government relations):

(14) *Per questa ragione$_i$, ha detto che se ne andrà e_i.

       for this reason   he said   that he will leave

This is so because the CLLD phrase has no inherent quantificational force (contains no bare quantifier of the appropriate kind), nor is the semantics of the construction capable of contributing such quantificational force, unlike in topicalization. Since adjuncts, unlike (certain) complements, cannot enter a long-distance binding chain either, no well-formed derivation will be available to (14).

Under the amalgamation hypothesis, the presence of a negation taking the EC in its scope radically changes the situation. Here, a null operator O is licensed because, being in the exclusive scope of *non*, with which it can amalgamate (at LF), it receives from it the required quantificational force:

(70) Per questa ragione^k, O_i^k credo che non se ne andrà e_i.

Given the identity of (superscript) coindexing between O and the phrase in Top, which here expresses the fact that the former is essentially a "placeholder" for the latter (see Chomsky 1977), the phrase in Top itself will be under the scope of the negation and will thus ultimately amalgamate with *non* to give an LF representation of the form (71):[29]

(71) Non + per questa ragione$_i$ [credo che se ne andrà e_i]

This amalgamation hypothesis in fact receives independent support. It makes a number of predictions that turn out to be correct, allowing us at the same time to account for some otherwise curious properties of the construction.

If being in the scope of clausal negation may license a null operator via amalgamation (a process that therefore turns a non-*Wh*-Movement construction into a *Wh*-Movement construction), it is predicted that when an object is in the exclusive scope of negation and can amalgamate with it, then it will no longer need to be locally bound by a clitic, since it may function as a variable bound by the null operator.

We have seen that quantified NPs, as opposed to (certain) bare quantifiers, cannot function as inherent operators binding a variable and therefore need to be resumed by a clitic because of the non-*Wh*-Movement status of CLLD. See, for example, the contrast between (72) and (73):

(72) a. Qualcosa, farò.
         something I will do
     b. Qualcuno, troverò di sicuro che mi aiuti.
         someone I'll surely find   who will help me

(73) a. *Pochi soldi, di sicuro guadagna.
         little money he surely earns
     b. *Molti amici, ha invitato,   che io sappia.
         many friends he has invited as far as I know

Interestingly, if the IP-internal EC is in the scope of clausal negation, the ungrammatical (73a–b) become grammatical (as originally pointed out to me by Mauro Scorretti):

(74) a. Pochi soldi, di sicuro non guadagna.
         little money surely   he does not earn
     b. Molti amici, non ha invitato,   che io sappia.
         many friends he has not invited as far as I know

Even certain classes of nonquantified NPs, which also require a resumptive clitic when clitic left dislocated, are less than totally unacceptable if in the scope of a clausal negation:

(75) a. ?Questo, Gianni non farà mai.
          this   Gianni will never do
          (versus
          *Questo, Gianni farà sempre.
           this   Gianni will always do)

b. ??Gianni, credevo   che non vedessi.
    Gianni I thought that you did not see
    (versus
    *Gianni, credevo   che vedessi.
    Gianni I thought that you saw)

c. ??Il suo libro, non leggerò.
    his book,   I will not read
    (versus
    *Il suo libro, leggerò.
    his book   I will read)

We may interpret their marginality as a consequence of the marginal capacity "names" have to amalgamate with a negation at LF.

The amalgamation hypothesis also crucially predicts that all those constituents that may be clitic left dislocated only in the presence of clausal negation can be interpreted only under the scope of this negation. That is indeed what we find, although this state of affairs is in no way logically necessary.

Take for example (74b). Alongside 'The friends that he has invited are not many', one might well expect it to have a reading such as 'The friends that he has not invited are many'. But this is not so. Only the former reading is possible, with the quantifier *molti* 'many' under the scope of *non*. This is all the more surprising, a priori, as the sentence acquires such a reading when a clitic locally binds the object EC:

(76) Molti amici, non *li* ha invitati,   che io sappia.
     many friends he *them*-hasn't invited as far as I know

All this is of course expected if a prerequisite for the absence of the object clitic is that the object EC be in the exclusive scope of the negation so that a null operator may be licensed, as the amalgamation hypothesis predicts.

The same holds for non-NPs. Consider the contrast between (77) and (78). In (78) the fronted phrase is necessarily understood in the scope of the negation:

(77) a. *In un modo diverso, Carlo si comporterà.
         in another way   Carlo will behave

     b. *Andato a casa, Gianni è.
         gone home   Gianni has (lit. *is*)

     c. *Fredda, Ivo l'ha mangiata.
         cold   Ivo has eaten it

(78) a. In un modo diverso, Carlo non si comporterà.
         in another way   Carlo will not behave

b.   Andato a casa, Gianni non è.
     gone home   Gianni has (lit. *is*) not
c.   Fredda, Ivo non l'ha mangiata.
     cold   Ivo has not eaten it

We also expect that, whenever some other phrase is in the scope of clausal negation, CLLD of the constituents in (74) and (78) will be impossible— once again, a correct prediction. See (79), where the overt contrasts show that a phrase other than the EC is under the scope of the negation:

(79) a. *Molti amici$_i$, *non* ha invitato e_i *per lettera*, ma per telefono.
          many friends he has not invited by letter   but by phone
     b. *In un modo diverso$_i$, *non* si è comportato *alla festa* e_i,
          in another manner   he did not behave   at the party
          ma per strada.
          but in the street
     c. *Andato a casa$_i$, *non* è e_i *in macchina*, ma a piedi.
          gone home   he has not by car   but by foot

A related case is (80):

(80) *In un modo diverso$_i$, *non* ho promesso
      in another manner   I did not promise
      che mi sarei comportato e_i.
      that I would behave

Here, although the EC associated with the fronted phrase is c-commanded by the negation, it is not in its scope. This is because the negation belongs to a superordinate clause, and the scope of the negation is clause-bound in the general case (that is, abstracting from limited cases of "Neg-raising," as in *In un modo diverso$_i$, non credo che si comporterà* e_i 'In another manner, I don't think that he will behave').

Consider, now, how the amalgamation hypothesis dissolves the second puzzle: the fact that adverbial adjuncts appear to be extractable from Ross's negation island, in apparent violation of Rizzi's (1990) Relativized Minimality account of it, whereby in a structure like (81), e_i fails to be antecedent-governed by *in che modo*, owing to the intervention of the potential $\bar{\text{A}}$-antecedent *non*:

(81) *[$_{CP}$[$_{PP}$ In che modo]$_i$ [$_{IP}$ NP [non si comporterà e_i]]]?
          in which manner   will he not behave

Consider, now, the corresponding well-formed CLLD case:

(82) [$_{CP}$[$_{PP}$ In un modo diverso]$_i$ [$_{IP}$ NP [non si comporterà e_i]]].
          in another manner   he will not behave

In this case, even if the null operator moving from e_i is directly extracted from the government domain of *non*, Relativized Minimality will not be violated. *Non* does not qualify here as an *intervening potential $\bar{A}$-antecedent* preventing e_i from being antecedent-governed by the fronted operator. Since the two are coindexed, *non is* the closest antecedent governor of *e*.

One may ask, incidentally, what prohibits coindexing *non* with the adverbial operators in ordinary *Wh*-Movement constructions, thus voiding the effect of Relativized Minimality on negation islands altogether. My tentative answer is that overt *wh*-operators and the focus operators of the cleft and topicalization constructions are semantically incapable of amalgamating with a negation. This seems to be confirmed by the fact that even such quantifiers as *molti* 'many' and *tutti* 'all', which can normally amalgamate with a clausal negation, do not when they are focused (heavily stressed) in situ. For example:

(83) Franco non ha colpito $\begin{cases} \text{MOLTI BERSAGLI} \\ \text{TUTTI I BERSAGLI} \end{cases}$.

Franco did not hit $\begin{cases} \text{many (focus) targets} \\ \text{all (focus) targets} \end{cases}$

(83) can only mean that 'The targets that he did not hit (which he missed) were many/all'. Note also that the negation in *How many targets didn't you hit?* has the verb, not the interrogative quantifier, in its scope (= How many targets did you miss (= not hit)?).

Thus, far from constituting a problem, the apparently surprising behavior of CLLD phrases under negation turns out to provide interesting confirmation for the idea that the construction per se is not endowed, unlike topicalization, with a null operator moving to Spec CP.

2.5 Two Additional Constructions: Resumptive Preposing and Adverb Preposing

The claim that CLLD does not involve *Wh*-Movement except in the presence of (certain) bare quantifiers, or clausal negation, is prima facie contradicted by the unexpected well-formedness of two other classes of cases:

(84) a. Allo stesso modo,   si comportò suo figlio.
         in the same manner behaved his son
     b. Arrestati per ubriachezza, sono stati anche loro.
         arrested for drunkenness   were they too

    c. Fredda, credo che l'abbia mangiata solo lui.
       cold   I think that only he ate it

(85) a. Domani, mi ha promesso che verrà.
       tomorrow he promised me that he will come

    b. Ad Aiaccio, credo che sia nato Napoleone.
       in Aiaccio   I think that Napoleon was born

    c. Per divertirsi,   mi chiedo
       to amuse themselves I wonder
       se siano andati a Coney Island.
       whether they went to Coney Island

(84a–c) contain left-dislocated constituents construed with ECs that can only enter chains of antecedent government relations. If such sentences were instances of CLLD, their well-formedness would be problematic, since the ECs could only be antecedent-governed if the successive cyclic movement of a null operator were involved. But CLLD does not involve any such movement, except under the special circumstances noted above, and not verified here.

There is, however, evidence that these cases are instances not of CLLD but of a separate (*Wh*-Movement) construction, subject to somewhat different contextual conditions. The need to recognize the existence of such a construction alongside CLLD is in fact pointed out in Cinque 1978b, fn. 71 and 1983c, fn. 25 and is more amply motivated in Benincà 1988.

The first piece of evidence is that, despite their formal (and intonational) similarity with CLLD sentences, (84a–c) are felt to belong to a more literary, or recherché, style.

Second, the pragmatic conditions under which (84a–c) are well formed are different and much more restricted than those governing CLLD. The fronted phrase must either directly resume an identical phrase in the immediately preceding discourse or be inferentially linked to such a phrase (much as in the English VP-Preposing construction: . . . *and kill himself he did*). For some unclear reason, such preposing in Italian is almost obligatorily accompanied by inversion of the subject.[30] For example, (84a–c) become totally unacceptable if the subject is preverbal, in striking contrast to CLLD structures, for which no such condition holds:

(86) a. *Allo stesso modo, suo figlio si comportò.
       in the same manner his son behaved

    b. *Arrestati per ubriachezza, anche loro sono stati.
       arrested for drunkenness they too were

    c. *Fredda, credo   che lui l'abbia mangiata.
       cold   I think that he ate it

Of particular relevance here is the fact that such constructions show every diagnostic of *Wh*-Movement, in systematic contrast to CLLD. For example, under the peculiar pragmatic and formal restrictions just noted, it is possible for an object not to be resumed by a clitic (87) and to license parasitic gaps (88). Moreover, the construction is (again unlike CLLD, and like topicalization) incompatible with another *Wh*-Movement construction (89). Compare (89a–b) with (90), in which CLLD can unproblematically cooccur with a *wh*-interrogative construction. These are all expected properties, if *Wh*-Movement of a null operator is indeed involved.[31]

(87) ...e questo disse anche il Sottosegretario.
       and this said   the Vice Minister too

(88) La stessa cosa negò ____ senza commentare ____ il suo avvocato.
      the same thing denied   without commenting   his lawyer

(89) a. *...e la stessa cosa,   a chi disse   suo figlio?
           and the same thing to whom said his son
      b. *QUESTO, a chi disse   suo figlio?
          this (focus) to whom said his son

(90) Questo, a chi   *l'*ha detto suo figlio?
      this   to whom *it* said   his son

We may also note that the only apparent exceptions to Belletti and Rizzi's (1981) and Rizzi's (1982, chap. 4) observation that a preverbal subject N̄ associated with an indefinite specifier cannot be pronominalized with *ne* appear to obey the peculiar pragmatic conditions of this construction. For example:

(91) a. ...e una ne cadde   anche il giorno dopo.
           and one of-them-fell the day after too
      b. ...e molti ne furono pubblicati   anche l'anno seguente.
          and many of-them-were published the year after too

We can thus interpret them as well-behaved cases of successive cyclic *Wh*-Movement of a QP from a postverbal position (92), rather than as ill-behaved cases of Clitic Movement from a preverbal subject (93):

(92) ...[[$_{QP}$ una]$_k$ [$_{CP}$[$_{IP}$ pro ne$_i$ cadde $t_k t_i$...]]]

(93) ...[$_{IP}$[$_{NP}$ una t_i] [$_{\bar{I}}$[$_I$ ne$_i$ cadde] [$_{VP}$...]]]

This conclusion is supported by the structure's sensitivity to weak islands, which would be unexpected if (93) rather than (92) were the appropriate analysis of (91a). See (94), which contains a negative island:

(94) *...e una non ne cadde   neanche il giorno dopo.
       and one not of-them-fell the day after either

Finally, consider the dislocation of idiom chunks. Benincà (1988, 151) observes that this is in general possible only when the idiom chunk resumes an idiom mentioned in the (immediately) preceding discourse. See (95a–b) (= Benincà's (133a–b)):

(95) a. Quando gli hai detto che saresti partito,
          when you told her   that you would have left
          Maria è cascata dalle nuvole,
          Maria (lit.) fell from the clouds (showed ignorance of the fact)
          e dalle nuvole è cascata anche sua madre,
          and from the clouds fell her mother too
          che pure doveva saperlo.
          who should have known

      b. Tutti a quel punto   sono rimasti di sasso,
          everybody at that point was left (lit.) of stone (staggered)
          ma di sasso è rimasto soprattutto Giorgio.
          but of stone was left above all Giorgio

This appears to suggest that idiom chunks, which ordinarily cannot enter binding chains because of their general nonreferential character, cannot be clitic left dislocated either. When they appear to be, as in (95a b), they are instead examples of distinct *Wh*-Movement constructions such as Resumptive Preposing.[32]

Being in the scope of a negation licenses a null operator in CLLD, and in fact this is another means to dislocate an idiom chunk. See (96), which may well be uttered *ex abrupto*, thus failing to qualify as a case of Resumptive Preposing:[33]

(96) Nel pallone,   non ci vai mai, tu?
      (lit.) in the balloon not there you ever go
      'Don't you ever get confused?'

If so, (84a–c) cease to be problematic for the non-*Wh*-Movement analysis of CLLD and are in fact entirely natural given the evidence for the *Wh*-Movement nature of Resumptive Preposing.

Let us turn now to the second class of potentially problematic cases, (85a–c), repeated here:

(85) a. Domani, mi ha promesso che verrà.
          tomorrow he promised me that he will come

   b. Ad Aiaccio, credo che sia nato Napoleone.
      in Aiaccio   I think that Napoleon was born
   c. Per divertirsi,   mi chiedo
      to amuse themselves I wonder
      se siano andati a Coney Island.
      whether they went to Coney Island

All of these sentences involve a fronted adverbial that is construed with the embedded, not the matrix, clause, thus suggesting the presence of *Wh*-Movement from the embedded clause to the Spec CP of the matrix clause.

If these were instances of CLLD, they would represent an anomaly for the non-*Wh*-Movement analysis of the construction. But there is some indication that they too belong to a distinct construction. This indication comes from a peculiar restriction to which all such cases are subject: unlike what happens in ordinary *Wh*-Movement constructions, the fronting of the adverbial preserves only an embedded IP-initial interpretation of the adverbial, not the VP-internal interpretation.

Before we discuss this restriction, a brief digression is in order concerning the fundamental syntactic distribution of temporal, locative, and reason adverbials. Characteristically, these adverbials occupy either an IP-initial or an IP-final position.[34] Often, depending on which of the two positions the adverbial occupies, the sentence differs in meaning (that is, in the scope properties of the adverbial), even though this may not always be easy to express with precision. Consider, for example, such pairs as these:

(97) a. In 1821, Napoleon died.
     b. Napoleon died in 1821.

(98) a. At the restaurant, please eat!
     b. Please eat at the restaurant.

(99) a. To amuse myself, I went to Coney Island.
     b. I went to Coney Island to amuse myself.

The two sentences of each pair differ systematically in meaning. For example, as pointed out by Kuno (1975), (97a) says something about the year 1821. It says that something notable happened—namely, Napoleon's death. (97b), on the other hand, says something about Napoleon—namely, that his death occurred in 1821. The same is true for (98a–b), as observed by Geis (1986b). The force of the request conveyed by *please* affects only the verb in (98a) and only the adverbial in (98b).[35] Finally, (99a) says that, to amuse myself, I did something (namely, go to Coney Island), rather than stay home and listen to music, whereas (99b) says that the reason I went to Coney Island was to amuse myself, rather than to visit relatives. Such differences are all a function of the different scopes of the adverbial, which modifies the entire IP in the (a) cases and only the VP in the (b) cases.[36]

There are essentially two ways of accounting for (97)–(99). One is to relate the IP-initial position and IP-final (VP-adjoined) position via *Wh*-Movement, in the same vein as the Adverb Preposing analysis of the sixties (see Ross 1986, 179ff.). In this case the different scope properties of the adverbials would presumably be a function of the different structural positions that they occupy at S-Structure. The other way to account for (97)–(99) is simply to base-generate the adverbial independently in either IP-initial or IP-final position (in the latter case, either adjoined to VP or directly under IP). The difference in scope between the adverbials would again follow from the different structural positions that they occupy (now, at all levels of representation).

There are reasons to favor the base-generation over the movement analysis. The first has to do with the inability of the adverbial in IP-initial position to preserve the scope that the adverbial has in IP-final (VP-adjoined) position: a property that is entirely unprecedented for ordinary *Wh*-Movement constructions. As (100a–c) demonstrate, a topicalized, questioned, or clefted adverbial may generally retain the scope of the VP-internal trace. (In fact, ordinarily it must, as we will see.)

(100) a. NEL 1821,   è morto Napoleone!
          in 1821 (focus) Napoleon died
      b. In quale anno è morto Napoleone?
          in which year did Napoleon die
      c. E' nel 1821 che Napoleone è morto.
          it is in 1821 that Napoleon died

This property can be made more visible by having two quantifiers interact with each other. Compare (101a–c) with (102), the Adverb Preposing case:

(101) a. In quale città del sud ognuno di loro è nato?
          in which southern city was every one of them born
      b. IN UNA CITTA' DEL SUD, ognuno di loro è nato.
          in a southern city (focus)   every one of them was born
      c. E' in una città del sud che ognuno di loro è nato.
          it's in a southern city that every one of them was born

(102) *In una città del sud, ognuno di loro è nato.
          in a southern city   every one of them was born

In (101a–c) the fronted indefinite phrase can be in the scope of the universal distributive quantifier *ognuno di loro*, so that the southern city may well be different for each of the persons involved. For example, one might answer (101a) with "Pasquale was born in Naples, Nicola in Bari, and Letterio in Messina." In (102), on the other hand, *in a southern city* is not under the scope of the universal quantifier. There is just one city involved for everybody, whence the strangeness of the sentence with the distributive quantifier in subject position distributing over no set.

Given that the same scope relations are preserved under embedding (*In quale città del sud credi che ognuno di loro sia nato?* 'In which southern city do you think that every one of them was born?'), the possibility of having the fronted indefinite phrase under the scope of the embedded IP subject must be due to its VP-internal trace being under the scope (c-command domain) of the subject. The absence of such scope interaction in (102) in turn indicates that no VP-internal trace is available in Adverb Preposing cases (we will shortly consider a possible reason for this).

A second reason to favor a base-generation over a movement analysis of the IP-initial/IP-final adverbial pairs is provided by the observation that, at least in some cases, base generation is the only option. If so, unless a movement analysis is needed to account for other things (which it is not), it becomes redundant.

What are the adverbial cases that can only be base-generated in IP-initial position? One example is provided by a particular reason adverbial in Italian, the conjunction *siccome* followed by a clause. This adverbial is found only in IP-initial, never in IP-final, position, so that here there is no question of an IP-final source for the adverbial. In this connection, it is interesting to compare the distribution of *siccome* (+ CP) with two other causal conjunctions in Italian, *perché* and *poiché* (see Gruppo di Padova 1974):

(103) a. Me ne vado { *siccome / perché / poiché } ho sonno.

      I leave   because   I am sleepy

     b. { Siccome / *Perché / Poiché } ho sonno, me ne vado.

         because   I am sleepy I leave

(103a) shows that *perché* and *poiché*, but not *siccome*, may appear in IP-final position; (103b) shows that *perché* may not appear in IP-initial position (which is again problematic for a movement (but not a base-generation) analysis of the construction).[37]

A quite different argument that certain adverbials must be able to originate in IP-initial position rather than being moved there from an IP-final position is provided by Longobardi (1983). Longobardi notes that if such strong and weak crossover cases as (104a–b)

(104) a. *[Di parlare a [che ragazzo]$_i$]$_k$[$_{IP}$ pro$_i$ vi ha chiesto t_k]?
to speak to   which boy   did he ask you

 b. *?[Di parlare a [che ragazzo]$_i$]$_k$[$_{IP}$ vi ha chiesto t_k sua$_i$ madre]?
to speak to   which boy   did his mother ask you

are a function of the obligatory presence of a trace within the associated IP, the fact that no strong or weak crossover effects are found with the apparent fronting of adverbial adjuncts as in (105a–b) suggests that no IP-internal trace should be postulated in such cases:

(105) a. Dopo aver presentato Maria a che ragazzo$_i$,
after presenting Maria   to which boy
lui$_i$ vi si è dimostrato riconoscente?
he was grateful to you

 b. Dopo aver presentato Maria a che ragazzo$_i$,
after presenting Maria   to which boy
sua$_i$ madre vi si è dimostrata riconoscente?
his mother was grateful to you

Rather, Longobardi concludes, the adverbial adjunct must have moved from an IP-initial position, where it was base-generated.[38]

On the basis of this evidence I conclude that no actual grounds exist for the classical analysis of Adverb Preposing. On the contrary, reasons exist for base-generating the adverbials directly in IP-initial position (possibly, Top) and in (at least) two distinct IP-final positions, one under VP and one outside VP, with the ensuing differences concerning their semantic scope.

After this digression, we may return to the peculiar restriction to which all of the cases in (85), repeated here, appear to be subject:

(85) a. Domani, mi ha promesso che verrà.
tomorrow he promised me that he will come

 b. Ad Aiaccio, credo   che sia nato Napoleone.
in Aiaccio   I think that Napoleon was born

 c. Per divertirsi,   mi chiedo
to amuse themselves I wonder
se siano andati a Coney Island.
whether they went to Coney Island

Although the fronted adverbial must be construed with the embedded clause, the only possible interpretation is the one that corresponds to the embedded IP- (or CP-) initial scope, never the one corresponding to the embedded VP scope. Thus, (85a–c) are synonymous with (106a–c), not with (107a–c) (in the reading with no pause before the IP-final adverbial):

(106) a. Mi ha promesso, domani,   che verrà.
          he promised me tomorrow that he will come

      b. Credo, ad Aiaccio, che sia nato Napoleone.
          I think in Aiaccio   that Napoleon was born

      c. Mi chiedo, per divertirsi,
          I wonder   to amuse themselves
          se siano andati a Coney Island.
          whether they went to Coney Island

(107) a. Mi ha promesso che verrà domani.
          he promised me that he will come tomorrow

      b. Credo che Napoleone sia nato ad Aiaccio.
          I think that Napoleon was born in Aiaccio

      c. Mi chiedo se siano andati a Coney Island
          I wonder   whether they went to Coney Island
          per divertirsi.
          to amuse themselves

This contrasts with what we find in ordinary *Wh*-Movement constructions, including Resumptive Preposing and the limited *Wh*-Movement instances of CLLD when the dislocated phrase is in the scope of negation or is itself a bare quantifier. For all of these the scope of the fronted adverbial can be (in fact, must be)[39] the VP-internal one. Consider (108a–c), the fronted adverbials of which share the scope of (107a–c), not that of (106a–c):

(108) a. DOMANI,   mi ha promesso che verrà.
           tomorrow (focus) he promised me that he will come

      b. AD AIACCIO,   si dice   che Napoleone sia nato.
           in Aiaccio (focus) they say that Napoleon was born

      c. *PER DIVERTIRSI,   mi chiedo
           to amuse themselves (focus) I wonder
           se siano andati a Coney Island.[40]
           whether they went to Coney Island

This suggests, then, that we are confronted with a quite special, construction-specific, instance of *Wh*-Movement, which only affects IP-initial adverbials. I will call it *Adverb Preposing*, modifying in part the original usage of the term.[41]

2.6 Implications for an Analysis of *Wh*-Movement

To recapitulate the point of the discussion so far, it appears that, factoring out certain only apparent instances of CLLD, a substantial number of rather subtle and seemingly unrelated properties of the CLLD construction can be tied together and simply viewed as different manifestations of a single, abstract property: the absence of *Wh*-Movement.[42] That conclusion appears to be strengthened by the systematic and coherent contrast observed for each such property between CLLD and topicalization, a construction that differs minimally from CLLD precisely in having *Wh*-Movement.

If correct, this conclusion has some nontrivial implications for a number of general issues. First, given that CLLD displays Connectivity, in the sense illustrated above, it follows that Connectivity cannot be made to depend on, or correlate with, Move α. Second, given that CLLD is sensitive to (strong) islands, it seems that this property can no longer be interpreted as a diagnostic criterion for *Wh*-Movement but can instead be interpreted as a property of chains, whether these are created by movement, as in standard *Wh*-Movement constructions, or base generation, as in CLLD.

The properties of the construction in fact suggest a more abstract way of looking at *Wh*-Movement, since certain instances of CLLD were seen above to involve *Wh*-Movement—at first sight a rather paradoxical situation. We observed that the construction appears to acquire the properties of successive cyclic *Wh*-Movement (the ability to enter into government chains) only under particular conditions: when some nonreferential operator is involved (either a dislocated bare quantifier, which necessarily enters into government chains, or a negation taking scope over the dislocated phrase).

A more accurate characterization of CLLD would then seem to be that the construction is not endowed with a (null) operator; hence, it lacks the properties that go with it (the ability to enter into government chains).

In a more general vein, the observed properties of CLLD make it tempting to interpret *Wh*-Movement as an epiphenomenon, in that, as CLLD shows in a particularly clear way, its defining properties are not always found together, do not single out a homogeneous class of constructions, and in fact may lead separate lives, as it were.

(109) *Defining properties of* Wh-*Movement* (see Chomsky 1977)
   a. It obligatorily leaves a gap.
   b. It is subject to long movement, under certain conditions.

    c. It is subject to successive cyclic movement, under certain other conditions.

    d. It obeys strong islands.

    e. It obeys weak islands (when it applies successive cyclically).

It appears that property (109a) is found only when an operator is involved (whether overt or null, whether referential or nonreferential). Since CLLD (as opposed to topicalization) is not endowed with a (null) operator of either kind, it will lack property (109a), though it shows properties (109b) and (109d) (unless the dislocated phrase is itself an operator intrinsically):

(110) a. Gianni, *(lo)   incontro domani.
          Gianni (him) I meet   tomorrow

      b. Mario, non so   perché lo abbiano invitato.
          Mario I don't know why they invited him

      c. *A Franco, non concluderai nulla
          to Franco you will conclude nothing
          senza parlargli.
          without speaking to him

Properties (109b) and (109d) thus lead an independent life from the others (though I have suggested they are associated with binding chains). When an intrinsic operator is dislocated, the construction acquires property (109a), and given that non-*wh* intrinsic operators are apparently only of the nonreferential type, it further acquires the linked properties (109c) and (109e), binding being unavailable:

(111) a. Qualcosa, credo   che (*lo) farà. (see section 2.2.2)
          something I think that (s)he will do (it)

      b. *Qualcosa, mi chiedo chi potrà fare.
          something I wonder who will be able to do

      c. *Qualcosa, se ne è andato senza fare.
          something he left   without doing

Topicalization may instead show the clustering (109a), (109b), (109d), because it contains a (null) operator that (as a function of its ultimate antecedent in Top) may qualify as a referential operator and thus enter into a binding chain (see (112)), although it may show the previous clustering (again depending on the ultimate antecedent of the null operator; see (113)):

(112) a. QUESTO, mi chiedo se (*lo) desiderino.
          this (focus) I wonder if they want

    b. *FRANCO,   credo che, invitando, facciano
        Franco (focus) I think that inviting   they commit
        il più grave errore della loro vita.
        the worst error   of their life

(113) a.   NESSUNO,   credo che (*lo) abbiano visto.
        nobody (focus) I think that they saw (him)

    b. *NESSUNO,   mi chiedo
        nobody (focus) I wonder
        perché abbia visto. (see section 1.4.1)
        why he saw

    c. *NESSUNO,   se ne è andato per invitare.
        nobody (focus) he left   to invite

Under a conception of *Wh*-Movement as a primitive and monolithic cluster of properties, it would be hard to make sense of the different arrangements that the properties in (109) may assume, and in particular of the character of CLLD, which would sometimes qualify as a *Wh*-Movement construction and sometimes as a non-*Wh*-Movement construction. The defining properties of *Wh*-Movement are thus better seen as separate defining properties of the two types of operators isolated in chapter 1, or of the absence of an operator.

Chapter 3

Ā-Bound Pro versus Variable

3.1 Introduction

In this chapter we will look at evidence that points to two distinct, though interrelated, conclusions.

The first is that in the currently assumed class of variables (roughly, NP ECs locally Ā-bound by an operator) two separate subclasses should be recognized. One subclass is represented by parasitic gaps (1a), gaps of apparent (NP-) extraction from islands (1b), and gaps of *complement object deletion* (COD) constructions (1c):

(1) a. (?)The article that we filed without reading *e*...
    b. (?)The article that we went to England without reading *e*...
    c. The article was too long for us to read *e*.

The other subclass is represented by the remaining *wh*-traces (as found, for example, in interrogative and relative constructions, clefts, and topicalizations). As it turns out, the gaps in the first subclass share properties not shared by the gaps of the second.

The second general conclusion is that the partially different syntactic behavior of the two subclasses of gaps may be accounted for by analyzing the gaps in (1) not as pure variables (Ā-bound [−pronominal, −anaphor] elements) but as *pronominal variables* (Ā-bound [+pronominal, −anaphor] elements), entering what may be conceived of as a kind of (empty) resumptive pronominal strategy (see Chomsky 1982).

The two conclusions are logically independent, though, at least in part. Even if the second proved wrong, the first could still be right.

In sections 3.2 and 3.3 I will discuss the conceptual and empirical evidence that appears to support the distinction, and the particular interpretation of it that I will propose. In section 3.4 I will address the deeper question of which principles determine the (essentially complementary) distribution of pronominal and pure variables in different constructions.

Apparently, a simple answer is available. The (resumptive) Ā-bound pro strategy is always possible as a more marked option alongside the ordinary movement strategy, but it is the only option available whenever Move α is excluded on independent grounds, as is arguably the case in the three constructions illustrated in (1).

3.2 The Unitary Analysis of *Wh*-Constructions

3.2.1 COD Gaps, Parasitic Gaps, and Gaps of Apparent Extraction from Islands as *Wh*-Traces

At least since Chomsky 1977, the notion of *wh*-construction has had a unitary and well-defined characterization. In essence, every construction (A) sensitive to island conditions and (B) containing an EC free in a precise local domain (its governing category) is analyzed as a *wh*-construction (Chomsky 1977, 86). The EC in question is the trace of an overt (or null) *wh*-phrase moved in the syntax to Spec CP. Such an EC, a [−pronominal, −anaphor] element, is further interpreted in LF as a variable bound by the (quasi-quantifier) phrase in Spec CP. Under this characterization, not only standard relative and interrogative constructions, but also cleft, topicalization, comparative, and related structures are analyzed as involving *Wh*-Movement, with enlightening results (Chomsky 1977, 1982). Along with topicalization, the constructions illustrated in (1) are also analyzed as involving an abstract application of *Wh*-Movement, since they conform to properties (A) and (B) (although concerning the former, matters are somewhat more complex, as we will see).

There is substantial evidence that COD constructions such as (1c) contain a variable Ā-bound by an abstract operator at S-Structure, as indicated in (2):[1]

(2) The book$_i$ was too long [O_i for [us to read e_i]].

These constructions not only apparently meet conditions (A) and (B) but also show other properties shared only by other *wh*-constructions. First, as Chomsky (1982, 45) notes, the EC of (2) is able to license parasitic gaps, a prerogative of *wh*-traces, not NP-traces:

(3) This book$_i$ is too interesting [to put e_i down [without having finished e_i]].

Second, it appears to create crossing effects with other Ā-bound ECs:[2]

(4) a. Who$_j$ is that book$_i$ too boring to send e_i to e_j?

   b. *What$_i$ is John$_j$ too boring to send e_i to e_j?

Third, it behaves, in dative contexts, just like a *wh*-trace. A dative object cannot be *Wh*-Moved, as originally noted by Fillmore (1965) (though it can be NP-Moved):

(5) a. Who$_j$ did you give the book to e_j?

   b. *Who$_j$ did you give e_j the book?

   (Compare *I gave John the book*.)

Nor can a dative object be the complement object EC of the constructions in (2). See for example (6a–b), drawn from Lasnik and Fiengo 1974:

(6) a. John$_j$ is not easy [to give presents to e_j].

   b. *John$_j$ is not easy [to give e_j presents].

If COD constructions involve abstract *Wh*-Movement from the position of the EC, the ungrammaticality of (6b) can be traced to the same principle that rules out (5b).[3] All in all, the analysis of these constructions as covert *Wh*-Movement constructions thus appears well motivated.

Similar considerations apply to parasitic gap constructions and constructions displaying apparent extraction from islands. Their gaps license parasitic gaps:[4]

(7) a. ?Il ragazzo che hanno convinto *e* [di poter aiutare *e*
        the boy   who they convinced   they were able to help
        [pur senza coinvolgere *e* nelle loro attività]]...
        without even involving in their activities

   b. ?Il professore che se ne sono andati via [senza neppure salutare *e*
        the teacher   who they went away   without even greeting
        [dopo aver sfruttato *e* per i loro interessi]]...
        after exploiting   for their own interests

Like *wh*-traces (and unlike NP-traces), neither can occupy the dative object position of the dative construction:

(8) a. *The man we invited *e* [without giving *e* the invitation]...

   b. *The boy who we went to the party [without giving *e* the invitation]...

Furthermore, even if parasitic gaps and extraction from island gaps are characteristically found embedded within an island, as in (9a) and (10a), they show sensitivity to further embeddings in islands, as noted by Kayne (1983), Longobardi (1983), and Chomsky (1986b). See (9b–e) and (10b–e), respectively:

(9) This is the man O_i John interviewed t_i ____

    a. [before giving the job to e_i].

    b. [before asking [which job to give to e_i]].

    c. [before announcing [the plan to speak to e_i]].

    d. [before reading [the book you gave to e_i]].

    e. [before expecting you to leave [without meeting e_i]].

(10) This is the man O_i John went away ____

    a. [without saying goodbye to e_i].

    b. [without asking [which job to give to e_i]].

    c. [before announcing [the plan to speak to e_i]].

    d. [without reading [the book you gave to e_i]].

    e. [instead of staying [without speaking to e_i]].

So, for these constructions too, a *Wh*-Movement analysis would seem to be well motivated.[5] Chomsky's (1986b) analysis of extraction from island gaps, such as that in (10a) and (11), which is limited to NPs, is that NPs, but not non-NPs, are allowed to adjoin to the adjunct PP, thus voiding its barrierhood (and, indirectly, that of IP):

(11) ?Who$_i$ did [$_{IP}$ you [$_{VP}$ leave [$_{PP}$ without [$_{CP}$[$_{IP}$ speaking to t_i]]]]]?

Chomsky (1986b) also analyzes parasitic gap constructions such as (12a) as containing an instance of null operator movement, as indicated in (12b),[6]

(12) a. The article which$_i$ you filed t_i before reading e_i...

    b. The article which$_i$ you filed t_i [before [O_i [[reading t_i]]]]...

where the chain of the parasitic gap and that of the real gap are assumed to give rise to a *composed chain*, a specific construct that is associated with parasitic gap structures and yields their interpretation (also see Browning 1987).

The question of the conditions under which parasitic gaps are licensed (compare (12a) with (13)) may then be regarded as the question of the conditions under which chain composition is permitted (at S-Structure):

(13) *The article which was filed before we could read...

Chomsky (1986b) considers two possibilities. One assumes the correctness of the anti-c-command requirement of earlier work and derives it from general principles applied to the composed chain.[7] The other imposes a specific condition on chain composition: the head of the parasitic gap chain must be 0-subjacent to the final element of the real gap chain. Chomsky essentially leaves the choice open (though in section 11 he discusses some theory-internal evidence that appears to favor the approach based on the anti-c-command requirement).[8]

The second approach, based on 0-Subjacency, requires the null operator in (12b) and similar cases to adjoin to the adjunct PP:

(14) ...[$_{PP}$ O_i [$_{PP}$ before [$_{CP}$ t_i [$_{VP}$ reading t_i]]]]]

3.2.2   One Conceptual Problem

Even though the *Wh*-Movement analysis of the three constructions in (1) has the advantage of expressing in a unified way the properties they share with ordinary *wh*-constructions, it fails to explain one of their characteristic properties. Whereas in ordinary *wh*-constructions *Wh*-Movement applies in principle to any maximal projection, in parasitic gap constructions, constructions with apparent extraction from islands, and COD constructions *Wh*-Movement appears to be strictly limited to NPs. Thus, parasitic gaps of a category other than NP are quite generally impossible:[9]

(15) a. *[$_{AP}$ Quanto importanti] si può diventare t [senza sentirsi e]?
            how important   can one become   without feeling
      b. *[$_{PP}$ A chi]   hai lasciato la lettera t [dopo esserti rivolto e]?
            to whom did you leave the letter after turning
      c. *[$_{QP}$ Quanti]   ne hai presi t [senza pagarne e]?[10]
            how many did you get of-them without paying of-them
      d. *[$_{VP}$ VENUTO A CASA] era t [senza che fosse e suo padre].
            come home (focus)   he had without his father having
      e. *[$_{AdvP}$ Quanto gentilmente] si è comportato t con te
            how kindly   did he behave   with you
          [senza comportarsi e coi tuoi amici]?
          without behaving   with your friends?

Under the 0-Subjacency approach sketched above, this could be accounted for by appealing to the same general condition that prevents extraction of non-NPs from adjunct islands (NPs, but not non-NPs, may adjoin to the adjunct PP) so that any (empty) non-NP in the parasitic gap structure would fail to become 0-subjacent to the real gap:

(16) *Quanto importanti$_i$ si può diventare t_i [$_{PP}$ senza [$_{CP}$ O_i sentirsi t_i]]?
          how important   can one become   without   feeling

A barrier (PP) intervenes.

Under the alternative approach based on the anti-c-command requirement, on the other hand, it is not entirely clear why the sentences in (15) should be impossible.

In any event, even if the alternative based on 0-Subjacency were to prove superior, the question would still remain why only NPs should be able to adjoin to an adjunct.

The same asymmetry arises in the case of extraction from islands. (17) exemplifies the adjunct case, (18) the complex NP case of the N complement type, and (19) the complex NP case of the relative clause type:[11]

(17) a.   Anna, che me ne sono andato via
          Anna who I went away
          senza neanche salutare, . . .
          without even saying goodbye to

     b.   *Anna, con la quale me ne sono andato via
          Anna with whom I went away
          senza neanche parlare, . . .
          without even speaking

(18) a.   Gianni, che pure abbiamo escluso la possibilità di ammettere
          Gianni who we excluded   the possibility of admitting
          nel nostro club, è molto bravo.
          to our club   is very clever

     b.   *Gianni, di cui abbiamo escluso   la possibilità
          Gianni about whom we excluded the possibility
          di parlare con loro, è peraltro molto bravo.
          of talking with them is nonetheless very clever

(19) a.   I Rossi,   che dubito   ci sia qualcuno   disposto a rivedere
          the Rossis who I doubt there is anybody willing to see again
          dopo quanto è successo, . . .
          after what happened

     b.   *I Rossi,   in cui dubito   ci sia qualcuno
          the Rossis in whom I doubt there is anyone
          disposto a confidare, dopo quanto è successo, . . .
          willing to confide   after what happened

Finally, COD constructions present a similar picture (only NP gaps are possible there), though additional factors may be involved in preventing *Wh*-Movement of non-NPs, as we will see in section 3.4.

To summarize, under the unitary *Wh*-Movement analysis of these constructions, the general question remains why they display their particular asymmetry between NPs and non-NPs. It would be nice if this asymmetry could be attributed to some independent principle, or if it were a consequence of a particular aspect of the analysis of these constructions. In the next section we will consider a small number of properties that appear to distinguish the gap in these constructions from the gap in ordinary *Wh*-Movement constructions. A systematic difference will emerge about which the unitary *Wh*-Movement analysis once more has nothing to say.

3.2.3 Some Empirical Problems

3.2.3.1 Nonreferential Complement NPs   One factor distinguishing the constructions in (1) from ordinary *wh*-constructions is a peculiar restriction that affects the former.

Recall the earlier observation that NPs, but not non-NPs, can apparently be moved in the constructions of (1). It turns out, however, that not all kinds of NPs can be extracted in these constructions:

(20) a. *Quanti chili   pesa *t*   [senza credere   di pesare *e*]?
         how many kilos does he weigh without believing he weighs
     b. *Quanti chili   ha smesso di mangiare
         how many kilos did he stop eating
         [pur senza pesare *e*]?
         without even weighing
     c. *Cento chili   sono difficili [da pesare *e*] per tutti.
         one hundred kilos are difficult to weigh   for everybody

(21) a. *Quante settimane ha passato *t* a Berlino
         how many weeks did he spend in Berlin
         [senza aver voluto passare *e* a Londra]?
         without wanting to spend   in London
     b. *Quante settimane se ne è andato via [senza passare *e*
         how many weeks did he go away   without spending
         a Londra]?
         in London
     c. *Una settimana è difficile [da passare *e* digiuni].
         one week   is difficult to spend   without eating

This contrasts with the possibility of *Wh*-Moving the same NPs in ordinary *Wh*-constructions:

(22) a. Quanti chili   dice   di pesare *t*?
         how many kilos does he say he weighs
     b. I chili   che dice   di pesare *t* non sono pochi.
         the kilos that he says he weighs are not few
     c. CINQUANTA CHILI, dice   di pesare *t*.
         fifty kilos (focus)   he says he weighs

(23) a. Quante settimane passerai *t*   a Berlino?
       how many weeks will you spend in Berlin
   b. Le settimane che passa *t*   fuori casa   sono troppe.
       the weeks   that he spends away from home are too many
   c. TRE SETTIMANE, ho passato *t* da loro.
       three weeks (focus) I spent   at their place

Neither *quanti chili* nor *quante settimane* in (20)–(23) is an *adjunct* NP. In
these environments both admit *ne*-cliticization, which is a clear test for
structural objecthood in Italian (Belletti and Rizzi 1981, Burzio 1981,
1986):

(24) a. Quanti   ne   pesavi allora (di chili)?
       how many of-them did you weigh (of kilos)
   b. Quante   ne   hai passate lì   (di settimane)?
       how many of-them did you spend there (of weeks)

Thus, the ill-formedness of (20)–(21) cannot be attributed, like that of the
adjunct NPs in (25a–c), to a violation of the ECP (under Chomsky's
(1986b) Minimality Condition):[12]

(25) a. *The way he fixed my car *t* [*t* [after [*t* [fixing his *t*]]]]...
   b. *The way he decided to stop [*t* [after [*t* [fixing the car *t*]]]]...
       (Compare *He decided to stop after fixing the car that way.*)
   c. *?That way may be hard [to fix the car *t*].

It appears that under the *Wh*-Movement analysis for (1), the restriction
observed in (20) and (21) can be made to follow if only a subset of NPs,
possibly only "referential" NPs, are allowed to adjoin to the adjunct PP;
though this again raises the question of why there should be such a
restriction.[13]

3.2.3.2 The Subject of Tensed Complement CPs

A second property dis-
tinguishing the gap of the constructions in (1) from regular *wh*-gaps is that
the former (though not the latter) are apparently marginal in the subject
position of complementizerless tensed sentences (in English). Compare (26)
with the perfect acceptability of (27), which contains an ordinary *wh*-trace
in the same position:[14]

(26) a. *?Someone who John expected [*e* would be successful though
         believing [*e* is incompetent]]...
   b. *?The student that Susan left because John said [*e* was
         intelligent]...
   c. *?Mary is hard for me to believe [*e* kissed John].

(27) Someone who we expected [*e* would be successful]...

Chomsky (1982, 55, 1986b) notes that (26a) in fact becomes worse if *that* is present in the C of the more deeply embedded clause (and the same seems to be true for (26b–c):

(28) a. *Someone who John expected [*e* would be successful though believing [that *e* is incompetent]]...

   b. *The student that Susan left because John said [that *e* was intelligent]...

   c. *Mary is hard for me to believe [that *e* kissed John].

We are thus faced with a three-way distinction. Chomsky's (1982) analysis draws the dividing line between (27) on one hand and (26)/(28) on the other, thus failing to account for the contrast between (26) and (28). Chomsky's (1986b) analysis instead makes a principled distinction between (28) on one hand and (26)/(27) on the other. The (slight) contrast between ordinary *wh*-gaps and gaps of the type found in (1) ((27) versus (26)) thus remains to be expressed.[15]

3.2.3.3 The Subject of Certain Infinitival CPs

A context providing a clearer contrast between parasitic gaps, extraction from island gaps, and COD gaps on one hand and ordinary *wh*-traces on the other is the subject position of certain infinitival clauses in French and Italian. As is well known, the French and Italian counterparts of the English sentence (29a) are ungrammatical:

(29) a. I believed John to be intelligent.

   b. *Je croyais John être intelligent.

   c. *Io ritenevo John essere intelligente.

The contrast is standardly attributed to the fact that English *believe*, but not French *croire* or Italian *ritenere*, is an exceptional Case marking V inducing the deletion (or transparency) of the complement CP boundary (see Chomsky 1981, 303 and passim). As a result, the NP *John* is Case-marked in (29a) but not in (29b–c)—whence a Case Filter violation.

The grammaticality of (30a–b), which is at first sight surprising,

(30) a. L'homme que je croyais être intelligent...

   b. L'uomo   che ritenevo   essere intelligente...

   the man   that I believed to be intelligent...

can instead be accounted for if we assume, following Kayne (1984, chap. 1),[16] that *croire/ritenere*, though unable to govern and Case-mark the embedded subject position (across two sentential boundaries), can govern and assign Case (across a single sentential boundary) to a (*wh-*) NP in the adjacent Spec CP moved successive cyclically to the higher Spec CP:[17]

(31) L'homme [NP$_i$ que [je croyais [t_i [t_i être intelligent]]]]...

This is one context where successive cyclic movement is required by Case considerations alone.

In the present context it is interesting that, unlike ordinary *wh-*constructions, the constructions of (1) apparently cannot avail themselves of the successive cyclic derivation of (31):[18]

(32) a. *?L'homme que nous appréciions *e* sans croire [*e* [*e* être
   intelligent]]...
   b. *?L'uomo che apprezzavamo *e* pur senza ritenere [*e* [*e* essere
   intelligente]]...
   the man who we appreciated without even believing to be
   intelligent

(33) a. *?La seule personne que nous avons été récompensés
   pour avoir cru [*e* [*e* être intelligente]]...
   b. *?L'unica persona che siamo stati ricompensati
   per aver ritenuto [*e* [*e* essere intelligente]]...
   the only person who we have been rewarded
   for considering to be intelligent

(34) a. *?Cet homme est facile à croire [*e* [*e* être intelligent]].
   b. *?Quest'uomo è facile da ritenere [*e* [*e* essere intelligente]].
   this man is easy to believe to be intelligent

Each example in (32)–(34) should also be contrasted with extraction from the minimally different subject position of a small clause (which does not require a successive cyclic derivation):

(35) a. L'homme que nous appréciions sans croire [*e* intelligent]...
   b. L'uomo che apprezzavamo pur senza ritenere [*e*
   intelligente]...
   the man who we appreciated without believing intelligent

(36) a. ?La seule personne que nous avons été récompensés
   pour avoir cru [*e* intelligente]...
   b. ?L'unica persona che siamo stati ricompensati
   per aver ritenuto [*e* intelligente]...
   the only person who we have been rewarded
   for considering intelligent

(37) a. (?)Cet homme est facile à croire [e intelligent].

     b. (?)Quest'uomo è facile da ritenere [e intelligente].

       this man is easy to believe intelligent

The three constructions in question appear once more to pattern alike and to contrast with ordinary wh-constructions. In fact, under a Wh-Movement analysis for them, the ungrammaticality of (32)–(34) is entirely unexpected.[19]

3.2.3.4 The Second Object of the Dative Construction

A fourth context in which the gap of the constructions in (1) appears to behave differently from ordinary wh-traces is provided by the dative construction in English.

We have seen that the Wh-Movement analysis of parasitic gaps, apparent extraction from islands, and COD constructions accounts for the ungrammaticality of such forms as (38a–c):

(38) a. *The man we invited t [without giving e the invitation]...

     b. *The man we went away [without giving e the invitation]...

     c. *John is not easy [to give e presents].

Under such an analysis, their ungrammaticality can be reduced to that of (39),

(39) *Who$_i$ did you give t_i those books?

in which a wh-trace is found in the first object position of the dative construction.

The constructions in (1), however, are characterized by another (albeit less severe) restriction in dative contexts, which is not shared by ordinary wh-constructions.

Let us begin with the COD case, for which the restriction has been explicitly noted in the literature. As Lasnik and Fiengo (1974) observe, the second object of the dative construction can be a wh-trace unproblematically, but a COD gap only marginally:

(40) a.   What$_i$ did you give that man t_i?

     b.   The book (which$_i$) I gave that man t_i...

(41) a.   *?Books$_i$ are not easy [to give (even) that man t_i].

     b.   *?Those books$_i$ are too boring [to give (even) that man e_i].

     c.   *?Those books$_i$ are interesting enough [to give (even) that man e_i].

     d.   *?He bought some books$_i$ [to give (even) that man e_i].

Judgments concerning (41) vary from speaker to speaker, ranging from "slightly marginal" to "quite marginal." I have uniformly adopted the grammaticality judgments indicated in Lasnik and Fiengo's (1974) discussion of these facts. But they should be taken in their contrastive rather than their absolute value. What is at stake here is not the actual degree of deviance of the forms but the reality of the contrasts indicated.

Though the judgments are again rather delicate, it seems that a contrast comparable to that between (40) and (41) is also found in the parasitic gap case and the case of apparent extraction from islands. Compare (42) and (43) with (1a) and (1b), respectively:

(42) *?The book$_i$ that we filed t_i instead of giving that man e_i...

(43) *?The book$_i$ that we left the library without giving that man e_i...

If so, we have one more property that unites the constructions in (1) and opposes them to ordinary *wh*-constructions—and another contrast on which the unitary *Wh*-Movement analysis is silent.

3.2.3.5 Adjuncts within Adjuncts A pure *Wh*-Movement analysis for the constructions in (1) raises one additional question. If *Wh*-Movement can extract NPs (though not non-NPs) out of adjuncts, as in (44), obeying 0-Subjacency,

(44) The article$_i$ [$_{CP}$ NP$_i$ that [$_{IP}$ we [$_{VP}$ went to England] [$_{PP}$ t_i [$_{PP}$ without [$_{CP}$ t_i [$_{IP}$ PRO I [$_{VP}$ t_i [$_{VP}$ reading e_i]]]]]]]]]...

why is there such a serious decrease in acceptability when an NP is "extracted" out of two adjuncts, as in (45)?

(45) *The book$_i$ that we left Russia [without being arrested [after distributing e_i]]...[20]

The *Wh*-Movement analysis appears to offer no internal answer. A derivation exists for (45) that meets 0-Subjacency:

(46) The book$_i$ [$_{CP}$ NP$_i$ that [$_{IP}$[...] [$_{PP}$ t_i [$_{PP}$ without [$_{CP}$ t_i [$_{IP}$ VP [$_{PP}$ t_i [$_{PP}$ after [$_{CP}$ t_i [$_{IP}$ I [$_{VP}$ t_i [$_{VP}$ distributing e_i]]]]]]]]]]]]...

Similar remarks could be made with respect to parasitic gaps and COD gaps. As noted by Longobardi (1983), a parasitic gap cannot be embedded within an adjunct that is part of another adjunct (though it can be embedded within a single adjunct):

(47) ?I capi di bestiame che abbiamo eliminato t [senza neppure cercare
        the head of cattle that we have eliminated   without even trying
        di salvare e]...
        to save

(48) *I capi di bestiame che abbiamo eliminato *t* [senza neppure cercare
       the head of cattle that we have eliminated   without even trying
       di chiamare il veterinario [prima di abbattere *e*]]...
       to call the vet   before killing

COD gaps also appear to be able to occur inside one but not two adjuncts:

(49) a. ?John is too nice for us to ask for money after helping *e*.
       b. *John is too rich for us to go away without asking for money
            after helping *e*.

The ungrammaticality of (48) and (49b) is again unexpected within a
Wh-Movement analysis of parasitic gaps and COD gaps. 0-Subjacency is
met throughout. A comparable problem is raised by repeated extraction
of NPs from CNPs, as we will see in Section 3.3.4.

3.3   A Nonunitary Analysis of *Wh*-Constructions

3.3.1   Pure Variables and Pronominal Variables

We now turn to consider a (partial) alternative to the unitary *Wh*-
Movement analysis that may express the observed differences between the
two types of gaps while retaining the basic insights and explanatory power
of the former analysis. This alternative represents a partial return to, and
an extension of, the analysis of parasitic gaps and gaps of apparent extraction from islands proposed by Chomsky (1982). It provides a unified
answer to the conceptual and the specific empirical problems noted earlier,
as well as to four additional properties distinguishing the gaps in (1) from
ordinary *wh*-traces. New problems also arise in relation to the selective
island violations that these constructions permit and the vacuous movement
hypothesis of Chomsky (1986b).

   The basic idea to be developed is that the gap in the constructions in (1)
is not a pure variable (a *wh*-trace created by an application of Move α) but
a pronominal variable (a base-generated pro that comes to be Ā-bound by
an operator at S-Structure). This implies interpreting such constructions
as obligatorily instantiating this sort of resumptive pronoun strategy. I will
turn in section 3.4 to the factors that give rise to such a situation by ruling
out ordinary *Wh*-Movement in these constructions.

   Along with pure variables (*wh*-traces), pronominal variables share the
property of being Ā-bound by an operator. I will accordingly suggest that
all the properties that the two types of variables have in common derive
from this very feature. The properties that distinguish them will instead
follow from their different intrinsic makeup.

As noted, this analysis recalls Chomsky's (1982) proposal concerning parasitic gap constructions and constructions displaying apparent extraction from islands. There Chomsky analyses these gaps, under the functional definition of ECs, as empty pronominal elements [+pronominal, ±anaphor] at D-Structure and as variables [−pronominal, −anaphor] at S-Structure, as a result of their coming to be Ā-bound by some operator (in the former case, the operator binding the real gap; in the latter case, a base-generated operator). They cannot remain pronominals (PRO or pro) at S-Structure, because the governed status of the EC excludes PRO and the apparent impossibility of (locally) determining its pronominal features excludes pro. Furthermore, operators base-generated in Ā-position are crucially assumed not to be able to bind an EC at S-Structure, except under special conditions met by the construction of apparent extraction from islands.

Here we will pursue a slightly different variant of that approach, extending the analysis in the following ways. First, we will assume that parasitic gaps and gaps of apparent extraction from islands (as well as COD gaps) are pros, not only at D-Structure, but also at S-Structure, where they come to be Ā-bound. Second, we will assume that operators base-generated in Ā-position are indexed freely, not only at LF but also at S-Structure (perhaps throughout).

These are the minimal, or least costly, assumptions, in any event.[21] But they raise two questions, one relating to the consequences of free indexing and the other to the content determination of pro at S-Structure.

As already noted, Chomsky (1982) takes indexing of categories base-generated in Ā-position to be generally impossible at S-Structure (an exception being made for such cases as (1b)). There are two reasons for this. First, to admit free indexing at S-Structure in such configurations as (50)

(50) $\alpha_i [\ldots e_i \ldots]$

would seem to allow one "to form constructions freely violating island conditions, in effect treating base-generated PRO as a resumptive pronoun" (p. 59). I defer a detailed discussion of this issue until section 3.3.4, simply noting here that this consequence might in fact be welcome if some island condition violations are indeed attested (for NP gaps) and if the remaining overgeneration could be restrained by some independent principle.

The second reason relates to the fact that lexical resumptive pronouns would be expected to license parasitic gaps, contrary to fact (see Chomsky

1982, 58). Chomsky reports the following contrast in Spanish, already mentioned in chapter 2:

(51) a. El reloj de que me hablaste, el qual han conseguido arreglar t
       [sin mover e], ha quedado muy bien.

   b. *El reloj de que me hablaste, que lo han conseguido arreglar [sin
       mover e], ha quedado muy bien.
       'The clock you spoke to me about, which they got to fix (it)
       without moving, now works very well.'

(51a) and (51b) differ in that the first contains a real gap, left by syntactic movement of *el qual* into Spec CP, which comes to $\bar{\text{A}}$-bind the parasitic gap at S-Structure, whereas the second is not derived by movement but simply contains a lexical resumptive pronoun. If a base-generated null operator could $\bar{\text{A}}$-bind the "parasitic" gap at S-Structure in (51b), then the relative unacceptability of the sentence would go unexplained.

The case of (51b) is in fact not qualitatively different from the case of extraction from adjuncts such as (1b). Since the latter is relatively acceptable, owing to the possibility of either base-generating a null operator in Spec CP (Chomsky 1982) or directly extracting a null NP from the adjunct (Chomsky 1986b), the unacceptability of (51b) must be attributed to some additional factor.

One difference between (51b) and (1b) is that the variable inside the adjunct is preceded by a coindexed pronominal in (51b), though not in (1b). The contrast between (1b) and (51b) is thus reminiscent of that between (52) and (53) (the latter an instance of backward pronominalization):

(52)   They managed to fix the wall without moving the clock.

(53)   *They managed to fix it$_i$ without moving the clock$_i$.

It is not unreasonable to think that whatever renders (53) relatively unacceptable will also account for the relative unacceptability of (51b).[22] This appears to be indirectly supported by the following observation. Certain backward pronominalization cases in which the pronoun is more deeply embedded are acceptable. Interestingly, cases corresponding to these, in which the antecedent is a variable, are also acceptable:

(54) a. Dovranno convocare anche   il poliziotto   che lo$_i$ ha arrestato
       they will also have to summon the policeman who arrested him
       prima di poter   interrogare Gianni$_i$.
       before they will be able to interrogate Gianni

    b. Gianni$_{i,}$, che dovranno convocare anche   il poliziotto
       Gianni   who they will also have to summon the policeman
       che lo$_i$ ha arrestato prima di poter   interrogare e_i, ...
       who arrested him   before they will be able to interrogate

In such contexts as (54b), lexical resumptive pronouns do appear to license parasitic gaps, contrary to what appeared to be the case in (51b). In either case, though, this is a misleading characterization of the facts. What licenses the parasitic gap in (54b) is whatever licenses the gap in (1b). Note that there is no reason to think that the parasitic gap of (51b) should not be analogously licensed. The reason for its unacceptability is instead to be ascribed to independent factors (the poorly understood conditions on backward pronominalization).

If the foregoing considerations are essentially correct, the original motivation for disallowing free indexing at S-Structure of categories base-generated in Ā-position becomes less compelling.[23]

Consider next the content determination of pro at S-Structure. In Chomsky 1982 the relevant requirement imposed on such determination is that some coindexed nominal element be present in the (local) context at S-Structure that can identify the pro in terms of the pronominal features of person and number (and perhaps gender and Case): the ϕ-features. The prototypical context considered there is that of Agr governing the subject pro in the tensed sentences of pro-drop languages.

Consider, however, the case of an operator Ā-binding a pro in A-position at S-Structure. In such a context the pro qualifies as a variable, under any current definition.[24]

Variables have ϕ-features at S-Structure (Chomsky 1981, 322ff.).[25] If the ϕ-features of standard variables are determined (or checked) by the Ā-antecedent (or a more remote antecedent when the local antecedent is a null operator; Chomsky 1982, 85), then it is perhaps not unnatural to regard the feature content of the gap of the constructions in (1)—a pronominal variable at S-Structure, under this analysis—as analogously determined by its "acquired" antecedent (which would then authorize the pro).

It might be objected that the way in which the ϕ-features of variables are determined by the antecedent is by being "left behind" under movement (Chomsky 1981, 323). As the pro would not be related to its acquired antecedent via movement, no ϕ-features could possibly be "left behind" on it.

As a matter of empirical fact, however, parasitic gaps, extraction from island gaps, and COD gaps do have ϕ-features. This can be seen in (55), where they appear to govern agreement of a predicate adjective (in Italian):

(55) a. (?)La person*a*   che hanno assunto *t*
        the person (+ fem, + sing) who they have employed
        pur senza considerare   [*e* adatt*a*
        even without considering   suitable (+ fem, + sing)
        per quel lavoro]...
        for that job
     b. (?)Giann*a*,   che persino l'avvocato della difesa
        Gianna (+ fem, + sing) who even the defense counsel
        ha esitato prima di definire [*e* inferm*a* di mente]...
        hesitated before defining   mentally ill (+ fem, + sing)
     c.   Quest*a* macchin*a*   non è facile da rendere
        this car (+ fem, + sing) is not easy to render
        [*e* competitiva   sul mercato].
          competitive (+ fem, + sing) on the market

If the ϕ-features of pro cannot have been "left behind" by movement, they must have been base-generated there, a possibility independently made available by the theory.[26]

Having ϕ-features, however, does not per se authorize an EC:

(56) *I filed that book without reading   *e*   .
                                        (3rd pers, +sing, Acc)

Apparently, what distinguishes (56) from the (relatively) well formed (57), and the like,

(57) (?)Which book did you file *t* without reading   *e*   ?
                                                     (3rd pers, +sing, Acc)

is the fact that the ϕ-features of *e* are "determined" (in the sense of 'rendered visible', 'identified') by some antecedent that overtly matches those features at S-Structure in (57), but not in (56). This amounts to saying that *which book* in (57), but not *that book* in (56), can qualify as an antecedent for *e*. I suggest that this is because the relation between *which book* and *e* in (57) satisfies the general and independently needed definition of variable, whereby *which book* becomes an ($\bar{\text{A}}$-) antecedent of *e*, in turn coming to identify its ϕ-features.[27] In (56), instead, *e* can be neither a (pronominal) variable, nor PRO, nor NP-trace. It can only be pro, co-indexed with *that book* in A-position. But, at least under the "intrinsic" definition of ECs, no independent definition of pronominal is available that crucially refers to the notion of A-antecedent.[28] We may assume, then, that *e* (= pro) in (56) does not "acquire" any antecedent capable of rendering its ϕ-features visible at S-Structure.

In this light, the Ā-antecedent of the pro in the constructions of (1) serves a purpose similar to that of Agr in a pro-drop language. It provides the overt grammatical indication needed for the ϕ-features of pro. Let us suppose, then, that alongside identification of pro via Agr (in the tensed sentences of pro-drop languages) there is a second way to identify pro, namely, via Ā-binding at S-Structure.[29] If so, the gaps in (1) can be [+pronominal, −anaphor] elements at S-Structure (in fact, throughout), as desired in the minimal assumption approach mentioned above.

3.3.2 A Unified Answer to the Conceptual and Empirical Problems

We have seen that a *Wh*-Movement analysis of the constructions in (1) leaves one conceptual problem unanswered: Why should *Wh*-Movement in such constructions be restricted to NPs only? Note that the limitation cannot be attributed to the empty character of the operator.[30] Ordinary *wh*-constructions such as regular relatives, topicalizations, and clefts show instances of empty operator movement too. Nonetheless, we have repeatedly seen a systematic contrast between such cases of empty operator movement and the constructions in (1). The answer must be found elsewhere. I suggest that it lies in the fact that (for reasons to be discussed in section 3.4) overt *Wh*-Movement is uniformly excluded from the constructions in (1). Thus, the gap of these constructions can only be of category NP because, *Wh*-Movement being unavailable, only NP, and no other category, has access to a second strategy, in essence an (empty) resumptive pronominal strategy. This is because NP is the only category that has an empty pronominal form (pro or PRO). In this view, (1a–c) are blocked, as instances of the ordinary movement strategy, just like the forms in (58):

(58) a. *How tired can one feel without being?
     b. *The man to whom I went away without speaking is there.
     c. *The man was too boring to whom to speak.

However, they are acceptable (marginally in the (a) and (b) cases) as instances of the resumptive pronominal strategy.

This is the central insight of Chomsky's (1982) analysis of parasitic gaps and extraction from island gaps. As noted, I depart here from that analysis in taking the structures in (1) to have a base-generated empty operator in Spec CP, coindexed with (hence, Ā-binding) at S-Structure a base-generated pro. Thus, the latter is authorized by being identified in its ϕ-features by the operator at S-Structure. Both the base generation of operators in Spec CP and the base generation of pros in A-positions are independently justified;[31] hence, their combination should not be unexpected.

What is crucial, in the present analysis, is that coindexing between the two (hence, more generally, indexing of categories in $\bar{\text{A}}$-positions) is possible at S-Structure. If that were not so, pro would fail to be identified at that level, since it would not qualify there as a (pronominal) variable.[32] Accordingly, (59a–c) will be the S-Structure representations of (1a–c),

(59) a. The article [[O_i that [we filed t_i [without reading pro$_i$]]]] . . .
     b. The article [[O_i that [we went to England [without reading pro$_i$]]]] . . .
     c. The article was too long [O_i for [us to read pro$_i$]].

where O in Spec CP is a [−pronominal, −anaphor] NP, a nonargument in a $\bar{\theta}$-position. The contrast between (1) and (58), then, will simply follow from the fact that non-NPs have no access to the (empty) resumptive pronominal strategy—a natural consequence of the fact that only NPs are defined in terms of the features [±pronominal, ±anaphor] (that is, only NPs can be empty pronominals).[33]

Pending a reconsideration of the selective island violations of "NP extraction", postulating an empty pronominal variant of the resumptive strategy may offer an additional advantage: it apparently allows Chomsky's (1982) stringent requirement on the nature of the analysis for parasitic gaps (and extraction from island gaps) to be retained. Given their marginality, Chomsky notes, "one would not expect that the parasitic gap phenomenon is sanctioned by special properties of U [niversal] G [rammar]" (p. 39). Rather, its basic properties should follow from principles of UG that are independently motivated, and any difference among languages in this area should reduce to independent differences holding among the languages in question (for work substantiating the latter desideratum, roughly within Chomsky's (1982) approach, see Felix 1985, Bennis and Hoekstra 1984–85, Koster 1984, 1987, and Engdahl 1985).

It is not yet clear how the notion of chain composition and especially the 0-Subjacency requirement on it (if that should prove superior to the anti-c-command requirement) may follow from independent principles of UG, though that is surely possible. If, on the other hand, UG quite generally allows pros to be identified by an operator $\bar{\text{A}}$-binding them at S-Structure, then the basic properties of parasitic gaps virtually follow (in interaction with the principles characterizing their selective violation of island conditions).

Turning to the empirical differences between ordinary *wh*-traces and the gaps of the constructions in (1), we will see that the same assumption providing a solution to the conceptual problem will provide a unified and simple account of these as well.

We have seen that not all bare (complement) NPs can enter into the parasitic gap construction, be extracted from islands, and qualify as acceptable COD gaps (see (20)–(21)), although the same NPs can be *Wh*-Moved in ordinary *wh*-constructions (see (22)–(23)). Though unclear under a unitary *Wh*-Movement analysis, the asymmetry seems to follow from the hypothesis that the gaps of the constructions in (1) are not regular *wh*-traces but are Ā-bound pros. If these gaps are indeed Ā-bound pros, it becomes possible to relate the ungrammaticality of (20)–(21) to that of the forms in (60), which show that the NPs in question cannot in general be resumed by (overt) pronominals (presumably because they are not fully referential):

(60) a. *Lui vorrebbe pesare   cento chili   perché *li* pesa
       he would like to weigh one hundred kilos since *them* weighs
       il suo attore preferito.
       his favorite actor (since his favorite actor weighs them)

   b. *Ho passato tre settimane a Berlino
       I spent   three weeks   in Berlin
       prima che *le* passasse Gianni.
       before Gianni spent *them*

Incidentally, this indicates that the crucial contrast is not between complement and adjunct (as suggested in Stowell 1986), but between being compatible and not being compatible with resumption by a pronominal form. (61)–(62) represent a minimal contrast in Italian:

(61) Ho passato tre settimane a Londra.
     I spent   three weeks   in London

(62) Sono rimasto tre settimane a Londra.
     I stayed   three weeks   in London

As Belletti and Rizzi (1981) demonstrate, *tre settimane* is a complement NP (a direct object) in (61) and an adjunct NP in (62). This can be seen, for example, from the fact that the former, though not the latter, admits *ne*-cliticization (Belletti and Rizzi 1981, Chomsky 1981, 300ff.):

(63) a. Ne ho passate tre   a Londra.
       ne I spent   three in London
   b. *Ne sono rimasto tre   a Londra.
       ne I stayed   three in London.

Now, despite the complement/adjunct distinction, both NPs yield ill-formed results when they appear as parasitic gaps, gaps of extraction from islands, or COD gaps:

(64) a. *Quante settimane trascorrerai *t* a Londra
          how many weeks will you spend in London
          prima di passare *e* a Parigi?
          before spending   in Paris

     b. **Quante settimane ti fermerai *t* a Londra
          how many weeks will you stop in London
          prima di rimanere *e* a Parigi?
          before staying   in Paris

(65) a. *TRE SETTIMANE, me ne sono andato
          three weeks (focus)   I left
          per non dover passare *e* lì.
          not to spend there

     b. **TRE SETTIMANE, me ne sono andato
          three weeks (focus)   I left
          per non dover rimanere *e* lì.
          not to stay there

(66) a. *Una settimana è difficile da trascorrere *e* digiuni.
          one week   is difficult to spend   without eating

     b. **Una settimana è difficile da rimanere *e* digiuni.
          one week   is difficult to stay   without eating

What the two NPs appear to have in common, if not their thematic status, is their nonreferentiality and consequent incompatibility with resumption by a pronominal form. This is shown, for overt pronominals, by (67)–(69):

(67) a. *Quante settimane trascorrerai *t* a Londra
          how many weeks will you spend in London
          prima di passar*le*   a Parigi?
          before spending *them* in Paris

     b. **Quante settimane ti fermerai *t* a Londra   prima di rimaner*le*
          how many weeks will you stop in London before staying *them*
          a Parigi?
          in Paris

(68) a. *TRE SETTIMANE, me ne sono andato
          three weeks (focus)   I left
          per non dover*le* passare lì.
          not to have to spend *them* there

b. **TRE SETTIMANE, me ne sono andato
three weeks (focus)   I left
per non dover rimaner*le* lì.
not to have to stay *them* there

(69) a. *Una settimana è difficile da trascorrer*la* digiuni.
one week   is difficult to spend *it*   without eating
b. **Una settimana è difficile da rimaner*la* digiuni.
one week   is difficult to stay *it*   without eating

If the gap in (64)–(66) is pro, the ungrammaticality of those forms can be related to that of (67)–(69), quite apart from the complement/adjunct distinction between the (a) and (b) cases. The extra deviance of the (b) forms appears imputable to the fact that although object pronominals are at least possible with the transitive *passare/trascorrere* in referential contexts (70a), there is no context in which an object pronominal can cooccur with the intransitive *rimanere* (70b):

(70) a.   Ci rimarrò   tre settimane. Spero di passarle
I will stay there three weeks   I hope I will spend *them*
in allegria.
being jolly

b.   **Ci rimarrò   tre settimane. E spero   di rimaner*le*
I will stay there three weeks   and I hope I will stay *them*
in allegria.
being jolly

Earlier we considered Taraldsen's observation that parasitic gaps are marginal in the subject position of a complementizerless tensed CP (the observation extends to extraction from island and COD gaps). This property is not shared by ordinary *wh*-traces. Compare (26) and (27), repeated here:

(26) a. *?Someone who John expected [*e* would be successful though
believing [*e* is incompetent]]...
b. *?The student that Susan left because John said [*e* was
intelligent]...
c. *?Mary is hard for me to believe [*e* kissed John].

(27) Someone who we expected [*e* would be successful]...

As noted, the reason for the (relative) contrast between (26) and (27) remains unclear under the unitary *Wh*-Movement analysis. Successive cyclic movement should be as fully available in (26) as it is in (27).

The reason why it is not, I suggest, is that no *Wh*-Movement is possible in such constructions on independent grounds (as we will see in section 3.4), so that the option will be the base generation of a pro in subject position and an operator in the highest embedded CP, $\overline{\text{A}}$-binding the pro. But pro must be formally licensed by a head, and C, we may assume, is not an appropriate licenser (just as it is not an appropriate head governor in English or Italian—see chapter 1 and Rizzi 1990, chap. 2). If pro raises to the Spec position of the first CP dominating it, it could be formally licensed by the upper V:

(71) $\ldots \text{V} [_{\text{CP}} \text{pro}_i [_{\text{IP}} t_i \ldots]] \ldots$

Nonetheless, the structure will be excluded because the ϕ-features of pro fail to be identified. We have claimed that the pro of the constructions of (1) is authorized at S-Structure because pro concomitantly becomes a variable at that level by acquiring an $\overline{\text{A}}$-antecedent (which in turn identifies its ϕ-features, as required). In (71), however, pro cannot be interpreted as a variable by the general definition of variable, since it is not in an A-position. Hence, its ϕ-features cannot be identified either.

One final possibility is left: namely, that a coindexed EC is base-generated in the Spec position of the first CP dominating pro, thus permitting Agr to fill the C position licensing pro (72a), by analogy with ordinary extractions of tensed CP subjects (72b) as analyzed by Koopman and Sportiche (1988) and Rizzi (1990), where Agr in C head-governs the variable:

(72) a. $O_i \ldots \text{V} [_{\text{CP}} \text{EC}_i \text{ Agr}_i [_{\text{IP}} \text{pro} \ldots]] \ldots$
      b. $\text{Who}_i \ldots \text{think} [_{\text{CP}} e_i \text{ Agr}_i [_{\text{IP}} e_i \ldots$

In this case, however, as in the case discussed in note 15 (modulo the formal licensing versus head government requirement), the EC in the Spec CP will receive no interpretation at LF, in violation of Chomsky's (1988) economy requirements, as discussed by Rizzi (1990). Interestingly, the grammaticality judgments of (26a–c) appear to match that of (i) of note 15, repeated here as (73):

(73) Who do you wonder whether we believe [*t* can help us]?

At least (26a) and (26c) cannot be reduced to the account of (73), since no island intervenes between the operator and the variable there. The fact that a stronger violation occurs if *that* is present in the C adjacent to the pro (Chomsky 1986b) also follows. If *that* fills C, Agr cannot. Hence, pro will end up not being formally licensed.

The (b) cases of (32)–(34), repeated here in (74), illustrate another context where the constructions in (1) appear to differ from ordinary *wh*-constructions in not having access to the successive cyclic derivation normally open to *Wh*-Movement:

(74) a. *?L'uomo che apprezzavamo *t* pur senza ritenere
   the man who we appreciated without even believing
   [*e* [*e* essere intelligente]]...
      to be intelligent

   b. *?L'unica persona che siamo stati ricompensati
   the only person who we have been rewarded
   per aver ritenuto [*e* [*e* essere intelligente]]...
   for considering   to be intelligent

   c. *?Quest'uomo è facile da ritenere [*e* [*e* essere intelligente]].
   this man   is easy to believe   to be intelligent

I suggest that these cases are amenable to exactly the same account as (26). The two properties in fact turn out to be simply two distinct manifestations of the same deeper cause: lack of *Wh*-Movement in the constructions of (1).

A similar argument from Dutch for Chomsky's (1982) nonderivational analysis of parasitic gaps (and the extension suggested here) is discussed by Bennis and Hoekstra (1984–85, 67–68) (also see Bennis 1986, 52–54). Bennis and Hoekstra present evidence that in Dutch extraction from sentential complements is possible only via successive cyclic movement, and they attribute that property to the fact that the complement clause to the right of the matrix verb is not *canonically* governed.[34] As they note, the derivational approach to parasitic gaps predicts that a parasitic gap should be found in a complement clause within an adjunct, since it may resort to the successive cyclic strategy like ordinary *Wh*-Movement. As (75) shows, the prediction turns out to be incorrect (for more careful discussion, see Bennis and Hoekstra 1984–85):

(75) *Welke boeken heb je   [zonder te weten [dat je *e*
   which books   have you without to know that you
   mocht bekijken]] *t* doorgebladerd?
   could inspect   browsed through

The last contrast noted earlier between ordinary *wh*-traces and the gaps of the constructions in (1) concerns the second object of the dative construction in English. It can be a *wh*-trace unproblematically, (as in (76)) but a COD gap, a parasitic gap, or an extraction from island gap only marginally (see (41)–(43), repeated here as (77)–(79), bearing in mind the cautionary note on the relevant acceptability judgment in section 3.2.3.4):

(76) a.   What$_i$ did you give that man e_i?
      b.   The book$_i$ (which$_i$) I gave that man e_i...
      c.   My book$_i$ [O_i [I won't give that man e_i]].

(77) a.   *?Books$_i$ are not easy [to give (even) that man e_i].
      b.   *?Those books$_i$ are too boring [to give (even) that man e_i].
      c.   *?Those books$_i$ are interesting enough [to give (even) that man e_i].
      d.   *?He bought some books$_i$ [to give (even) that man e_i].

(78) *?The book$_i$ (that) we filed e_i instead of giving that man e_i...

(79) *?The book$_i$ (that) we left the library without giving that man e_i...

As occasionally noted, this property recalls a property characteristic of NP-Movement, rather than *Wh*-Movement, in dative contexts. See the marginality of (80), where the second object has been NP-Moved under Passive (the grammaticality judgment is again that of Lasnik and Fiengo (1974)):

(80) *?The book$_i$ was given that man e_i.

On the basis of this similarity it might be suggested that COD constructions share properties of both *Wh*-Movement and NP-Movement (see Condon 1982). But this would be a rather curious and unprecedented state of affairs.

There is another possibility to consider. Dative constructions are characterized by a further well-known restriction: their second object can be a pronominal only very marginally (if at all). For example:

(81) *I gave that man it/them.

If the EC of the constructions in (1) is an $\bar{A}$-bound pronominal (pro) rather than a *wh*-trace, the possibility arises of relating the marginality of (77)–(79) to that of (81) (despite, perhaps, their different degree of deviance, to which we will return). Indirect evidence supporting this idea is provided by the following observation. Such forms as (81) are substantially improved if the dative object is itself a pronominal. See (82a–b), drawn from Oehrle 1976:

(82) a.   ?Gimme it.
      b.   ??I gave 'im THEM.

It turns out that such cases as (77)–(79) are also improved (becoming, in fact, unexceptionable) when the dative object is itself a pronominal. This would be rather strange if the EC were a real *wh*-trace but is understandable if it is a pronominal (in view of (81)–(82)).

(83) a. Books$_i$ are not easy [O_i [to give him e_i]].
    b. Those books$_i$ are too boring [O_i [to give him e_i]].
    c. Those books$_i$ are interesting enough [O_i [to give him e_i]].
    d. He bought those books$_i$ [O_i [to give him e_i]].

(84) The book$_i$ (that) we filed t_i instead of giving him e_i...

(85) The book$_i$ (that) we left the library without giving him e_i...

The similarity of the two cases, if real, could hardly be accidental. However, something must be said about their different degree of deviance—a potentially disturbing factor.

A possible solution to this problem is suggested by the nature of the restriction on pronominals in the dative construction. In his discussion of this peculiarity of the construction, Oehrle (1976) proposes a general output condition, which requires of the rightmost of the two objects that it be "heavier" or "more prominent" (along a certain scale of "prominence") than the leftmost, noting further that what is involved is a computation of the *relative* "prominence" of the two objects.[35]

In addition to an intrinsic "measure" of prominence, whereby, for example, full NPs are by definition more prominent than pronominals, one must take into account a number of external means for rendering a category more or less prominent (for example, by stressing or destressing it, respectively). Though clear in its general outline, the condition is not easy to render fully explicit, given the many factors involved. Oehrle proposes (86) (his (13) of part II) as a first approximation to a "measure" of (relative) prominence, noting the "descriptive" character of the condition and the possibility that "future insights into the English intonational system may allow us to dispense with it" (p. 169):

(86) a. The following surface structure is ungrammatical if NP$_1$ is higher on the scale of prominence than NP$_2$:

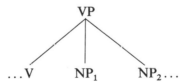

    b. *Prominence* is defined with respect to the following hierarchy, where a lower number reflects lower prominence:
      1. Cliticized pronouns
      2. *Me, it*
      3. *Us, you*

    4. Other third person pronouns

    5. Everything else

Going back to the different degrees of deviance of *I *gave that man them*, ??*Those books$_i$ are not easy to give that man e$_i$*, and *What$_i$ did you give that man e$_i$?*, we may note that the EC in the second sentence falls somewhere between the first (pure overt pronominal case) and the third (pure variable case), since it qualifies as a pronominal variable. Thus, it is perhaps not surprising that the grammaticality judgment of the second case also falls between those of the first and the third. No doubt, under the unitary *Wh*-Movement analysis, each of the differences so far reviewed between *wh*-traces and the gaps of (1) is amenable to separate treatment. What is interesting is that the $\bar{\text{A}}$-bound *pro* analysis appears to provide a unified solution.

3.3.3 Some Additional Evidence

3.3.3.1 A Property of the CLLD construction One particularly clear piece of evidence for the pronominal nature of the gaps in (1) derives from a peculiarity of the CLLD construction examined in chapter 2. There we observed that CLLD, unlike topicalization, does not involve *Wh*-Movement of a null operator—hence the possible occurrence of resumptive clitics, generally prohibited in ordinary *wh*-constructions (topicalization included):

(87) A Gianni, (gli) scriveremo   domani.
      to Gianni we (to-him) will write tomorrow

(88) a. A chi   (*gli) scriverete   domani?
          to whom will you write (to-him) tomorrow

      b. A GIAṆNI,   (*gli) scriveremo   domani.
          to Gianni (focus) we (to-him) will write tomorrow

We also saw that the obligatoriness of the clitic for dislocated NPs (see (89)), a particularly clear indication of the absence of a null operator, has one interesting exception. No clitic is required (in fact, possible) when the NP happens to be a bare quantifier (such as *qualcosa* 'something or other', *qualcuno* 'someone'; see (90)):

(89) Gianni, non *(lo) abbiamo visto.
      Gianni we not (him) have seen

(90) Qualcosa, (*lo) farò *e* anch'io, da grande.
      something I will do (it) when I grow up

A natural account of this complex (and apparently capricious) pattern of optional, obligatory, and impossible resumptive pronouns in CLLD in Italian seems to involve the proper definition of variable. If we assume that a variable must be (locally Ā-bound and) operator-bound and that only NPs in Spec CP or bare quantifiers such as those in (90) qualify as operators, then we have a simple account for the contrast between (89), where the clitic is required, and (90), where it is not only not required but in fact impossible. Only in (90) does the empty NP qualify as a variable,[36] a conclusion confirmed by the fact that a resumptive clitic is actually impossible in (90), just as it is in ordinary *wh*-constructions such as (88) and (91):

(91) a. Che cosa (*1') ha fatto/a *e*?
      what   did he do (it)
   b. La cosa *O* che (*1') ha fatto/a *e*...
      the thing   that he did (it)

If (90) is indeed correctly analyzed in terms of the same operator/variable configuration at S-Structure found in (91), an unexpected asymmetry emerges. Whereas *wh*-phrases can in general license a parasitic gap, besides authorizing their real gap (see (92)), the bare quantifiers of the CLLD quite clearly can authorize only their real gap. See the contrast between (90) and (93):

(92) (?)Quali libri   hai preso *t*   senza pagare *e*?
     which books have you taken without paying

(93) a. *Qualcosa ho fatto *t* anch'io pur senza finire *e*.
      something I did too   even without finishing
   b. *Qualcuno forse   licenzieranno *t* dopo aver assunto *e*.
      someone perhaps they will fire   after having employed

The unacceptability of (93a–b) (versus the relative acceptability of (92)) is rather surprising if bare quantifiers can indeed identify as a variable a [−pronominal, −anaphor] EC that they Ā-bind at S-Structure, entering into an Ā-chain with it.[37]

Under a movement analysis of parasitic gaps, it is not clear why a null operator cannot move from the adjunct clauses in (93) whereas it can in (92). The bare quantifier and the matrix object gap form an Ā-chain that should permit chain composition. A solution for this contrast is available, however, if we assume that parasitic gaps are pros throughout. We know that bare quantifiers such as those in (90) and (93) cannot be resumed by an overt pronominal either within the same (complex) sentence or across discourse (presumably owing to their nonreferential status). For example (recalling that *qualcosa*, as a quantifier, is masculine):

(94) *Qualcosa,   farò anch'io. Ma non so   se
      something or other I will do too but I don't know whether
      far*lo* oggi.
      to do *it* today

In this light, the ungrammaticality of (93) is entirely parallel to that of (95), where the parasitic gap has been replaced by an overt pronoun, a possibility generally open to ordinary parasitic gaps of the adjunct type, as shown by the minimal pair (92) and (96), but not here:

(95) a. *Qualcosa, ho fatto *e* anch'io pur senza finir*lo*.
     b. *Qualcuno forse licenzieranno *e* dopo aver*lo* assunto.

(96) (?)Quali libri   hai preso *t*   senza pagar*li*?
      which books have you taken without paying *them*

The contrast can reasonably be attributed to the fact that *wh*-phrases like *quali libri* do retain some referential force, unlike the bare quantifiers of (90), (93), (94), and (95). For example, they can be resumed by a pronominal across discourse (*Quali libri hai preso? Li hai pagati?* 'Which books have you taken? Have you paid for them?').

Some *wh*-phrases do not seem to be as open to a referential reading as the *wh*-phrase in (92) and (96). For example, *che* in (97) cannot be resumed by a pronominal:

(97) Speaker A: Che farai   stasera per cena?
                 what will you do tonight for dinner
     Speaker B: *Non so,   ma *lo/la* farò   volentieri.
                 I do not know but I will do *it* willingly

Interestingly, just like bare quantifiers, these *wh*-phrases appear not to be able to $\bar{\text{A}}$-bind a parasitic gap:

(98) *Che posso fare *t* stasera per cena
      what can I do   tonight for dinner
      senza essere in obbligo di mangiare *e*?
      without having to eat

This is again expected if parasitic gaps are pronominal (variables). To put it differently, parasitic gaps appear to display here a property more typical of pronominals than of pure variables (they cannot be linked to a non-referential operator).[38]

3.3.3.2 Montalbetti's Facts Additional evidence for the pronominal nature of the Ā-bound EC in parasitic gap, extraction from island, and COD constructions, at S-Structure and LF, can be constructed on the basis of work by Mario Montalbetti.

Montalbetti (1983, 1984) points out some coherent facts of Spanish indicating that an overt pronominal (in positions where it can alternate with an empty variant) can be bound only to a bound pronominal, not to a formal variable (a QR or *wh*-trace). For example, (99) in Spanish cannot be understood as in (100a), which represents the bound interpretation of *ellos*, but only as in (100b), which represents its coreferential reading:

(99) Muchos estudiantes piensan que ellos son inteligentes.

     many students think   that they are intelligent

(100) a. (Many x: x a student) x thinks x is intelligent $\neq$ (99)

     b. (Many x: x a student) x thinks they are intelligent

This is apparently related to the fact that *ellos* in (99) can alternate with pro, given the pro-drop nature of Spanish. It is (99) with pro substituted for *ellos* that receives interpretation (100a).

Simplifying somewhat, it seems that where there is a choice between the overt and the empty variant of a pronominal, the overt variant "specializes" for the coreferential reading, and the empty one for the bound reading. This follows if we assume (101) (= (34) of Montalbetti 1984, chap. 4; see also Higginbotham 1983):

(101) *Overt Pronoun Constraint* (OPC)

     Overt pronouns cannot link to formal variables if the alternation overt/empty obtains.

Principle (101) rules out interpretation (100a) for (99) on the basis of the fact that *ellos* is bound to a formal variable at LF (the trace of *muchos estudiantes* left by an application of QR). Identical effects obtain with *wh*-traces and with NP-traces of quantificational NPs in place of QR traces.

(102) contrasts with (99) in allowing a bound interpretation of the overt pronominal apparently because the latter has an intermediate nontrace antecedent (pro):

(102) Muchos estudiantes$_i$ dijeron que pro$_i$ piensan

     many students said   that they think

     que ellos$_i$ son inteligentes.

     that they are intelligent

(102) can thus be interpreted as (103):

(103) (Many x: x a student) x said x thinks x is intelligent

Whenever the overt/empty alternation is not available, an overt pronominal can be bound to a formal variable. For a more careful discussion of these findings and further evidence for the existence of something like principle (101), see Montalbetti 1983, 1984. Montalbetti's observations appear to extend to Italian, though the judgments are often delicate.

Montalbetti notes that if only a bound pronominal (not a formal variable) can license the bound interpretation of an overt pronoun, then we have a rather strong diagnostic for the pronominal/nonpronominal nature of certain controversial empty categories. Thus, "if an overt pronoun is linked to an empty category whose nature is uncertain, then, if the pronoun can be interpreted as a bound variable, the empty category in question cannot be trace, but a pronominal" (Montalbetti 1983, 23).

Applying this test to parasitic gaps and the EC of COD constructions, as in (104a–b) (= (36) and (40) of Montalbetti 1984, chap. 4),

(104) a. A quiénes contrató t_i el director sin persuadir e_i
         who   did the director hire   without persuading
         de que ellos$_i$ viajen   a Lima?
         that they should travel to Lima

      b. Muchos estudiantes$_i$ son faciles de convencer e_i
         many students   are easy   to persuade
         de que ellos$_i$ viajen   a Lima.
         that they should travel to Lima

Montalbetti notes that both are found to license the bound interpretation of the overt pronominal (*ellos*), which in turn suggests that they are not formal variables.

This conflicts with the fact that such gaps can themselves license a parasitic gap, just like ordinary *wh*-phrases. Consider, for example, (105) (= (50) of Montalbetti 1983):

(105) Esta teoria$_i$ es dificil de explicar e_i sin conocer e_i.
      this theory is hard to explain   without knowing

Montalbetti's suggestion for resolving the apparent paradox is to deny such ECs the status of formal variables. If formal variables are defined as in (106) (= (34) of Montalbetti 1984, chap. 2; also see Higginbotham 1983),

(106) *Formal variable*
      v is a formal variable iff (i) v is an empty category in an argument position; and (ii) v is linked to a lexical operator in a nonargument position.

then the parasitic and COD gaps of (104) are not formal variables, because their binders are not lexical. Hence, they do not fall under the OPC.

Even if we ignore the question of why ECs locally bound by lexical operators should differ in such a way from ECs bound by null operators, we are still confronted with a problem. Not all ECs Ā-bound by a null operator can bind an overt pronoun. For example, the EC of ordinary tensed relative clauses in Italian (and Spanish) can be Ā-bound by a null operator yet cannot bind an overt pronoun:

(107) Gli studenti$_i$ O_i che non siamo riusciti a convincere t_i
     the students   who we could not convince
     che loro$_i$ avrebbero superato l'esame   non si sono presentati.
     that they would have passed the exam didn't show up

The bound interpretation of *loro* is not available in (107). A possible way out would be to stipulate that in tensed relative clauses the null operator acts like a lexical one (see Stowell 1986); but this would not be particularly enlightening. Instead, I suggest that no such stipulation is needed and that parasitic and COD gaps can license the bound interpretation of the overt pronominal precisely because they *are* (bound) pronominals, not *wh*-traces, just like the pro of (102).

3.3.3.3 Vergnaud's Idiom Argument

Noting the implication for the Ā-bound pro analysis, Jean-Roger Vergnaud (personal communication) has observed that in French bare NPs that are part of an idiom appear to resist extraction out of islands that (marginally) admit extraction of other bare NPs. His observation extends to Italian. Compare (108) and (109), which involve the idiom *avere una parte in qualcosa* 'to play a role in something':

(108) a. Che parte$_i$ ha avuto t_i nella destituzione del re?
       which role did he play in the destitution of the king
   b. La parte$_i$ che ha avuto t_i nella destituzione del re
       the role   that he played in the destitution of the king
       è tutt'altro che trascurabile.
       is anything but negligible

(109) *La parte$_i$ che non si è ancora pentito per aver avuto t_i
     the role   that he has not yet repented for playing
     nella destituzione del re   è tutt'altro che trascurabile.
     in the destitution of the king is anything but negligible

(Compare

?La sola persona$_i$ che non si è ancora pentito   per aver trattato t_i
the only person who he has not yet repented for treating
in quel modo è Carlo.

like that   is Carlo)

Comparable effects appear to hold for the corresponding parasitic gap and COD cases (though the judgment is less firm for the former; see the discussion below):

(110) ??La parte$_i$ che ha avuto t_i anche senza desiderare di avere e_i
the role   that he played even without desiring to play
nella destituzione del re   è stata peraltro trascurabile.
in the destitution of the king was in any event negligible

(111) *Una parte decisiva$_i$ è stata tutt'altro che facile da avere e_i
a decisive role   was anything but easy   to play
nella sua riabilitazione.
in his rehabilitation

These facts are not expected under a pure *Wh*-Movement analysis of these constructions. Suppose, however, that the $\bar{\text{A}}$-bound pro strategy were the only option available. Here, the ungrammaticality of these forms does not arise from the unavailability of a pronominal form resuming the idiom chunk (*la parte*). Albeit marginally, the idiomatic NP can apparently be resumed by a pronoun:

(112) Speaker A: So   che ha avuto una parte importante
I know that he played an important role
nella sua destituzione.
in his destitution

Speaker B: ??No! *L*'ha avuta solo nella destituzione
no! he played it only in the destitution
del suo predecessore
of his predecessor

Rather, it seems that these constructions are ill formed because the idiom NP (*la parte*) is not contiguous to the remaining part of the idiom at D-Structure (in fact, it is not contiguous at any level of representation), violating the general condition on idiomatic expressions discussed by Chomsky (1980b, 149–153). This appears true at least for (109) and (111), where, if no *Wh*-Movement derivation is available, the idiom NP must be base-generated in its left-peripheral position and be construed with a base-generated pro.

This may also explain the less severe violation found in the parasitic gap case. There, the idiom NP *is* related via *Wh*-Movement to the position of the real gap, so that it may be assumed to be contiguous to the remaining part of the idiom at D-Structure (Vergnaud 1974, 1985). Thus, no comparable violation of the condition on idiomatic expressions is involved in the parasitic gap case—whence its contrast with (109)/(111). Once again a significant property of these constructions follows from interpreting them as instances of the resumptive pro strategy.

3.3.3.4 Longobardi's Scope Argument One additional argument for the pronominal nature of the gap resulting from apparent extraction from islands is explicitly suggested by Longobardi (1986), who argues as follows:

Quantified NPs that have been *wh*-extracted from a nonisland (and accordingly may bind a real gap, in our terms) retain the ability to enter into scope relations with other quantified NPs in the CP from which they were extracted. For example:

(113) Quanti pazienti   ritieni
      how many patients do you think
      [che debba visitare *t* ogni medico]?
      that each doctor should visit

Quanti pazienti can still be understood in the scope of *ogni medico* ('For each $x : x$ a doctor, how may $y : y$ a patient, you think that x should visit y'). This property should follow from an appropriate theory of "reconstruction," which should be able to draw the relevant parallelism between (113) and (114):

(114) Ritengo che ogni medico debba visitare trenta pazienti.
      I deem   that each doctor should visit   thirty patients

Quantified NPs that have been *wh*-extracted from a position inside CP occupied by an overt resumptive pronominal cannot enter into scope relations with other quantified NPs inside the same CP. For example:

(115) ?Quanti pazienti   ritieni
      how many patients do you deem
      che ogni medico *li* debba visitare?
      that each doctor should visit *them*

In (115) *quanti pazienti* cannot be understood as falling in the scope of *ogni medico*.

Quantified NPs that appear to have been extracted from a strong island behave with respect to scope relations like quantified NPs resumed by a pronominal (as in (115)), not like those binding a real variable (as in (113)):

(116) Quanti pazienti$_i$ te ne sei andato prima che ogni medico
      how many patients did you go away before   each doctor
      potesse visitare t_i?
      could visit

In (116) the only possible (albeit marginal) reading is 'How many are the patients such that you went away before they could be visited by each doctor?', in which *quanti pazienti* is not within the scope of *ogni medico*.[39]

This is reminiscent of the analogous failure of scope Reconstruction into weak islands noted by Longobardi (1987b), which we interpreted in section 1.4.2 as an indication that nonreferential operators can enter only into government chains, not binding chains. Government chains are also blocked by strong islands, so that no scope reconstruction is expected to obtain here either. Failure of scope Reconstruction is then compatible with the interpretation of the CP-internal EC as either a trace of binding or a pro. Strong islands, however, block binding chains, as we saw in chapter 1. Thus, we conclude that the CP-internal EC must be pro.[40]

3.3.4 On the Selective Island Sensitivity of Ā-Bound Pro

If the gaps of the constructions in (1) are base-generated pros at D-Structure and remain pros at S-Structure, their distribution should be unaffected by the theory of bounding, which is taken to pertain to movement only. In other words, the gaps of the constructions in (1) should be immune to island conditions. But this is not true—at least not entirely true, as many authors have pointed out. Thus, although parasitic and extraction from island gaps are found in (some) adjunct and complex NP islands (see (117)–(119)), they cannot occur in all types of islands. For example, they are not found in subject islands (Kayne 1984, chap. 8), as (120) illustrates:

(117) a. ?L'articolo che abbiamo messo t via [senza fotocopiare e]...
          the article that we put away   without copying
      b. ?L'articolo che ce ne siamo andati via [senza fotocopiare e]...
          the article that we went away   without copying

(118) a. ?Carlo, che abbiamo ricoverato t [con la speranza
          Carlo who we hospitalized   with the hope
          di poter salvare e],...
          of being able to save
      b. ?Carlo, che abbiamo discusso più volte
          Carlo who we discussed   several times
          [la possibilità di ammettere e nel nostro club],...
          the possibility of admitting   to our club

(119) a. ?E' un uomo che [chiunque incontri *e* una volta]
      he is a man whom those who meet once
      non può dimenticare *t*.
      cannot forget

    b. ?Carlo, che spero di trovare qualcuno [che sia disposto
      Carlo who I hope to find someone who is willing
      ad ospitare *e* per questa notte], . . .
      to put up for the night

(120) a. *Piero, che abbiamo convinto *t* che [invitare *e*]
      Piero who we convinced that to invite
      ci è impossibile, . . .
      is impossible for us

    b. *Piero, che me ne andai prima che [invitare *e*]
      Piero who I went away before inviting
      divenisse necessario, . . .
      would become necessary

Moreover, even their ability to violate certain types of islands is severely limited. In general, they seem to be able to violate one, but not more than one, island at a time. See for example (121), where the gap is embedded within two adjuncts (see Longobardi 1983), and (122)–(123), where the gap is embedded within two complex NPs (see Chomsky 1982, 1986b):

(121) a. *I capi di bestiame che abbiamo eliminato *t*
      the head of cattle that we have eliminated
      [senza cercare di chiamare un veterinario
      without even trying to call a vet
      [invece di abbattere *e*]]
      instead of slaughtering

    b. *Una persona che me ne vado [senza aspettarmi
      a person that I go away without expecting
      alcuna riconoscenza [dopo aver aiutato *e*]] è Mario.
      any gratitude after helping is Mario

(122) a. *Carlo, che abbiamo ricoverato *t* [con la speranza
      Carlo who we hospitalized with the hope
      di aumentare [le probabilità di salvare *e*]], . . .
      of increasing the probabilities of saving

    b. *Carlo, che ci siamo presentati [con la speranza di aumentare
      Carlo who we turned up with the hope of increasing
      [le probabilità di salvare *e*]], . . .
      the probabilities of saving

(123) a. **E' una donna   che [chiunque conosca [qualcuno che ama *e*]]
          she is a woman that whoever knows   someone who likes
          non può non considerare *t* fortunata.
          cannot but consider lucky

      b. *Mario, che non conosco [nessuno disposto ad aiutare
          Mario who I don't know anybody willing to help
          [quelli che vogliono rovinare *e*]], . . .
          those who want   to ruin

This is particularly striking in the case of apparent extraction from islands. If the Adjunct and CNP Conditions can be violated once in a sentence, why can they not be violated twice or more?

On a purely observational level, any adequate analysis must apparently derive the fact that the bounding conditions on the constructions in (1a–b), though similar to those of ordinary *wh*-constructions, are "weaker," in some sense to be made more precise.

Besides the conceptual and empirical problems already noted, a unitary *Wh*-Movement analysis is apparently unable to characterize the partially different nature of the bounding conditions that hold of the two classes of constructions. See, for example, the contrast between (118b) and (124):

(124) *Carlo, con cui   abbiamo discusso più volte   la possibilità
       Carlo with whom we discussed   many times the possibility
       di stare *t*, . . .
       of staying

I will thus continue to pursue the hypothesis that attributes no *syntactic* movement to the constructions in (1). This of course requires a different account of their partial island sensitivity. In Cinque 1983a I adopted the idea that pros, as ECs, should fall under the Connectedness Condition (CC) (Kayne 1984, chap. 8). This immediately accounted for the ungrammaticality of the subject condition cases of (120a–b). However, the classical formulation of the CC was unable to draw the appropriate distinction between such cases as (117)–(119), which contain a single violation of the Adjunct or CNP Condition, and (121)–(123), which contain two such violations, one embedded inside the other. The CC treats the two classes of cases alike, since in both the antecedent is contained in a g-projection of the governor of the gap, and each intermediate maximal projection is on a right branch.

As Longobardi (1983, 1985a) observes, for parasitic gaps, it is possible to draw the appropriate distinction between a single violation and two or more repeated violations of the Adjunct Condition, by tightening the formulation of the CC. In essence, he suggests requiring that each intermediate maximal projection not only be in a canonical government configuration (on a right branch in right-branching languages and on a left branch in left-branching languages) but also be properly governed.[41] Abstracting from the directionality issue, this is in fact a partial return to Kayne's (1984, chap. 3) extended notion of the ECP.

Consider how the contrast between (117a) and (121a), repeated here, follows from this stricter notion of the CC:

(117) a. ?L'articolo che abbiamo messo *t* via [$_{PP}$ senza fotocopiare *e*]...
          the article that we put away   without copying

(121) a. *I capi di bestiame che abbiamo eliminato *t*
          the head of cattle that we have eliminated
          [$_{PP}$ senza cercare   di chiamare un veterinario
          without even trying to call   a vet
          [$_{PP}$ invece di abbattere *e*]]...
          instead of slaughtering

(117a) is still permitted. Although the g-projections of the governor of the parasitic gap would, on their own, stop at the adjunct PP, since it is a non-properly governed constituent, they have the option of extending upward to the antecedent by "connecting" with those of the real gap (the adjunct PP is immediately dominated by a node that is in the g-projection path of the governor of the real gap). On the other hand, (121a) is correctly excluded since the g-projections of the governor of the parasitic gap stop at the first adjunct PP, as before, but have no way to extend upward by "connecting" to those of the governor of the real gap. This is due to the absence of a coindexed gap in the immediately higher adjunct. Since these g-projections do not contain the antecedent, the structure is correctly ruled out.

Nonetheless, even this modification of the CC fails to account for extraction from island gaps, where a similar contrast obtains between one and two compounded violations of the Adjunct Condition:

(125) a. ?I dolci   che è scappato   [$_\alpha$ dopo aver rubato *e*] erano pochi.
          the sweets that he ran away   after stealing   were few
      b. *I dolci   che è scappato   [$_{\alpha'}$ dopo esser stato sgridato
          the sweets that he ran away   after being scolded
          [$_\alpha$ per aver rubato *e*]] erano pochi.
          for stealing   were few

Whereas the classical CC predicts the (relative) well-formedness of (125a–b), leaving the ill-formedness of (125b) unaccounted for, the stricter

CC seems capable of ruling out (125b) but now leaves the relative well-formedness of (125a) unaccounted for. The g-projections of the governor of *e* stop in both (125a) and (125b) at α, which does not contain the antecedent of *e*. Unlike what happens in the parasitic gap case, here α is not able to "parasitically" connect to some other g-projection path that leads to the common antecedent.

To sum up, the (relative) well-formedness of (125a), in opposition to the clear ill-formedness of genuine extraction out of adjuncts (*The man to whom I went away without speaking...*)still remains to be accounted for, even under the proposed modification of the CC.[42] In addition, the CC approach raises a more general, conceptual problem. The (revised) CC and the bounding condition on movement are very close to each other, yet distinct. The bounding condition on movement requires essentially that all intermediate maximal projections be θ-marked by a [+V] head (directly or not, depending on whether an adjunct or a complement is moved). The (revised) CC essentially demands that all intermediate maximal projections be governed by some head (a weaker condition, apparently). Ideally one would like to be able to unify them. Longobardi (forthcoming) makes an interesting attempt in this direction. Here, I will suggest that the partially different bounding conditions holding of *wh*-traces and pro not only can be unified but in fact are the same. They only *appear* to be distinct because of the option of pied piping (at LF), a condition governed by the CC, as Kayne (1983) argues (or by the revised CC, as I will suggest).

In other words, by assuming that a pro unmoved in the syntax must move at LF, either by itself or within a larger phrase under pied piping (governed by the CC), we will derive the fact that in general one island, and not more than one island, can be "suspended."

To see this, we may begin by observing the similarity between the constructions in (1) and pied piping (in relatives). It has been noted that the constructions in (1) are best when the gap is found in a nonfinite clause (finiteness rendering the sentence relatively unacceptable).[43] A similar restriction has been observed for pied piping. Nanni and Stillings (1978) and Cinque (1981–82, 273ff.) report contrasts like these:

(126) a.   Mario, aver scritto al quale,   credo sia stato un errore, ...
           Mario to have written to whom I think was a mistake
      b. *?Mario, che abbiano scritto al quale,
           Mario that they wrote   to whom
           credo sia stato un errore, ...
           I think was a mistake

(127) a.   The elegant parties, to be admitted to one of which was a
           privilege, had usually been held at Delmonico's.
      b.   *They bought a car, that their son might drive which, was a
           surprise to them.

The similarity between the constructions in (1) and pied piping in fact
runs much deeper. Like the gaps in (1), the *wh*-NP within a pied-piped
clause cannot occur in subject position. Kayne (1983) offers the following
examples:

(128) a.   *John Smith, the possibility of who(m) marrying you became a
           reality only yesterday, . . .
      b.   *I suoi studenti, non essere i quali stati promossi, . . .
           his students   not having which been passed

Furthermore, like a locally governed gap in (1), a locally governed *wh*-NP
in a pied-piped constituent cannot occur embedded within a clause that
constitutes a left branch (in a right-branching language):

(129) a.   *Mario, prima che [vedere il quale] ci fosse impedito
           Mario before   seeing whom   was prohibited
           entrammo, . . .
           we entered
      b.   *Mario, che entrammo   prima che [vedere *e*]
           Mario who we entered before   seeing
           ci fosse impedito, . . .
           was prohibited

These similarities, and the others pointed out in note 43, thus make it
plausible that some common principle is involved in pied piping and in the
constructions in (1). I will suggest that this is simply the fact that pied
piping is necessarily involved in the constructions of (1).

Such cases as (128a–b) led Kayne (1983) to propose that pied piping is
constrained by the same notion of g-projection that figures in the CC. His
proposal essentially consists in the following two assumptions:[44]

(130) a.   The Comp of a relative clause can be filled by a
           complementizer or a *wh*-phrase (and by nothing else).
      b.   If B is a *wh*-phrase and Z is a g-projection of B, then Z is a
           wh-phrase.

This amounts to saying that only *wh*-phrases or g-projections of
wh-phrases can be found in Spec CP.

The hypothesis accounts for the ill-formedness of (128a–b) in the following way. The *wh*-phrase is ungoverned, so it has no g-projections (apart

from itself). Consequently, the constituent in Spec CP does not qualify as a *wh*-phrase, and (128a–b) violate (130a).

The hypothesis also predicts the ill-formedness of (129a), which thus lends support to Kayne's original insight. Since only a substring of the constituent in Spec CP (the subject clause) qualifies as a g-projection of *il quale* (hence, as a *wh*-phrase), (129a) also violates (130a).

If pied piping is to be characterized in terms of the CC notion of g-projection, then we have some evidence that the CC should be tightened along the lines suggested by Longobardi—namely, by imposing a proper government requirement on each g-projection of the governor of the gap. Only such tightening appears to be able to draw the appropriate distinction between the well-formedness of the (a) cases in (131)–(133) and the ill-formedness of the (b) cases:

(131) a.   Carlo, affezionati al quale non erano, . . .
           Carlo fond of whom   they were not
      b.   *La sconfitta, arrabbiati per la quale   non saranno, . . .
           the defeat   angry   because of which they will not be
           (Compare *Arrabbiati per la sconfitta, non saranno.*)

(132) a.   La Russia, l'attacco   alla quale fu un disastro, . . .
           Russia   the attack on which was a disaster
      b.   *L'inverno successivo, l'attacco alla Russia durante il quale
           the following winter   the attack on Russia during which
           fu un disastro, . . .
           was a disaster
           (Compare *L'attacco alla Russia durante l'inverno fu un disastro.*)

(133) a.   Gianni, per poter   dire   di aver superato
           Gianni in order to be able to say they had overtaken
           il quale truccarono la gara, . . .
           whom   they fixed the competition
      b.   *Gianni, dopo essere arrivati prima del quale si fermarono
           Gianni after arriving   before whom   they stopped
           tutta la notte, . . .
           the whole night

Under the classical notion of g-projection figuring in the CC and the pied-piping convention, the constituents in the Spec CP of both the (a) and (b) cases above qualify as g-projections of the governor of the *wh*-NP since each intermediate maximal projection is on a right branch (the adjuncts are also governed, though not properly governed). By contrast, under the stricter definition of g-projection proposed by Longobardi, only the constituents in Spec CP in the (a) examples qualify as g-projections of the *wh*-phrase (hence as *wh*-phrases). Those in the (b) examples do not, since the g-projections of the *wh*-phrases stop at the internal adjunct phrase or clause, which is not properly governed. As a result, these examples violate (130a).[45] I will thus tentatively conclude that the notion of g-projection used in the CC and pied piping must be revised accordingly.[46]

The constructions in (1), as well as pied piping, appear to be characterized by yet another condition: namely, a condition on tense. If pied piping reduces to the upward percolation of the [+wh] feature of a *wh*-NP, then we might express the observed tense effect as a condition on (upward) percolation:

(134) Tensed I weakly blocks the (upward) percolation of features.

However, this leaves open the question why tensed I has that effect on percolation.

As I will suggest, the tense effect found in the constructions of (1) can possibly be seen as a function of pied piping playing a role in their derivation. The tense condition expresses the apparently ineliminable difference between the constructions in (1) and pied piping on one hand and ordinary *Wh*-Movement on the other, which is not sensitive to that effect (and appears in fact to obey more stringent bounding conditions).[47]

The stricter formulation of g-projection plus the tense condition thus derive the essential properties of pied piping. Let us now consider how the interplay of pied piping and movement at LF may account for the observation that one, but not more than one, island can be violated in the constructions of (1). We will look first at the most striking case: apparent extraction from islands. I suggest that the pro unmoved in the syntax must move at LF (in effect treating it as some kind of abstract *wh*-phrase).[48]

In (125a–b), repeated here,

(125) a. ?I dolci   che è scappato [$_\alpha$ dopo aver rubato *e*] erano pochi.
            the sweets that he ran away   after stealing   were few
      b. *I dolci   che è scappato [$_{\alpha'}$ dopo esser stato sgridato
            the sweets that he ran away   after being scolded
            [$_\alpha$ per aver rubato *e*]] erano pochi.
            for stealing   were few

if pro, in the position of *e*, were to move by itself, replacing the abstract operator binding it, there would be no well-formed derivation. Both binding and government are blocked there by the intervening barrier α.

Consider now the other possibility: that movement affects not pro directly, but a phrase larger than pro under pied piping (much as the movement of a *wh*-phrase allows the option of moving not the *wh*-phrase itself but a larger phrase). If the "larger phrase" can only be a g-projection of the governor of pro (or the *wh*-phrase, respectively), in the spirit of Kayne's (1983) analysis of pied piping, then (125a–b) are correctly distinguished. In both cases the features of pro percolate upward to α, the highest g-projection of pro (via the pied-piping convention (130b)). Subsequent movement of α then gives a well-formed derivation in (125a), though not in (125b). In the latter case another barrier for binding and government intervenes, namely, α'. This two-step process thus appears able to circumvent exactly one (adjunct) island, but not two, as desired.

This analysis treats (125a–b) as the LF counterparts of the overt syntactic movement found in (135a–b):

(135) a.   I dolci,   [$_\alpha$ dopo aver rubato i quali] è scappato t,
the sweets   after stealing which   he ran away
erano pochi.
were few

 b. *I dolci,   [$_\alpha$ per aver rubato i quali] è scappato
the sweets   for stealing   which   he ran away
[$_{\alpha'}$ dopo esser stato sgridato t, erano pochi.
after being   scolded   were few

Perhaps the marginality of (125a), as opposed to the full grammaticality of (135a), can be interpreted as a consequence of a general principle attaching some cost to LF movement when a corresponding movement in "overt syntax" is possible, along lines possibly reminiscent of Chomsky's (1988) analysis.

Does movement of the larger phrase containing pro under pied piping create a binding or a government chain? Given the adjunct status of α, the framework developed in chapter 1 leads us to expect the creation of a government chain. This in turn predicts that movement of α in LF will be blocked not only if α is embedded in a strong island, as in (136), but also if it is embedded in a weak island, as in (137). To judge from the ill-formedness of (137a–c), the prediction appears to be borne out:

(136) a. *Mario, che abbiamo pianto [$_{PP}$ dopo esser partiti
Mario who we wept   after going away
[$_\alpha$ senza salutare e]], . . .
without greeting

b. *Mario, che [$_{CP}$ partire   [$_\alpha$ senza salutare e]]
   Mario who   going away   without greeting
   ci rovinerebbe, ...
   would ruin us

c. *Mario, che rimprovero sempre [$_{NP}$ quelli [$_{CP}$ che se ne vanno
   Mario who I always scold   those   who go away
   [$_\alpha$ senza salutare e]]], ...
   without greeting

(137) a. *Mario, che mi chiedo [$_{CP}$ da quanto tempo siano partiti
         Mario who I wonder   since when   they went away
         [$_\alpha$ senza salutare e]], ...
         without greeting

b. *Mario, che *non* me ne sono andato via che ieri
   Mario who I didn't go away   but yesterday
   [$_\alpha$ senza[49] salutare e], ...
   without greeting

c. *Mario, che mi sono reso conto [$_{CP}$ che sono partiti
   Mario, who I realized   that they went away
   [$_\alpha$ senza salutare e]], ...
   without greeting

A similar analysis extends to parasitic gaps (of the adjunct type). Consider an example of the relevant contrasts pointed out by Longobardi (1983, 1985a):

(138) I capi di bestiame che abbiamo eliminato t
      the head of cattle that we have eliminated
      [$_\alpha$ senza far soffrire e] ...
      without having to suffer

(139) *I capi di bestiame che abbiamo eliminato t
      the head of cattle that we have eliminated
      [$_{\alpha'}$ senza cercare di chiamare un veterinario
         without trying to call a vet
      [$_\alpha$ invece di abbattere e]] ...
         instead of slaughtering

Here too, if pro itself moves at LF from the position of e to the operator position, there is no well-formed derivation in either (138) or (139), owing to the presence of the barrier α. If the pied-piping option is chosen, however, there is a possible derivation for (138), though none for (139), as desired. The largest phrase obtainable via the pied-piping convention is α, in both (138) and (139) (it is the first nonselected XP dominating the governor of the gap, which blocks any further upward percolation of features). Now, movement of α will be unproblematic in (138), but it will be blocked by a barrier, α', in (139).

As with the case of apparent extraction from islands shown in (137), it is not surprising that an intervening weak island renders the parasitic gap constructions of the adjunct type impossible:

(140) a. *Il tuo libro, che mi chiedo   da quanto tempo
            your book   which I wonder since when
            abbiano ricevuto t [$_\alpha$ senza leggere e], . . . (OK: *legger*lo)
            they received   without reading
       b. *Il tuo libro, che non ho ricevuto t che ieri
            your book   which I haven't received but yesterday
            [$_\alpha$ senza dover pagare e], . . . (OK: *pagar*lo)
               without having to pay
       c. *Il tuo libro, che mi ha dato fastidio leggere t
            your book   which bothered me   to read
            [$_\alpha$ senza capire e], . . . (OK: *capir*lo)
               without understanding

This is because the weak island blocks the successive cyclic LF movement of the adverbial α.

Possible evidence confirming the LF movement of the adverbial α in (138) (and (139)) is provided by a significant correlation noted by Lonzi (1988). In her study of gerund types in Italian, Lonzi points out that only gerunds that can be *Wh*-Moved in "overt syntax" (for instance, manner gerunds) admit parasitic gaps:

(141) a.   E' [cullandolo]   che l'ho addormentato t.
            it is by rocking him that I managed to put him to sleep
       b.   Il bambino che ho addormentato t [cullando e]. . .
            the baby   that I put to sleep   by rocking

(142) a. *E' [trovandolo stanco]   che lo avevo addormentato t.
            it is having found him tired that I put him to sleep
       b. *Il bambino che ho addormentato t [trovando e stanco]. . .
            the baby   that I put to sleep   having found tired

The second property reduces to the first (itself plausibly a consequence of lack of head government for gerunds generated as IP adjuncts; see chapter 1).

In this analysis, the tense effect found in extraction from island constructions and parasitic gap constructions is attributed to the workings of the pied-piping (percolation) convention, whose application is needed to circumvent a bounding violation.[50]

Let us now consider the case of apparent CNP violations with parasitic gaps and extraction from island gaps (which are slightly more marginal than the adjunct cases so far considered). To begin with, they too seem to show a tense effect, as indicated by the contrast between the (a) and (b) forms of (143)–(144):

(143) a. ?Un libro che [quelli [interessati a leggere *e*]]
          one book that those interested in reading
          potranno trovare *t* presso la segreteria del dipartimento...
          will be able to get from the secretary of the department

      b. ???Un libro che [coloro [che desiderano leggere *e*]]
          one book that those who want to read
          potranno trovare *t* presso la segreteria del dipartimento...
          will be able to get from the secretary of the department

(144) a. ?E' un libro   che dubito esista [qualcuno
          it's that kind of book that I doubt there is someone
          [interessato a tradurre *e* in italiano]].
          interested in translating into Italian

      b. ???E' un libro   che dubito che esista [qualcuno
          it's that kind of book that I doubt that there is someone
          [che riesca a tradurre *e* bene]].
          who can translate   well

Before considering how the proposed approach can be extended to this case, let us look at how a pure *Wh*-Movement analysis fares.

One advantage of the *Wh*-Movement analysis is apparently the fact that it provides, together with the so-called Vacuous Movement Hypothesis (VMH; see George 1980, Chomsky 1986b), an account of the contrast between (143)–(144) and the following completely ungrammatical cases in which a nonsubject is relativized within the relative clause island:[51]

(145) *Carlo è un tipo che non è facile trovare [le persone [alle quali
       Carlo is a guy who it is not easy to find persons   to whom
       poter presentare *e*]].
       you can introduce

(146) *This is a paper that we need to find [someone [that we can
       intimidate with *e*]].

Essentially, as a more marked option, the VMH allows a *wh*-phrase that would otherwise move vacuously to Spec CP (a subject) to remain in situ even in a language where *Wh*-Movement applies in the syntax. This implies that when subjects are targets of *Wh*-Movement, and only then, an addition "escape hatch" will be available for other *wh*-phrases: Spec CP, not yet filled at S-Structure by the subject *wh*-phrase. See the contrast in (147) (=(112) of Chomsky 1986b):

(147) a.   This is a paper [that we need to find [someone [[who understands *e*]]]].

      b.   *This is a paper [that we need to find [someone [that [we can intimidate with *e*]]]].

In (147a), though not in (147b), the VMH allows the relative operator to move to Spec CP before reaching its final position. In (147b) Spec CP is already filled by the fronted object, whose movement—being non-vacuous—must take place before S-Structure. A similar situation is found with subject parasitic gaps such as (148a–b) (=(134a–b) of Chomsky (1986b):

(148) a.   He's a man [that [everyone [[who gives presents to *e*]] likes *t*]].

      b.   *This is a book [that [any man [to whom [we'll give *e*]] will like *t*]]

Once again, in (148a), though not in (148b), the operator binding the parasitic gap can move first to the unfilled Spec CP and then to its final position adjoined to the operator binding the real gap (for more careful discussion, see Chomsky 1986b, secs. 9 and 10).

The *Wh*-Movement analysis of these CNP cases raises some questions, however. First, it is silent about the contrast in grammaticality between "extraction" of NPs (marginally acceptable) and extraction of non-NPs (unacceptable). Consider the following contrasts, some of which were discussed in chapter 1:

(149) a.   ?Carlo, che si è discusso   del [l'utilità
          Carlo who people have discussed about the usefulness
          [di cointeressare *e* all'affare]], . . .
          of associating   in the business

      b.   *Carlo, a cui   si è discusso   del [l'utilità
          Carlo to whom people have talked about the usefulness
          [di rivolgerci *e*]], . . .
          of turning

(150) a.   ?L'unica persona che non troveremo   [nessuno
          the only person that we won't be able to find anyone
          [che sia disposto ad ospitare *e* questa notte]] . . .
          who is willing   to put up   for the night

    b. *L'unica persona su cui   abbiamo trovato [qualcuno
       the only person on whom we found   someone
       [che sia disposto a contare *e*]]...
       who is willing   to count

(151) a. ?Un professore, che [quelli [che fossero interessati
       a professor   who those who are interested
       a conoscere *e*]] potranno trovare *t* nel suo ufficio,...
       in meeting   will be able to find in his office
    b. *Un professore, a cui   [quelli [che fossero interessati
       a professor   to whom those who are interested
       a parlare *e*]] potranno rivolgersi *t*,...
       in speaking will be able to turn

Here, no appeal can be made to the more ample adjunction possibilities open to NPs as opposed to non-NPs. The only intervening nodes in these cases are IP, CP, and NP, none of which permit adjunction in Chomsky's (1986b) system.[52]

Second, if extraction of (referential) NPs can violate the CNP and Adjunct Conditions through the VMH and intermediate adjunction to the adjunct PP, respectively, one could expect movement out of an adjunct inside a CNP or out of a CNP inside an adjunct to be at least marginally possible. Apparently, though, no compounding of the two islands is possible:

(152) a. *E' un esame che   [quelli [che si presentano
       it's an exam which those who sit
       [senza aver preparato *e*]]] di solito passano *t* lo stesso.
       without preparing   usually pass   nonetheless
    b. *E' un esame che non conosco   [nessuno [che sia svenuto
       it's an exam which I don't know anybody who fainted
       [prima di sostenere *e*]]].
       before sitting

(153) a. *Un libro che abbiamo ordinato *t* [anche senza conoscere
       a book   that we ordered   even without knowing
       [una persona   [che fosse interessata a leggere *e*]]]...
       one single person who was interested in reading
    b. *Un libro che mi sono stupito [per aver conosciuto
       a book   that I was astonished for meeting
       [qualcuno [che era interessato a leggere *e*]]]...
       someone   who was interested in reading

The contrast between NPs and non-NPs under "extraction" out of CNPs, as well as the impossibility of compounding island violations, may on the other hand be accounted for within the pro analysis of extraction from island gaps once we consider how the approach so far discussed, based on pied piping and LF movement, can be extended in general to the CNP case. CNPs must apparently qualify as g-projections of a category inside the embedded clause for pied-piping purposes.

That they do is directly suggested by their ability to occur in Spec CP under pied piping (recall (130)):

(154) a. Carlo, [$_{NP}$ il pensiero [$_{CP}$ di invitare il quale]]
           Carlo   the idea   of inviting whom
           non ci ha neppure sfiorato, . . .
           did not even come to our minds
      b. Maria, [$_{NP}$[$_{CP}$ chiunque fosse sinceramente interessato
           Maria   whoever was truly interested
           alla quale]] non lo farebbe, . . .
           in whom   would not do it

The question now concerns the very formulation of "g-projection" that may achieve that result.

Earlier we saw evidence supporting Longobardi's proposal to tighten the notion of "g-projection" so as to impose a proper government require-ment (essentially: selection by a head) on all intermediate maximal projec-tions. If this proposal is implemented, however, only CNPs of the *N-complement type* qualify unproblematically as g-projections of some cate-gory inside the complement clause. CNPs of the relative clause type will not, since the relative CP is not selected by the head NP. Consequently, the g-projections of the governor of a pro within the relative clause should not extend beyond CP. We may achieve the correct result if, following Longobardi (1985c), we permit a g-projection to extend past a nonselected XP under predication. See (155), based on Kayne's (1983) definition (8):

(155) Definition: Y is a g-projection of *X* iff
      a. Y is a projection of X (in the usual sense of $\overline{X}$-theory) or of a
          g-projection of X
      b. Y immediately dominates W and Z, where Z is a maximal
          projection of a g-projection of X, and Z is selected in the canonical
          direction by W, *or is predicated of W*.

This definition allows the g-projection of the governor of *la quale* in, say, (154b) to reach the NP immediately dominating the relative CP and its head, thus accounting for the ability of this phrase to occur in Spec CP, under Kayne's convention (130). This also allows the g-projection of the governor of pro in (144a) and similar cases to reach the complex NP, so that its subsequent movement at LF, under the analysis suggested above, will not violate bounding theory.

This same analysis will also account for the impossibility of compounding two islands, as in (152b) and (153b). The g-projection of the governor of pro will stop at the first island barrier, so that movement of this phrase at LF will cross the other island barrier.

This approach still fails to account for the contrasts illustrated in (147) and (148), repeated here:

(147) a.   This is a paper [that we need to find [someone [[who understands
           e]]]].
      b.   *This is a paper [that we need to find [someone [that [we can
           intimidate with e]]]].

(148) a.   He's a man that [everyone [[who gives presents to e]]] likes t.
      b.   *This is a book that [any man [to whom [we'll give e]]] will like t.

In both the (a) and (b) cases the relative CP is predicated of the head NP. Consequently, the g-projection of e should reach the complex NP in both cases, thus missing the contrast.[53]

A possible principled way to derive the contrast, if real, is the following. Suppose that for the CP to be coindexed with the head NP under predication, the CP must be headed by the *wh*-phrase. This means that the head must shift from C to Spec CP : $[_{NP}$ NP$_i$ $[_{CP}$[wh$_i$] C]]] (see Taraldsen 1986). This move, however, has the consequence that IP is no longer selected by the *head* of CP. It is selected by C, but C is no longer the head of CP, and the new head, Spec CP, does not select IP.

If selection by a head is needed for a g-projection to extend past IP, the g-projections of the governor of pro in (147b) will stop at IP, which is not properly governed:

(147) b.   *This is a paper$_i$ that we need to find [someone$_k$ $[_{CP}O_k$ $[_C$ that]
           $[_{IP}$ we can intimidate t_k with pro$_i$]]].

How, then, is (147a) possible?

(147) a.   This is a paper$_i$ that we need to find [someone [who
           understands pro$_i$]].

An answer is available if we adopt the VMH, according to which the relevant S-Structure representation of (147a) is (156):

(156) $[_{NP}$ someone$_i$ $[_{CP_i}[_{Spec\,CP}$ $][_{C_i}$ $][_{IP}$ who$_i$ I$_i$ [understands pro]]]]

This structure allows the g-projections of pro to reach CP because IP is c-selected by C, the head of CP. How can they extend to NP under predication? We may take the Spec/Head agreement between *who* and *I* and Head/Head agreement between I and C (Chomsky 1986b) to allow the index of *who* to be on CP independently of movement and choice of Spec CP as head of CP.[54]

From this point of view, nonvacuous movement of a subject as in (157) (=(16c) of Chung and McCloskey 1983)

(157) *This is a paper that we really need to find [someone$_i$ [who$_i$ we all can agree [t_i [t_i understands]]]].

is indistinguishable from movement of a nonsubject, since the extension of the g-projections from CP to NP cannot arise here through Spec/Head and Head/Head agreement as in (147a).[55]

Although CNPs of the relative clause type can qualify as g-projections of some category within the relative clause, as shown by pied piping (see (154b))—and apparent extraction (see, for instance, (147a))—it appears that g-projections are not able to extend beyond the CNP even if this is selected by a head. If they could, cases like (158a–b) would be good instead of bad:

(158) a. *Mario, [$_{NP}$ qualcuno [$_{AgrP}$ disposto ad aiutare [$_{NP}$ quelli
          Mario   someone   willing to help   those
          [$_{AgrP}$ interessati a rovinare il quale]]]] non c'è, ...
          interested in ruining   whom   does not exist
      b. *Mario$_i$, che conosco [$_{NP}$ qualcuno [$_{AgrP}$ disposto ad aiutare
          Mario   who I know   someone   willing to help
          [$_{NP}$ quelli [$_{AgrP}$ interessati a rovinare e$_i$]]]], ...
          those   interested in ruining

There is, however, a difference between the well-formed (154b) and the ill-formed (158). In (154b) the upward extension of the g-projections is sanctioned in all "steps" but the last by selection by a head. The last (the step from CP to the CNP) is sanctioned instead by predication: [[$_{NP}$ NP [$_{CP}$ C [$_{IP}$ I [$_{VP}$ V X]]]]]. In (158), for the higher of the two CNPs to qualify as a g-projection of a category within the most deeply embedded clause, the extension of the g-projections past the first CNP should be able to reactivate the formation of g-projections via selection by a head. Suppose, however, that in the upward extension of projections, which can be sanctioned either via selection by a head or via predication, the mode that was abandoned in favor of the other cannot be reactivated. Then the appropriate distinction is drawn between the case of a single CNP and that of one or more CNPs, one inside the other.[56]

The corresponding parasitic gap cases fall in part under the same explanation. Consider (159):

(159) ??Mario$_i$, che ci presenterà t_i [$_{NP*}$[$_{CP}$ solo chi apprezza e_i

      Mario   who will introduce to us   only he who appreciates

      veramente]],...

      really

      'Mario, who only he who really appreciates will introduce to

      us,...'

Here, NP* qualifies as a g-projection of the governor of e_i. Subsequent movement of NP* at LF to the operator binding the real gap is licit, as is its overt *Wh*-Movement counterpart in (160):

(160) Mario, [$_{NP}$ solo chi apprezza il quale]$_k$

      Mario   only he who appreciates whom

      ci presenterà Gianni t_k,...

      will introduce Gianni to us

The subject subcase is problematic, however. Consider (161a–b):

(161) a. Mario$_i$, che [$_{NP*}$ chi apprezza e_i]

      Mario who   he who appreciates

      ci presenterà t_i sicuramente,...

      will surely introduce to us

b. He is a man that [$_{NP*}$ anyone who talks to e_i] usually likes t_i.

Here too, NP* qualifies as a g-projection of the governor of e_i, so that NP* can be the target of movement under pied piping. Here, however, movement of NP* at LF should produce an ill-formed result since the position from which it is moved is not properly head-governed.

I suggest that this is a special subcase calling for Kayne's original Connectedness insight. Just as we would say that *who* does not move at LF in (162),

(162) I'd like to know where who hid what.

      (Compare *I'd like to know where who hid it.)

the structure being saved by "connecting" *who* to the path from *what* to *where*, I would like to suggest that NP* (the pied-piping "enlargement"of pro) analogously does not move in (161). Rather, it "connects" to the path from t to the operator.

This ends our discussion of the selective island violations found with apparent extraction and parasitic gaps. Although many questions have been left open, the analysis developed here at least shows that island sensitivity within these constructions is no decisive argument that they do not involve pro.

3.3.5 Ā-Bound Pro and Strong Crossover

If the gap of the constructions in (1) is (Ā-bound) pro rather than variable, one might expect it to differ from ordinary *wh*-traces with respect to so-called strong crossover. Strong crossover effects are standardly interpreted as violations of Principle C of the binding theory, which affects R-expressions (requiring them to be (A-)free)[57] but not pronominals. Nothing prevents the latter from being A-bound (as long as they are free in their governing category).

The gap of the constructions in (1), however, must apparently be (A-)free too, thus behaving more like a variable than a pronominal. Consider (163)–(165):

(163) *Who$_i$ did they find t_i hostile before he$_i$ realized they wanted to help e_i?

(164) *Who$_i$ did he$_i$ say that they went away without greeting e_i?

(165) *They$_i$ are too stubborn for us to expect them$_i$ to allow us to invite e_i.

Nonetheless, there is one reason independent of "strong crossover" considerations that accounts for why the gaps in (1) cannot be locally A-bound. Pro needs to be identified. When not governed by personal Agr in pro-drop languages (or directly by their NP antecedent, as we will see in section 3.4), pros can be identified only via Ā-binding, thus becoming (pronominal) variables. If they are locally A-bound, they cannot qualify as (pronominal) variables, thus failing, in turn, to be identified. Though they have the appearance of strong crossover violations, (163)–(165) can thus be interpreted as cases of unidentified pros.

3.3.6 Ā-Bound Pro and Weak Crossover

Stowell and Lasnik (1987) note several contexts (which they term contexts of *weakest crossover*) in which weak crossover effects, although predicted to occur by current treatments, do not arise. Among these are parasitic gap and COD constructions, illustrated in (166) and (167) ((166) and (167a) are from Stowell and Lasnik 1987):

(166)   Who$_i$ did you gossip about t_i despite his$_i$ teacher having vouched for e_i?

(167) a. John$_i$ should be easy to persuade his$_i$ mother to vouch for e_i.
    b. John$_i$ is too stubborn for his$_i$ mother to vouch for e_i.
    c. John$_i$ is not honest enough for his$_i$ mother to vouch for e_i.

After arguing against an LF' approach of the type suggested by Chomsky (1982), Stowell and Lasnik propose to relate the insensitivity of these constructions to weak crossover to an independent semantic property: namely, they propose that the overt pronoun in such cases is Ā-bound by a null operator ranging over a *singleton* set, not by a genuine quantifier. So, for example, the value assigned to the gap in the parasitic domain in (166) is identical to the value assigned to the licensing trace, whereas the value assigned to the gap in the COD domain in (167) is identical to *John*. Stowell and Lasnik further suggest that traces bound by nonquantificational operators are not true variables but (null) names. As such, not surprisingly, they are immune to weak crossover effects. I do not find their argument for the null name status of the gaps in parasitic gap and COD constructions decisive.[58] The immunity to weak crossover effects is also a prerogative of resumptive pronominals. For example:

(168) The boy$_i$ who$_i$ we don't know whether his$_i$ parents died after sending him$_i$ to college...

So the same result would apparently follow if one considered the gap of parasitic gap and COD constructions as a null resumptive pronominal, as I suggest here. Recall that the ungrammaticality of (163)–(165) in which the EC is Ā-bound outside its governing category should not be taken to indicate that the EC cannot be a pronominal (variable) but must be either a variable or a (null) name. As argued in the previous section, such cases are still compatible with the idea that the EC is an empty resumptive pronominal that requires local A-binding for its identification (this is also acknowledged in Stowell and Lasnik 1987, fn. 11).

    In conclusion, I take the absence of weak crossover effects in parasitic gap and COD constructions to be compatible with—in fact, expected under—an analysis that interprets their ECs as pronominal in nature.[59]

3.3.7 The Common Properties of Ā-Bound Pros and *Wh*-Traces

Besides the properties that differentiate the gap of the constructions in (1) from ordinary *wh*-gaps and that follow as suggested from the different status of the gap, there are some properties that are typical of both types of gaps. In the present framework, such properties will have to follow from some feature that both pure variables and pronominal variables share. I suggest that this feature is simply that they are $\bar{\text{A}}$-bound ECs (regardless of whether the $\bar{\text{A}}$ relation is brought about by movement or not).

The three main properties that unite the gaps of (1) and ordinary *wh*-gaps are (A) their ability to license parasitic gaps, (B) their sensitivity to crossing effects, and (C) their incompatibility with the first object of the dative construction in English. Concerning (A), if what authorizes a parasitic gap is merely the presence of an operator in $\bar{\text{A}}$-position locally binding the EC at S-Structure (whether the operator was moved to Spec CP as in ordinary *wh*-constructions or base-generated there as in the constructions in (1)), then it is understandable why both types of gaps should license parasitic gaps. Concerning (B) and (C), what suffices is that the principle(s) responsible for crossing effects and for the restriction observable in the dative construction in English apply to $\bar{\text{A}}$-dependencies in general. (For analyses that imply this conclusion, see Pesetsky 1982, Kayne 1984, chap. 9, fn. 19 and passim, and Kayne 1985a.)[60] If this proves tenable, the extent to which $\bar{\text{A}}$-bound pros and *wh*-traces differ, and the extent to which they behave alike, follows entirely from their intrinsic makeup in interaction with independent modules of UG.

3.3.8   On the Alternation of Overt and Empty Pronominals

Nothing else interfering, the analysis so far developed would lead one to expect an overt (resumptive) pronominal to alternate freely with the empty (resumptive) pronominal hypothesized in the constructions of (1). This indeed appears to be the case, with two interesting exceptions. If these exceptions can be shown to be only apparent—in effect, due to independent interacting factors—then the alternation between gaps and overt pronominals in the constructions in (1) will be complete (thus supporting the claim that the gaps at issue are indeed (empty) pronominals).

Let us consider the three constructions in turn.

It appears that the alternation is indeed possible in all of the COD constructions but one: the *easy-to-please* construction. Compare (169) with (170)–(173):[61]

(169) a. Il problema non è facile da risolver (*lo) subito.
     b. The problem is not easy to solve (*it) immediately.

(170) a. Me lo hanno dato da recensir(lo) per domani.
     b. They gave it to me to review (?it) by tomorrow.

(171) a. Questo libro è troppo di parte per adottar *(lo) noi.
     b. This book is too biased for us to adopt (?it).

(172) a. Questo lavoro non è abbastanza remunerativo per accettar
       *(lo) subito.
     b. This job isn't remunerative enough to accept (?it) straightaway.

(173) a. Me lo hanno comprato per indossar *(lo) stasera alla festa.
     b. They bought it for me to wear (?it) tonight at the party.

Easy-to-please constructions differ from the other COD constructions in
yet another respect. Apparently, the complement of the former, though
not that of the latter, must be an "open sentence" containing a free variable
(to be later predicated of an antecedent in A-position). Thus, if a "closed
sentence" is utilized, the result is ungrammatical in (169), though not in
(170)–(173):[62]

(174) *The problem is easy (for us to get through the exam).

(175) They gave it to me (for us to get through the exam).

(176) The coach is to incompetent (for the team to win any games).

(177) This job isn't remunerative enough (for us to get through the
      week).

(178) They bought it (for me to get through the exam).

Particularly significant in this respect is the minimal contrast between (174)
and (179):

(179) The problem is easy *enough* for us to get through the exam.

   It is natural to regard these two differences between *easy-to-please* constructions and the remaining COD constructions as two consequences of
a more basic difference: namely, the fact that "adjectives of the *easy*-
category never assign a θ-role to their matrix subject when they have clausal
complements" (Chomsky 1981, 312), whereas the matrix subject of the
other COD constructions is a regular θ-position. This entails that any
argument in the subject position of the *easy-to-please* construction will
have to enter into a chain with a θ-position. Chomsky suggests that such
a θ-position is the (empty) complement object Ā-bound by an empty
operator in Spec CP at S-Structure. The A-chain formation between the
matrix subject and the complement object is rendered possible by a process
of reanalysis applying at S-Structure, which, among other things, turns the
variable into an anaphor (for more detailed discussion, see Chomsky 1981,
sec. 5.4). Since the requirement that the complement contain an empty NP
position that can enter into a chain with the matrix subject of the adjective
is satisfied neither in (169) nor in (174), a violation of the θ-Criterion
ensues.

No comparable requirement is put on the other COD constructions, since their subject position is a θ-position—hence the observed differences. As for (179), given that the infinitival clause is a complement not of *easy* but of the adjective qualifier *enough*, there is no need for it to contain an empty NP position (namely, to be an "open sentence" in the strict sense).

If this is correct, the optionality of phonetic realization for the pronominal in the COD constructions can be maintained in full generality, the apparent exception provided by the *easy-to-please* case being explainable on different grounds.

As for the gap of apparent extraction from islands, it seems that the alternation is uniformly possible, as expected:

(180) ?La sola persona che ce ne siamo andati via
      the only person that we went away
      senza neppure degnar(la) di uno sguardo   è Maria.
      without even deeming (her) worthy of a glance is Maria.

(181) ?Questo è un libro che di sicuro non c'è nessuno
      this is a book   that surely   there is nobody
      che sarebbe disposto a comprar (lo) a un prezzo simile.
      who would be willing to buy (it)   at such a price

Finally, with respect to parasitic gaps the alternation appears possible in the adjunct case, but very marginal (if at all possible) in the subject case. Compare (182) and (183):

(182)   ?Le carte   che Gianni ha messo *t* via dopo aver (le) esaminate
          the papers that Gianni put away   after examining (them)
          con cura...
          carefully

(183) a. ?Una persona$_i$ che chiunque conosca e_i
          a person   who whoever meets
          non può non apprezzare t_i è Gianna.
          cannot but appreciate   is Gianna

      b. *?Una persona$_i$ che chiunque la_i conosca non può non
          apprezzare t_i è Gianna.

      c. *?Una persona$_i$ che chiunque conosca e_i non può non
          apprezzarla_i è Gianna.

Once again, however, there appear to be independent reasons for the absence of the overt variant of the pronominal in the subject case. The (relative) unacceptability of (183b) can in fact be seen as a consequence of weak crossover.

If weak crossover reduces to Koopman and Sportiche's (1982) Bijection Principle, the contrast between (183a) and (183b) "might indicate that the Bijection Principle applies 'more strongly' ... to overt pronouns at LF than to gaps" (Chomsky 1982, 44).[63] In accounts of weak crossover that do not assume the Bijection Principle a comparable distinction is made between overt pronouns and gaps (see Kayne 1983, Safir 1984). Some indirect evidence that the unacceptability of (183b) is to be ascribed to weak crossover comes from the following observation. It has been noted that weak crossover is fully operative in questions and restrictive relatives but is suspended in appositives. Higginbotham (1980b), Safir (1984, 608), and Saito (1985, 148, fn. 34) find a contrast between restrictive and appositive relatives such as these:

(184) a. *?Who$_i$ does his$_i$ mother love t_i best?

      b. *?Do you remember that guy$_i$ who$_i$ his$_i$ mother loves t_i?

(185)   ?John$_i$, who$_i$ his$_i$ mother loves t_i, is unpopular.

For the analogous contrast between free relatives (*Whoever his mother admires...*) and appositives, see May 1985, 24.

The subject case of parasitic gaps presents a similar situation. If an appositive is substituted for the restrictive in (183b), the result is virtually acceptable. Compare (183b) with (186).

(186) ?Gianna$_i$, che chiunque la$_i$ conosca bene
      Gianna   who whoever knows her well
      non può non apprezzare e_i, ...
      cannot but appreciate

The more serious ill-formedness of (183c), on the other hand, can be attributed to a violation of Connectedness (also see Safir's (1984) Parallelism Constraint on Operator Binding).

It therefore seems reasonable to conclude that the phonetic realization of the pronominal in the constructions of (1) is entirely optional. Where the optionality appears to fail, independent and principled reasons turn out to be involved.[64]

3.4   UG and the Distribution of Pure and Pronominal Variables

If correct, the analysis presented thus far attains at most the level of descriptive adequacy, in Chomsky's (1965) sense. So far I have merely presented evidence that certain ECs partake in the nature of variables and pronominals simultaneously and that their properties may be accounted for if they are regarded as $\overline{A}$-bound pros. But I have said nothing concerning the structure of UG that renders this analysis *necessary*.

To put it differently (exploiting the usual ambiguity of the term *UG*), how do children come to know when they are confronted with an $\overline{A}$-bound pro rather than with a variable in certain constructions? If the ECs of the constructions in (1) are indeed $\overline{A}$-bound pros, what is it, in the structure of UG, that rules out analyzing them as pure variables (and conversely, in other contexts)?

The answer, I suggest, has two parts: (A) Both the ordinary movement strategy and the (empty) resumptive pro strategy are available in principle for every construction, with their respective properties. The latter (at least in the languages considered here) is the more marked strategy. (B) The ordinary movement strategy is excluded from the constructions of (1) by "conspiring" independent principles of UG. A direct consequence of (A) is that the empty resumptive strategy will always be possible as a more marked "second" option wherever the ordinary movement strategy is possible: an essentially correct result, at least for Italian. (See Cinque 1978b, Belletti 1979, Rizzi 1982, chap. 4, and Longobardi 1986, fn. 5, for some discussion about the two strategies in relatives and *wh*-interrogatives in Italian.) A direct consequence of (B) is that, wherever the movement strategy is unavailable for some reason, the empty resumptive strategy will be the only accessible option. That is, I claim, the situation in the constructions shown in (1).

If this conclusion should prove correct, the proposed account will also attain explanatory adequacy.

What remains to be seen is the very nature of the UG factors that rule out a movement derivation of the constructions in (1), leaving them with the resumptive strategy as the only option. Consider first the COD constructions, whose abstract configuration at S-Structure is given in (187):

(187) $[\ldots NP_i \ldots [_{CP}[\ldots O_i \ldots] C [_{IP} NP V \ldots e_i]]]$

The point is this: Could the category in Spec CP have originated in the position of the EC at D-Structure and have moved from there to Spec CP? e_i in (187) is an empty NP. So O_i will also have to be an NP in order to be able to bind e_i. If we assume that deletion in Spec CP can be dispensed with in these cases (perhaps everywhere), following Chomsky (1981, chap. 2, fn. 32 and references cited there), then O_i must have originated as an EC in IP at D-Structure. What type of NP EC is it?

First, O_i cannot be [−pronominal, −anaphor], for that would violate the θ-Criterion at D-Structure (see Chomsky 1982). The position is a θ-role position with no argument to bear it.[65]

Can O_i be [+pronominal, +anaphor] (=PRO)? Here, there is no violation of the θ-Criterion at D-Structure. Nonetheless, unlike Chomsky (1981, chap. 6), I suggest that it cannot. A generalization that appears to hold quite generally for categories in an Ā-position peripheral to IP, and entering into an Ā-chain with an EC in IP, is that they behave with respect to the binding theory as though they occupied the IP-internal position of the EC (see Guéron 1979, 1984, Belletti and Rizzi 1981, and Cinque 1982). For example, in such cases as (188)

(188) a. ... and [$_{VP}$ kill himself]$_i$ [$_{IP^1}$ John thinks [$_{IP^2}$ Bill did t_i]].

    b. SE STESSO$_i$, [$_{IP^1}$ crede   [che [$_{IP^2}$ Gianni rovinerà t_i]]].

    himself (focus)   he thinks that   Gianni will ruin

it is the post-Reconstruction position within IP that matters for binding theory purposes (the precise implementation of the Reconstruction process not being crucial here; for discussion, see the references just cited and Van Riemsdijk and Williams 1981, Chomsky 1981, Burzio 1986, chap. 3, Williams 1986, and Barss 1986, 1988. *Himself* or *se stesso* in (188) can only be bound to the subject of IP^2, exactly as in (189):

(189) a. [$_{IP^1}$ John thinks [$_{IP^2}$ Bill killed himself]].

    b. [$_{IP^1}$ Crede   [che [$_{IP^2}$ Gianni rovinerà se stesso]]].

    he thinks that   Gianni will ruin himself

Thus, in both cases the correct result follows from taking IP^2, the embedded IP, as the governing category of the anaphor *himself/se stesso*.[66]

If correct, this will have the very general consequence that PRO in Spec CP will never be possible. It cannot be base-generated there for thematic reasons at D-Structure (assuming it to be an argument). It cannot arrive there via movement either, as it will then be subject to the binding theory in its reconstructed position within IP, in which it is governed, thus leading to a contradiction of Principles A and B of that theory.[67]

Can O_i in (187) be [+pronominal, −anaphor] (=pro)? Here again, the θ-Criterion is not violated at D-Structure. However, the answer is once again negative, this time because of the identification requirements on pro. If the ϕ-features of pro must be identified, and if they can be so identified either via Agr (in the pro-drop languages) or via a local Ā-antecedent, in the manner suggested above, then pro in the Spec CP of (187) will not be identified at all. It is not identified by Agr, nor can it be identified by qualifying as a pronominal variable since it occupies an Ā-position at

S-Structure: a condition incompatible with the requirement on variables that they occupy an A-position (at that level).

The only remaining possibility is that O_i is [−pronominal, +anaphor]. But even this case is excluded, if categories in positions peripheral to IP at S-Structure count as being reconstructed into IP for purposes of the binding theory. In that case the anaphor has a governing category (the IP containing its trace) within which it must be bound. If it is not so bound, the sentence will plainly be ungrammatical. If it is bound—say, by the subject of IP, as in (190)—

(190) *They were invited [O_i [PRO$_i$ to play with t_i]].

the structure will still be excluded. Apparently, there is no such thing as an $\bar{A}$-bound anaphor:

(191) a. *The man$_i$ O_i that I thought that pictures of himself$_i$ were hanging on the wall...

       b. *The man$_i$ O_i that I think that PRO$_i$ to leave now would be a pity...

Thus, the operator in Spec CP will quantify vacuously.[68]

If these considerations are correct, there is no way for the O_i of (187) to be related to the S-internal EC via movement. The only option left by UG, then, is the (empty) resumptive pronominal strategy, in which the EC is a pro throughout, $\bar{A}$-bound by an empty [−pronominal, −anaphor] NP base-generated in Spec CP . The latter qualifies as an operator, I assume, by virtue of the position it occupies. The θ-Criterion is fully satisfied since the IP-internal EC receives a θ-role and is an argument throughout (pro), and the operator is a nonargument in a $\bar{\theta}$-position (Spec CP). No $\bar{A}$-chain is involved here, unlike the movement case, nor is any form of Reconstruction, which I assume to be dependent on $\bar{A}$-chains. Lexical *wh*-phrases base-generated in Spec CP need not receive a θ-role (or Case, for that matter) if they too are taken to be non-arguments in $\bar{A}$-position (see Chomsky 1981). Independent support for the claim that COD constructions in general do not involve *Wh*-Movement is apparently provided by the ill-formedness of such forms as (192) (see Chomsky 1977, 100):

(192) a. *John is $\begin{Bmatrix} \text{too poor} \\ \text{poor enough} \end{Bmatrix}$ to whom to give presents.

       b. *John bought it with which/what to play.

       c. *John is hard to whom to talk.

Under a *Wh*-Movement analysis of these constructions, it is not immediately clear why they should be ill formed. One might appeal to obligatory deletion of the *wh*-phrase (again see Chomsky 1977), but this leaves one question unresolved. It is generally the case that deletion of *wh*-phrases is obligatory only *up to recoverability* (Chomsky and Lasnik 1977). For example:[69]

(193) a. I found a man$_i$ $\left\{\begin{array}{l}*\text{who}_i\\O_i\end{array}\right\}$ to talk to t_i.

b. L'uomo$_i$ $\left\{\begin{array}{l}*\text{il quale}_i\\O_i\text{ che}\end{array}\right\}$ avete invitato t_i...
   the man   that/∅   you invited

c. It is [to John]$_i$ $\left\{\begin{array}{l}*\text{to whom}_i\\O_i\text{ that}\end{array}\right\}$ we want to talk t_i.

But deletion becomes nonobligatory (in fact, impossible) whenever the deleted element is unrecoverable. Alongside (193), we find (194), with no deletion of the *wh*-phrase:[70]

(194) a. I found a man$_i$ $\left\{\begin{array}{l}\text{to whom}_i\\*O_i\end{array}\right\}$ to talk t_i.

b. L'uomo$_i$ $\left\{\begin{array}{l}\text{al quale}_i\\*O_i\text{ che}\end{array}\right\}$ ho parlato...
   the man to whom/that I talked

c. It is John$_i$ $\left\{\begin{array}{l}\text{to whom}_i\\*O_i\text{ that}\end{array}\right\}$ we want to talk t_i.

If this is so, we would expect such forms as (192), where the deletion of the *wh*-phrase is unrecoverable, to be just as possible as the grammatical variants of (194). But they are not.

Their ill-formedness is perhaps to be attributed to a general requirement on *wh*-relative phrases (and their empty counterparts) that they be found, at S-Structure, in the Spec CP adjacent to their antecedent (abstracting from relative clause extraposition):

(195) *The boy I think whom you saw...

The ill-formedness of (192) thus constitutes an even more general reason for not attributing a *Wh*-Movement derivation to COD constructions.

   Next consider the case of parasitic gaps and extraction from island gaps. For partly distinct reasons, neither type of gap can be directly related to its Ā-antecedent as a result of movement. In the latter case this is prevented by bounding theory, and in the former by the fact that its (acquired) Ā-antecedent originates in a distinct position (I assume no "split" or "across-the-board" origin for the Ā-antecedent).[71]

However, the reasons just invoked do not rule out more "local" movements such as those shown in (195):

(195) a. ?The book (which$_i$) we filed t_i without [O_i reading t_i]...

b. ?The book (which$_i$) we went away without [O_i reading t_i]...[72]

But these possibilities are excluded here too if the conclusions reached above for the null operator of COD constructions are correct. The same kind of argument extends to the case at hand. The null operator of (195) cannot be in Spec CP as a result of movement, since any value for the [±pronominal, ±anaphor] features causes a violation at either D- or (reconstructed) S-Structure, in the manner discussed above with COD constructions. That is, O qualifies as none of the possible NP types.

Note that the analysis suggested here should not be taken to preclude *Wh*-Movement of an empty category in general. Such movement in fact appears to be attested in other constructions: in particular, I assume, in relative, topicalization, and cleft sentences such as those illustrated in (196)–(198), which contain a real variable rather than a pronominal variable, to judge from the properties reviewed in sections 3.2 and 3.3:

(196) a. L'orologio$_i$ [O_i che [hai regalato t_i a Gianni]]...
           the watch   that you gave   to Gianni

b. L'orologio di Gianni$_i$, [O_i che   [io ho rotto t_i]], ...
           Gianni's watch   which (lit. *that*) I broke

(197)   [[L'OROLOGIO$_i$] [O_i [ho rotto t_i]]].
           the watch (focus)   I broke

(198)   E' L' OROLOGIO$_i$ [O_i che [ho rotto t_i]].
           it's the watch   that I broke (cleft reading)

What intrinsic feature content does O_i have in (196)–(198)? It cannot be [−pronominal, −anaphor] for θ considerations at D-Structure. It cannot be [+pronominal, +anaphor] (=PRO) or [−pronominal, +anaphor] either, for reasons relating to the binding theory applying to the reconstructed S-Structure. Can it be [+pronominal, −anaphor] (=pro)? I suggest that, unlike the ECs in (1), it can.[73] This is because here, plausibly, though not in the constructions of (1) (see (187) and (195)), the ϕ-feature content of pro can be identified in Spec CP. Following Browning (1987), we can assume that the identification of pro occurs via agreement between the head NP, CP, and C (by percolation), and Spec CP (by Spec-Head agreement), in which case the pro identification operative in (194)–(196) may be considered identical to that of Agr in pro-drop languages, both operating under agreement with the antecedent of pro.

Notes

Chapter 1

1. After the classical work of Chomsky 1981, see among others Kayne 1981b, 1983, Huang 1982, Aoun 1985, 1986, Aoun et al. 1987, Lasnik and Saito 1984, Longobardi 1985b, 1987b, Koster 1984, 1987, Bennis and Hoekstra 1984–85, Bennis 1986, Stowell 1981, 1985, Koopman and Sportiche 1985, 1986b, Sportiche 1988, Chomsky 1986b, Manzini 1988, and Rizzi 1990.

2. The term *weak* (versus *strong*) *island* is somewhat misleading. It originated from the rather "weak" ill-formedness produced by complement extraction from *wh*-islands. It is, however, inappropriate on at least two counts: (1) because weak islands (except for *wh*-islands, to a certain degree) are not islands at all for the extraction of complements; and (2), because, when they act as islands (for adjunct extraction, and so forth), they give rise to *strong* ill-formedness.

A more appropriate term would be Ross's (1984) notion of *inner* island, a term that singles out a smaller ("inner") domain within the domain identified by the classical notion of "island" (Ross 1967), which is, in essence, a sequence of clauses each of which is the complement of the predicate of the next higher clause.

For convenience, however, I will continue to use the more familiar terms *weak* and *strong*.

3. I omit here the further chain of definitions for the terms in (9)–(13). See Chomsky 1986b.

4. Chomsky (1986b, 83) suggests the possibility that "proper government" satisfy a relation to a (lexical) head over and above antecedent government. In this view, the ECP would consist of two separate clauses, which, in the terms of Rizzi (1986, 1990), we may refer to as the *formal licensing* requirement (ia), and the *identification* requirement (ib):

(i) a. A nonpronominal EC must be properly head-governed.

b. A nonpronominal EC must be θ-governed or antecedent-governed.

"Properly head-governed means governed by a head that qualifies as a governor in the language (see section 1.8). Jaeggli (1982), Stowell (1985), Johnson (1985), Koopman and Sportiche (1986b), Aoun et al. (1987), Longobardi (1987b), Rizzi (1990), and Browning (1989b), among others, provide additional evidence in favor of such a "conjunctive" formulation of the ECP.

5. Chomsky (1986b) briefly discusses the possibility of reducing the θ-government requirement of the ECP to the antecedent government requirement. Given that VP adjunction is always possible, the trace of a verb complement will always be properly governed via antecedent government, independently of θ-marking. Thus, it seems that, at least for verb complements, θ-government could be eliminated from the definition of proper government (p. 79). Whether or not this reduction can actually be carried out (see below and chapter 2 for discussion), it in no way affects the classes of elements that can undergo long and successive cyclic Wh-Movement, which will still be elements in A- and Ā-positions, respectively.

6. Note that this problem is not resolved by the reduction of θ-government to antecedent government, since the reduction is only partial, limited as it is to verb complements (see Chomsky 1986b, 79).

Another problem for an ECP-based explanation of the dichotomy between long and successive cyclic Wh-Movement is discussed by Koopman and Sportiche (1986b), on the basis of certain data in Vata, where the different locality requirements on complement and adjunct extraction do not appear to be derivable from the ECP.

In Vata, extraction of non-PP adjuncts, subjects, and verbs cannot be "long" (for example, out of a wh-island) even if the ECP is satisfied (the trace of a non-PP adjunct is properly governed by a special adjunct morphology on the verb, and the trace of subjects and verbs escapes the ECP because it is overtly spelled out). Consequently, Koopman and Sportiche conclude, a different principle must be involved that distinguishes positions that can undergo long extraction from those that cannot. They suggest (i) as such a principle:

(i) *Condition on Long Extraction*
    X is a possible long extraction site iff X is a θ-position.

Objects and subcategorized PPs in Vata can thus be long-extracted (from a wh-island) since they are θ-positions. Adjuncts and verbs cannot. Koopman and Sportiche's conclusion appears to be compatible with both Rizzi's (1990) approach and the refinement to be suggested here.

7. This sentence is also impossible (or quite marginal) under the agentive reading of *pesare*, for reasons that will become clear later.

8. Measure phrases and idiom chunks cannot ordinarily be resumed by object clitics in discourse:

(i) a. Speaker A: Io peso 70 chili.
                    'I weigh 70 kilos.'
       Speaker B: *Anch'io li peso.
                    'Even I weigh them.'
    b. Speaker A: Farà giustizia.
                    'He will do justice.'
       Speaker B: *Anch'io la farò.
                    'I will do it too.'

But this has to do with the clash between their nonreferential status and the referential status of object clitics. Where these are used nonreferentially (as in clitic left dislocation, in which they are simple placeholders of object positions; see chapter 2), they are perfectly compatible with measure phrases:

(ii) a. 70 chili, non *li* pesa.
    '70 kilos, he does not weigh *them*.'
  b. Giustizia, non *la* farà mai.
    'Justice, he will never do *it*.'

9. In addition (or as an alternative) to the barrierhood of the interrogative CP under the *Barriers* system, a potential Ā-antecedent—the *wh*-phrase in the embedded Spec CP—intervenes, causing a violation of Relativized Minimality, in Rizzi's (1990) terms. See also the discussion below.

10. As Giuseppe Longobardi (personal communication) points out, if all decreasing monotes must move to Spec CP at LF, such cases as (22) are excluded even if negation, in its base position, does not count as a potential Ā-antecedent.

11. For different views and further pertinent references, see Reinhart 1983, Hornstein and Weinberg 1988, May 1988, and Stowell 1989.

12. Indefinites are known to allow both referential and nonreferential readings (see Fodor and Sag 1982). For example, in (ia) the indefinite is used referentially, since it can be linked to the pronoun even if it does not c-command it. By contrast, (ib) has a reading in which the indefinite is used quantificationally ("nonreferentially," in the relevant sense) since it is under the scope of another quantifier:

(i) a. Carlo, se si innamora   di una/qualche ragazza,
    Carlo if he falls in love with a/some girl
    non la lascia in pace.
    does not leave her alone
  b. Ognuno di loro ha parlato male   di una/qualche ragazza.
    each of them   spoke disrespectfully of a/some girl

As we should expect, indefinites are not extractable from a *wh*-island and display clear weak crossover effects only when they are used nonreferentially (for instance, when they are under the scope of another quantifier). See (ii), which is compatible only with the wide scope (referential) reading of *una/qualche ragazza*, and (iiia–b):

(ii) Di una/qualche ragazza non capisco   perché ognuno di loro
    of a/some girl   I do not understand why each of them
    abbia parlato male.   ·
    spoke disrespectfully

(iii) a. Se anche i *suoi* migliori amici tradiscono *un/qualche ragazzo*,
        if even *his* best friends   betray *a/some boy*
        questi può rimanerne irrimediabilmente scioccato.
        he may be irremediably shocked
    b. *Di solito il *suo* autore vorrebbe presentare *un/qualche libro*
        normally *his* author   would like to submit *a/some book*
        ad ogni editore.
        to every publisher
        (under the interpretation in which the indefinite is under the scope of the universal quantifier)

I thank Giuseppe Longobardi for bringing the problem of indefinites to my attention.

13. In Italian, when a negative element appears to the right of I, it is doubled by a sentential negation, which disappears when the element is to the left of I. For example:

(i) a. Credo che *(non) abbia visitato *nessun* museo.
       I think that he has (not) visited no museum
    b. *NESSUN MUSEO*, credo che (*non) abbia visitato.
       no museum   I think that he has (not) visited

For different accounts of this asymmetry, see Rizzi 1982, chap. 4, Longobardi 1987a, and Zanuttini 1988, forthcoming.

14. As expected, this sentence has only one interpretation, the collective one, in which *tutti i musei* does not interact with the negation ($\forall x, x \ldots$ he has not visited x). The (noncollective) quantifier interpretation (Neg $\forall x \ldots$) available when *tutti i musei* is not fronted across a negation (*Non ha visitato tutti i musei*) is here filtered out by the weak island.

15. Recall that the construction is a non-*Wh*-Movement construction, or, more accurately, one not employing (movement of) an empty operator. It is thus interesting to observe that the only elements that can be clitic left dislocated are those that can enter a *binding* relation. In other words, no element that can only be moved via successive cyclic movement in *wh*-constructions can be clitic left dislocated (see section 1.4.6 and chapter 2 on this point). The construction is thus a "pure representation" of *binding* relations (also obtainable via long *Wh*-Movement).

16. Longobardi (1987b) notes the ungrammaticality of (i),

(i) *Qualcosa, ho mangiato di guasto.
     something I ate spoilt

taking it to follow from the fact that extraction of subparts of arguments must respect a successive cyclic derivation. The preceding discussion suggests that even under an analysis in which *qualcosa* and *di guasto* are reanalyzed as two independent constituents, *qualcosa* must still connect to the appropriate EC via a chain of antecedent government links, because of its strict nonreferential interpretation (contributed by the presence of *di AP*). See Cinque 1989.

17. As noted, D-linking is only one way in which a phrase can become referential. Reference to specific members in the mind of the speaker is another (recall the earlier discussion on left-dislocated bare quantifiers).

18. I thank Anthony Kroch for constructing these sentences for me.

19. See, among others, Rizzi 1982, chap. 2 for Italian, Maling 1978 for Scandinavian, and Rudin 1986 for Bulgarian.

20. See Chomsky and Lasnik 1977, 447. Less clear is how to handle such cases as (i), pointed out to me by John Frampton:

(i) I know of nobody that I really know how to talk to.

If they are better than the corresponding topicalization cases (see (ii)), then they might indeed confirm the suggestion put forth above that relative, as opposed to topicalization and interrogative operators, are referential (even if their antecedent is not):

(ii) Nobody, I really know how to talk to.

21. To render the definition of barrier more perspicuous, I have directly built into (59) the notion of "blocking category" that figures in Chomsky's (1986b, 14) definition of barrier (his (26)). *L-marking* means "direct θ-marking by a lexical head." See below for discussion.

22. As for VP, which is not the complement of a lexical category, its barrierhood is voided in Chomsky 1986b via adjunction to it—an option unavailable to maximal projections that are arguments of some head (in particular, CP, IP, and NP). See section 1.7.3 below, for discussion.

23. "α m-commands β iff α does not dominate β and every γ (γ a maximal projection) that dominates α dominates β" (see (13) of Chomsky 1986b and corresponding text).

"α excludes β if no segment of α dominates β" ($= (17)$ of Chomsky 1986b).

24. Chomsky (1986b) discusses two variants of the Minimality Condition: a narrower formulation, given here in (62), and a broader formulation, obtained from (62) by replacing *immediate projection* with *projection*. Beginning on page 44, Chomsky discusses some evidence pointing to the correctness of the narrower formulation (62).

25. Rizzi (1990) also notes that Chomsky's (1986b) absolute notion of minimality has certain undesirable consequences. The barrierhood of $\bar{V}$ ($\bar{A}$), $\bar{I}$, and $\bar{C}$ (which must not count as barriers for simple adjunct extraction) is voided in Chomsky 1986b in three distinct and unrelated ways, by stipulating that $\bar{V}$ (and $\bar{A}$) can be missing when no Spec is present, that $\bar{I}$ is defective, and that a lexical C may delete at LF.

26. Note that $\bar{C}$ presumably does not count as a minimality barrier, in any event, if e_i is featureless. See Chomsky 1986b, 47.

27. Later I discuss (and reject) the possibility that segments of adjoined categories (VPs) count as (weak) barriers. See note 32.

28. Citing the following VP-Preposing case as evidence,

(i) John wanted to fix the fender with a crowbar, and fix it that way, he did.

Chomsky (1986b, 20) also admits the possibility that adverbials can be adjoined to VP.

29. See Guéron 1980, Taraldsen 1981, Baltin 1982, and Koster and May 1982. Note that, unlike relative clause extraposition from a subject, which might be a PF phenomenon (Chomsky 1986b, 40ff.), relative clause extraposition from an object appears to apply in the syntax, since it moves with VP under VP-Preposing (unless VP-Preposing itself takes place at PF Chomsky 1988 fn. 42). See (i), from Cardinaletti 1987:

(i) $[_{VP}[_{VP}$ Presentato $[_{NP}$ qualcuno $t]$ a Gianni] $[_{CP}$ che volesse parlare
        introduced   someone   to Gianni   who wanted to talk
    con sua figlia]],   non aveva ancora.
    with his daughter he hadn't yet

whether relative clause extraposition involves movement or simply a predication structure is still an open question. For relevant discussion and for arguments that it should be treated separately from PP and sentential complement extraposition from NP, see Johnson 1985, sec. 3.3.3.

30. Note that one could not prevent adjunction of *to whom* or *con chi* to VP in (74b) and (76b) by stipulating that no further adjunction is possible to an adjunction structure, since this condition would exclude many well-formed cases such as (ia) and (ib):

(i) a. How$_i$ did [$_{IP}$ they [$_{VP}$ t_i [$_{VP}$[$_{VP}$ behave t_i] [$_{PP}$ after speaking to him]]]]?
   b. In che modo$_i$ [$_{VP}$ t_i [$_{VP}$[$_{VP}$ presenteresti qualcuno   a Gianni t_i]
      how   would you introduce someone to Gianni
      [$_{CP}$ che volesse parlare con sua figlia]]]?
      who wanted to talk with his daughter

31. On the basis of the well-formedness of such cases as *Which meeting were they too angry* [$_{CP}$ *to hold*]? (on the nonarbitrary control reading), Chomsky in fact concludes that Subjacency violations are triggered only by the crossing of two barriers, because these cases are fine even if they contain one barrier, CP. But, as already mentioned, such examples are not really representative, since they contain an NP gap. Only (77a–b) involve extraction of a non-NP, and they point, as observed, to the opposite conclusion. Note that nothing prevents adjunction to AP in (77a–b) (Chomsky 1986b, 34, 79).

32. To be sure that it fails, we must briefly consider another possibility suggested in the literature. We have noted that, in complement extraction from VP-adjoined adjuncts and extraposed relative and degree clauses, only one (inherent) barrier is crossed, since the extracted complement can then adjoin to VP and AP, respectively, thus preventing IP from inheriting barrierhood. However, if segments of categories also could inherit barrierhood (as proposed in Belletti and Rizzi 1988), then even the three cases just mentioned would involve the crossing of two barriers (and could thus be reconciled with the *Barriers* theory of bounding). See (ia–b), which represent the derivations in question, with details omitted:

(i) a. ...[$_{VP}$ t [$_{VP*}$[$_{VP}$ V ...][$_{CP*}$ ... V t]]]
   b. ...[$_{AP}$ t [$_{AP*}$ too A [$_{CP*}$ ... V t]]]

The starred CPs represent the inherent barriers, and the starred VP and AP the "segments" allegedly inheriting barrierhood. This proposal, however, would lead us to expect a comparable Subjacency violation in (ii), which exemplifies extraction of a complement from a weak island, a non-L-marked extraposed CP adjoined to VP (a structure of the type (ia)):

(ii) Gianni, col quale non ti danneggerebbe di certo [$_{CP}$ parlare
     Gianni with whom it wouldn't certainly harm you to talk
     dei tuoi problemi t], ...
     about your problems

But in fact such extraction is possible, in sharp contrast with complement extraction from the three constructions at issue here, which give rise to total ungrammaticality. See (73), (76b), and (77a–b). We thus have reason to think that segments of categories cannot inherit barrierhood, and that the strong islandhood of

VP-adjoined adjuncts and extraposed relative and degree clauses is caused by the presence of a single barrier.

33. This is true of the adjunct island, of the complex NP island, of the CP island of degree and comparative clauses, and of other strong islands that will be discussed below.

34. The argument is based on such contrasts as these:

(i) a. *Who$_i$ did you say t_k to t_i [that Bill was here]$_k$?
    b. Who did you yell to that Bill was here?

(ia) is arguably excluded by the principle that rules out the crossing of Ā-dependencies (here Wh-Movement and extraposition). The well-formedness of (ib) suggests, then that no such crossing is involved there, which in turn implies that the clause is generated higher than the prepositional dative.

35. The distribution of the infinitival complementizer di in Italian, which I claimed is a diagnostic of internal argumenthood for a CP, provides confirming evidence that the sentential subject of psych-verbs is generated, at D-Structure, as an internal argument. The verbs of this class do (optionally) select di as the head of their infinitival complement (even if the option of omitting it is perhaps preferred with most of them). For example:

(i) a. Non ti preoccupava per nulla (di) non poterla più vedere?
       didn't it worry you at all   not to be able to see her any longer
    b. Lo spaventava, più di ogni altra cosa,
       it frightened him more than anything else
       (di) non poter più uscire.
       not to be able to go out any more
    c. Mi angustiava soprattutto   (di) dovermi presentare alle 7 di mattina.
       it used to anguish me above all to have to turn up at 7 a.m.

The factor that prevents the infinitivals CP from remaining in situ between the verb and the accusative experiencer, as in (ii), is the same factor that prevents the theme NP from remaining in that position, as in (iii): presumably, the adjacency requirement on accusative Case assignment to the experiencer (see Belletti and Rizzi 1988):

(ii) *Angustia   [$_{CP}$ (di) dover prima o poi morire] un po' tutti.
     it anguishes   to have to die sooner or later   everybody

(iii) *Angustia   [$_{NP}$ un fatto] tutti noi.
      it anguished   a fact   all of us

36. (80) is essentially the proposal originally made in Cinque 1978a, where "successive cyclic" Wh-Movement and "apparent extraction of NP" were not considered, however. I leave open the question whether there is a single notion of canonical government for the language, or whether it should be relativized for each head.

37. The intermediate status of such cases as (81) has been noted by (among others) Longobardi (1987b), who analyzes them as involving successive cyclic movement of the wh-phrase through the specifiers of the lower and intermediate CPs.

Here, I take them to involve binding (long Wh-Movement), since (ia–b), where the specifier of the intermediate CP is occupied by another wh-phrase, seem to me to have a status comparable to (81), and to contrast sharply with cases of adjunct extraction, which can instead only move successive cyclically (see (iia–b)):

(i) a. ??La persona a cui$_i$ mi chiedo perché [$_{IP}$[$_{CP}$ parlare t_i oggi]
the person to whom I wonder why   to speak today
dovrebbe essere così difficile]...
should be so difficult

b. ??La persona a cui$_i$ non so   se   [$_{IP}$[$_{CP}$ riuscire
the person to whom I don't know whether   to be able
a parlare t_i oggi] sarà davvero possibile]...
to talk today   will be really possible

(ii) a. *Il modo in cui$_i$ credo che [$_{IP}$[$_{CP}$ comportarsi t_i con loro]
one way in which I think that   to behave with them
sarebbe imprudente]...
would be risky

b. *Una ragione per la quale$_i$ credo che [$_{IP}$[$_{CP}$ licenziarlo t_i oggi]
one reason for which   I think that   to fire him today
sarebbe imprudente]...
would be risky

The deviance of the cases with a *wh*-phrase in the intermediate Spec CP cited by Longobardi must, then, be due to interfering factors. I also find such cases as (iiia–c) with extraction from weak islands other than *wh*-islands to have the same status as (81)—an unexpected result, if successive cyclic movement were involved:

(iii) a. ??Gianni, a cui$_i$ *mi rammarico* che [$_{IP}$[$_{CP}$ parlare t_i oggi]
Gianni to whom *I regret*   that   to speak today
non sarà possibile], ...
will not be possible

b. ??Gianni, a cui$_i$ *non* penso   che [$_{IP}$[$_{CP}$ parlare t_i oggi]
Gianni to whom I do *not* think that   to speak today
sarà difficile], ...
will be difficult

c. ??Gianni, a cui$_i$ *ci preoccupa* che
Gianni to whom *it worries us* that
[$_{IP}$[$_{CP}$ parlare di queste cose t_i]] sia diventato così difficile, ...
to speak about such things has become so difficult

A successive cyclic analysis of (81) also raises a technical question: What is the head governor of the trace in the lower CP? The only candidate is the head of the intermediate CP, the complementizer *che*, which, however, must not count as a proper head governor in other contexts (**Non pretendo che nessuno venga* 'I don't pretend that anybody comes', where *nessuno* takes wide scope; for discussion, see Rizzi 1982, chap. 4, and 1990, chap. 2).

Indeed, I find such cases as (iv), with a non-θ-marked preposed adverbial, reported by Longobardi (1987b, fn. 21), definitely worse than (81):

(iv) *Gianni, al quale$_i$ penso   che [[$_{CP}$ parlando t_i oggi]
Gianni to whom I think that   speaking today
non otterremo nulla], ...
we will obtain nothing

38. Another case showing the relevance of the canonical direction requirement on the notion of barrier for binding is arguably extraction from Verb-second complements in German. Extraction of an object from a Verb-second complement such as (i) (with the structure indicated)

(i) Du glaubst [$_{CP}$ er [$_{\bar{C}}$ hat [$_{IP}$ ihn gesehen]]].
    you think   he has   him seen
    'You think he saw him.'

is well formed only if the clause becomes Verb-first, that is, if the Spec CP is empty. Compare (iia) and (iib):

(ii) a. Wen glaubst du   [$_{CP}$ [$_{\bar{C}}$ hat [$_{IP}$ er e gesehen]]]?
        whom do you think   has   he   seen
        'Whom do you think he saw?'
     b. *Wen glaubst du [$_{CP}$ er [$_{\bar{C}}$ hat [$_{IP}$ e gesehen]]]?

This curious restriction, and apparent violation of the Verb-second requirement, is immediately accounted for if one assumes that the Spec CP must contain the intermediate trace of *wen* (see Tappe 1981, Haider 1986), which in turn implies that the extraction must have necessarily applied in a strict successive cyclic fashion.

But why should the successive cyclic option be available here, but not the long extraction option? The answer appears to reside in the fact that the complement from which extraction takes place is on the noncanonical side with respect to the verb (as originally suggested by Richard Kayne in class lectures at the University of Venice, 1983).

Note that, if CP is not a barrier (as a matter of fact, the trace in its Spec must be head-governed from outside), and IP is not a barrier intrinsically (see below), then it would seem that the successive cyclic movement out of CP could skip Spec CP, contrary to fact. Having abandoned the notion of barrier by inheritance, we cannot take the CP in this case to inherit barrierhood from IP.

The necessary passage through Spec CP can be forced independently, however, if we assume, unlike Chomsky (1986b), that specifiers are always structurally present and that they qualify (whether overt or empty) as potential Ā-antecedents for Relativized Minimality. Hence, they cannot be skipped.

39. In discussing extraction from complex NPs of the N-complement type, Chomsky (1986b, sec. 7) notes the "intermediate status" of many such sentences. It should be noted that, in all the examples discussed there, the phrases extracted are NPs, which, in our terms, have access to another strategy as well (see chapter 3). Indeed, if non-NP extraction is considered, the result is clearly ungrammatical. In Chomsky's (1986b) framework of assumptions, this observation could be incorporated into the definition of blocking category by requiring L-marking by a [+V, −N]^0 (γ is a blocking category for β iff γ is not L-marked by a [+V, −N]^0 and γ dominates β").

40. The possibility of further extracting the constituent from a *wh*-island confirms that long extraction is involved:

(i) Gianni, al quale$_i$ non so   chi avesse l'impressione
    Gianni to whom I don't know who had the impression
    di aver già parlato t_i, .../che non volessimo parlare t_i, ...
    of having already spoken/that we did not want to speak

41. Ross attributed the original observation to George Lakoff. Also see Stowell 1981 and Aoun et al. 1987.

42. A comparable situation is found in Italian, modulo the more limited possibility of "complementizer deletion," which requires, among other things, that the V be in the subjunctive (see Rizzi 1982, chap. 3, Wanner 1981, Cinque 1981, fn. 12, and Scorretti, forthcoming:

(i) a. Credo   (che) sia già stato spedito.
         I believe (that) it was (subj.) already sent
     b. Là possibilità * (che) sia già stato spedito...
         the possibility   (that) it was (subj.) already sent

(ii) a. Ho l'impressione   (che) sia già stato spedito.
         I have the impression (that) it was (subj.) already sent
     b. L'impressione * (che) sia già stato spedito,   non l'ho.
         the impression   (that) it was (subj.) already sent I don't have

43. That reanalysis is optional may be indicated by the possibility of passivizing the nominal followed by its complement. See (i), from Ross 1967, 147:

(i) The claim that plutonium would not float was made by the freshman.

44. English displays a similar situation, if we abstract from gerundive CPs, as originally pointed out by Brame (1980) and Hantson (1980). (See also Stowell 1981, 391 and chap. 7.) The same is true of Dutch (Hoekstra 1984). Note that the verbs in (94)–(96) are all compatible with a propositional complement, either bare, as in (i), or "nominalized," as in (ii):

(i) Contavo che venisse.
     I counted that he came

(ii) L'ho detto dedotto dall'esser stato Giorgio più riservato   del solito.
     I deduced it   from Giorgio's having been more reserved than usual

45. This is apparently not true for nonsubcategorized Ps. For example:

(i) a. E' rimasto a casa *per* [gli amici].
         he stayed home   for his friends
     b. E' rimasto a casa *per* [ché voleva vedere   i suoi amici].
         he stayed home   because he wanted to see his friends
     c. E' rimasto a casa *per* [vedere   i suoi amici].
         he stayed home   in order to see his friends

(ii) a. E' venuto a trovarci *dopo* [il nostro invito].
         he came   to see us after our invitation
     b. E' venuto a trovarci *dopo* [che lo abbiamo invitato].
         he came   to see us after that we invited him
     c. E' venuto a trovarci *dopo* [essere stato invitato].
         he came   to see us after having been invited

46. This possibility is lexically restricted. Certain Vs/As do not admit it:

(i) a. La sua fortuna si può attribuire/è imputabile a questo/*a che
         her luck   can be attributed to this/to that
         ha sposato un uomo ricco/*ad aver sposato un uomo ricco.
         she married a rich man/to having married a rich man

47. The acceptable variant being *Sono contento che tu parta* (without *di*).

48. The only genuine exception being, now, the preposition *a* (subcategorized by certain predicates; recall note 46), at its peculiar stylistic level. At this level, *a* will subcategorize for a CP complement that can be both tensed and infinitival (in accord with the null hypothesis). The stylistic contrast between (97b) and (97c) can now be seen to follow from the fact that the *a* of (97c), but not that of (97b), can also be taken as an instantiation of the stylistically unmarked use of *a* as an infinitival complementizer. The fact that the choice of the complementizer matches the subcategorization requirements of the matrix V/A could possibly follow from the fact that C can be accessible to subcategorization requirements, as shown by Groos and Van Riemsdijk (1981) and by Hirschbühler and Rivero (1983). Reuland (1983, sec. 3.5) proposes that (ia) has the structure (ib):

(i) a. I am counting on him marrying Mary.

b. ...counting $[_{CP}[_C$ on$][_{IP}$ him...

In this light, the structure of (iia) could well be (iib) (see Brame 1980, Hantson 1980),

(ii) a. I hoped for you to go.

b. I hoped $[_{CP}[_C$ for$][_{IP}$ you to go$]]$

without losing Chomsky and Lasnik's (1977) insight that it should be related to *hope*'s property of subcategorizing for *for* complements.

49. I assume that the comparable French facts are amenable to a similar treatment.

50. Manzini (1980) judges extraction from *a che*... contexts to be ungrammatical. Longobardi (1983, fn. 37) reports the example of extraction in (i) to be marginally acceptable,

(i) L'occasione nella quale ho provveduto a che tu possa incontrare Maria
the occasion in which   I took care   that you could meet Maria
è delle più favorevoli.
is among the most favorable

but speakers I have consulted tend to regard it as impossible.

51. Further support, based on Aux-to-Comp phenomena and interpolation of adverbials, for the idea that the *a* and the *di* of (90) are, despite appearances, complementizers rather than heads of PPs is discussed in Cinque 1990c.

52. One piece of evidence is provided by such contrasts as the following (originally noted in Kayne 1981a):

(i) a. The only one who$_i$ we'd favor t_i studying linguistics is John.

b. *John is the one who$_i$ I'm counting on t_i marrying her.

They can be explained (in updated form) if the relevant structure is (iia–b), respectively,

(ii) a. ... favor $[_{CP} t_i [_C$ Agr$] [t_i$...

b. ... counting $[_{CP} t_i [_C$ on$] [t_i$...

with the latter violating the head government requirement much as (iii) does:

(iii) Who$_i$ would you prefer $[_{CP} t_i [_C$ for$] [_{IP} t_i$ to win$]]$?

See Rizzi 1990, chap. 2 and section 1.8 below for discussion.

53. Binding is, of course, possible across these indirect CP complements, since the CP is θ-marked by a [+V] category in the canonical direction. For example:

(i) a. Gianni, al quale$_i$ vi informo   che non potrete rivolgervi t_i, ...
       Gianni (to) whom I inform you that you cannot address

   b. Maria, con la quale$_i$ l'ho convinto   che non avrei parlato t_i, ...
       Maria with whom I convinced him that I wouldn't have talked

See also the well-formedness of (102a–c) under Reuland's (1983) analysis of their complements as indirect CP complements.

If an indirect CP complement is indeed a barrier for government, then Kayne's (1984) example (ii)

(ii) John, who I assure you [$_{CP}$ t [$_{IP}$ to be a nice fellow]], ...

must be a double object construction, with *you* and the CP forming a small clause, along the lines suggested by Kayne (1985a). This is because CP does not act there as a barrier for government. Possibly in support of this conjecture is the fact that in the corresponding Italian case the first object is an overt dative:

(iii) ?Gianni, che gli(dat.)/*lo(acc.) assicurai essere una gran brava persona, ...
       Gianni who I assured to him   to be a nice fellow

54. Things are no different if the I projection must be split into two separate projections of Tense (T) and Agr (Pollock 1989, Moro 1988, Chomsky 1988). In this case C may be taken to c-select AgrP, Agr TP, T VP (see Belletti 1988).

55. Note that this definition of barrier for government is both more and less restrictive than Chomsky's (1986b) definition. It is more restrictive in that it allows only heads nondistinct from [+V] to lift the barrierhood of their (direct) complement. (Reference to [+V] heads seems in fact pervasive. See the definitions of barrier for binding and of head government below.) It is less restrictive in that the notion of lexicality plays no role. C and I, which are not lexical, also lift the barrierhood of the (direct) complements IP and VP.

56. This also implies that the definition of proper head government (ECP), discussed in section 1.8, cannot be directional.

Given Giusti's (1989) arguments that *scheinen* 'seem' constructions in German involve raising, the impossibility of extraposing the infinitival complement of these verbs, as in (i),

(i) *Weil Johann scheint   ein guter Kerl zu sein, ...
     because Johann seems a good fellow to be
     'Because Johann seems to be a good guy, ...'

could be attributed to the incompatibility of the latter with the necessary clause union nature of the construction (rather than to head government from the non-canonical side).

57. This could perhaps be derived from a tightened version of the Structure-Preserving Hypothesis, whereby movement from an adjunction position to a Spec position (or vice versa) would count as "improper." However, this would still permit successive movements via adjunction. It may be tempting to view the general upward boundedness of rightward movements (in right-branching languages) as an indication that adjuncts can only adjoin a phrase to the immediately domi-

nating maximal projection (and no farther). See Johnson 1985 for arguments that no iterative adjunction should be allowed.

The only cases of unbounded movement to the right reported in the literature involve left-branching languages, possibly suggesting a movement via heads or specifiers (see Satyanarayana and Subbarao 1973, Kaufman 1974. See also the case of Tangale, a Spec-CP-final SVO language (Kenstowicz 1987), with possible instances of unbounded movement to the right (L. Tuller, personal communication).

Note also that the well-known contrast between *Wh*-Movement and Heavy NP Shift (*Who did you talk to t yesterday?* versus *I talked to t yesterday all the students who had not passed the exam*) could follow from the above theory of adjunction.

In this light, (the core cases of) extraposition from NP could be viewed as "reanalysis" of the relative CP followed by adjunction, rather than as actual extraction plus adjunction. See Johnson 1985 for relevant discussion, though various problems remain (see also Cardinaletti 1987 and references cited there).

58. Concerning Clitic Movement, which also appears to apply in a strict successive cyclic fashion, I assume that its trace, much like NP-traces, counts only as a subpart of a discontinuous constituent and not as a referentially autonomous XP, like variables, thus excluding binding. Kayne (1989b) derives the fact that clitic climbing is possible only in null subject languages essentially from the fact that VP is a (government) barrier and the fact that only in null subject languages does a strong I succeed in L-marking it and hence in voiding its barrierhood (adjunction of a clitic to VP being excluded, possibly because of the head nature of clitics).

The hypothesis that VP is not an inherent barrier to government thus appears to lose Kayne's results concerning clitic climbing. One way to retain these results, while denying the barrierhood of VP, is perhaps the following, which relates clitic climbing to another property of null subject languages: their apparent ability to permit moving V to (the more rich) infinitival Agr (see Pollock 1989, Chomsky 1988, Belletti 1988). If clitic climbing is a function of the movement of the embedded I (Agr) to (C to) matrix I (Agr), as Kayne argues, the impossibility of clitic climbing in non–null subject languages could be viewed as a consequence of the fact that a clitic cannot move to infinitival Agr either (nor can it go directly to C, because of Relativized Minimality).

59. Chomsky (1986b, 20) cites such cases as (i) as possibly supporting the assumption that I θ-marks VP, hence properly governing it, given that antecedent government is out of the question here:

(i) Fix the car$_i$, I wonder whether he will t_i.

As a matter of fact, forms such as (i) with *se* 'whether' are quite marginal in Italian (see (ii)) and become completely impossible with real *wh*-phrases in Spec CP (see (iii)), which suggests that long *Wh*-Movement is presumably unavailable. To the extent to which it is available, one is perhaps dealing with the same selective interpretation of Relativized Minimality discussed by Rizzi (1990, chap. 3, app. 1) and here in chapter 2, note 1. (See also Roberts 1989.)

(ii)   *?Aggiustato la macchina, mi chiedevo se avesse.
            fixed the car   I wondered whether he had

(iii) a. *Aggiustato la macchina, mi chiedo chi abbia.
      fixed the car   I wonder who has
   b. *Aggiustato la macchina, mi chiedo perché abbia.
      fix the car   I wonder who he did

Note also that, under the approach to long *Wh*-Movement advocated above (requiring referential traces), the assumption that I θ-marks VP would be compatible with Chomsky's (1986b) assumption (35): namely, that θ-marking can percolate from a category to its head. This is because, even though the trace of V- (or N-) Movement would be θ-governed, the movement still could not be "long," for failure to meet the referential requirement. Hence, Stowell's (1981) theory of complementizer "deletion" could still be upheld.

60. The term *properly* is meant to restrict reference to those heads that function as governors in a particular language: for example, lexical and functional heads, except C, in English (see Rizzi 1990, chap. 2). Although I will later introduce explicit reference to nondistinctness from [+V] in the definition of the ECP (thus ruling out N and P as head governors, on general grounds), I will retain the term *properly* because C, even though nondistinct from [+V], qualifies as a head governor only in certain languages, not including Italian or English (for extensive discussion, see Rizzi 1990, chap. 2).

If Koopman and Sportiche (1988) are right, exclusion of C from the class of proper head governors (in certain languages) is not a problem for the proposal that proper head governors must be nondistinct from [+V] categories; for, they argue, proper head governors must meet a further condition of "strong selection." See their section 3.2 for discussion.

The fact that C (as opposed to I) is not a proper governor in Italian may also be at the root of the impossibility of IP-Preposing (versus the possibility of VP-Preposing). Consider:

(i) a. *[$_{IP}$ Gianni sia partito]$_i$ non credo   che t_i.
      Gianni has left   I don't think that
   b. [$_{VP}$ Andato a casa]$_i$, non è t_i.
      gone home   he hasn't

61. Here, choosing NP as the target of extraction introduces no derivational ambiguity since the resumptive strategy open to NPs only is also excluded. See chapter 3.

62. Koster (1978, 80–81; 1984, 68) makes a similar observation concerning Dutch. PPs cannot be extracted from NP even though no other barrier is passed:

(i) *Wij hebben [t naar Hawaii [de reis t] geannuleerd t].
   we have   to Hawaii   the trip   canceled

Chomsky (1986b, 36 and sec. 11) mentions the possibility, originally suggested by Kayne (1981b), that N is not a proper governor. A similar suggestion is often made for P (again see Kayne 1981b).

63. Later, in fact, I will argue that whenever P may be nondistinct from [+V] (for example, in contexts where Case assignment is irrelevant), the same is true of Romance—whence the possibility of stranding prepositions taking PP complements.

64. See the definition of ECP (118), repeated here:

(118) A nonpronominal EC must be properly head-governed.

65. Presumably, the stipulation must be added that $\overline{P}$ and $\overline{Adv}$ are present *despite the absence of a specifier* (a condition, it may be recalled, that allows $\overline{V}$ to be absent in VP in the *Barriers* system (Chomsky 1986b, 4 and 47)). Alternatively, the stipulation could be added that an (empty) specifier is obligatory with such categories.

66. Kayne (1981b, fn. 25) conjectures that the apparent capacity of A(djectives) to govern for ECP purposes as in (i),

(i) John$_i$ is likely t_i to have left by now.

is "via *be* + A reanalyzed, rather than via A, so that A will be like N (but past participles will be like V)." If this is so, then [+ V] should be replaced by V in (133) and in the definitions of binding and government barriers. But consider constructions like (iia–b),

(ii) a. Anyone [PRO$_i$ likely [t_i to leave]] ...
 b. With [John$_i$ likely [t_i to leave]], ...

and also the fact that "reanalysis" per se possibly plays no independent role in preposition in stranding. See above and Rizzi 1990.

67. Concerning extraction from NP in English (more generally, Germanic), see Longobardi 1987b; in particular, Longobardi's suggestion that there may be no genuine extraction from NP in such language(s) where Spec is protected from government from outside. (In this connection, also see Bach and Horn 1976 and Chomsky 1977.) In fact, unlike what happens in Romance, neither (non-NP) complements nor subjects appear in general to be extractable in English:

(i) a. *The planet on which we saw a landing on TV ...
 b. *Of whom's did you read many books?
 (Compare *I read many books of John's.*)

Recall that the extraction of an NPs (*who$_i$ did you buy a picture of e$_i$?*) is no guarantee that real extraction (via long or successive cyclic *Wh*-Movement) has occurred. Like Koster (1987), and unlike Rizzi (1990, chap. 3, app. 2), I in fact take such cases to be instances of the $\overline{A}$-bound pro strategy to be discussed in chapter 3, movement (either long or successive cyclic) being blocked by the maximal projecton PP, which qualifies both as a binding and as a government barrier.

68. This may be superfluous for the NP-Movement case, if Grimshaw (1990) is right in arguing that "passive" nominals should not be analyzed as derived via NP-Movement that leaves a trace to be head-governed. The general argument takes the following form. First, through a variety of tests, Grimshaw demonstrates that nouns fall into two classes, only one of which (complex event nominals) has an argument structure comparable to that of verbs. Second, she provides evidence that (owing to the noun's defective θ-marking capacity) only XPs introduced by a preposition can fulfil the argument structure of complex event nominals. Neither a bare CP nor a bare NP (trace) can. This predicts that passive nominals will not show any of the diagnostic properties of argument-taking complex event nominals,

but that they will show only those of non-argument-taking result (and simple event) nominals, which cannot contain an NP-trace either.

The prediction is fulfilled in that, in all unambiguous cases of complex event nominals (gerundive nominals, nominals with event modifiers and adjuncts, and so on), passive is indeed impossible:

(i)　a.　*the tree's felling
　　　b.　*the city's destroying

(ii)　*the politician's frequent/constant nomination (under a passive reading)

(iii)　*the building's construction in three weeks

(iv)　*the book's translation to make it available to a wider readership

If NP-Movement is not at the basis of "passive" with nominals, then certain of its properties cease to be surprising, such as the peculiar fact than an A(P) must be able to bind an NP-trace (as in (v)) and the fact that NP-Movement within NPs is possible (in English) only with affected objects (cf. (vi)):

(v)　a.　the French$_i$ defeat t_i
　　　b.　la sua$_i$ decapitazione t_i
　　　　　his beheading

(vi)　a.　*the fact$_i$'s knowledge t_i
　　　b.　*the animal$_i$'s sight t_i

69. A problem remains concerning the apparent nonextractability of a PP complement of P (contrary to the Italian case discussed below):

(i)　*[Behind which car]$_i$ did they take a shot at him [$_{PP}$ from t_i]?

For discussion, see Van Riemsdijk 1978 and Koster 1987, 163ff.

Preposition stranding in Dutch (and certain regional varieties of German) appears to be more severely constrained: only NPs that receive a locative Case marking (*er, da* 'there') may extract. See Rizzi 1990, chap. 3, app. 2, for the suggestion that, as with extraction from NP in Romance, it is movement via Spec of the PP that renders P a proper head governor for the trace, though certain problems may remain here too concerning extraction of a locative NP from a PP itself the complement of another P. Extraction appears to be allowed only if the matrix P is a postposition (for discussion, see Bennis and Hoekstra (1984–85), Koster 1987, chap, 4).

70. The well-formedness of (i) is not problematic if the structure is as in (ii), parallel to (iii) (see Longobardi 1986):

(i)　Addosso, non gli è caduta.
　　　on　　　not to-him (she) has fallen
　　　'On she has not fallen to him.'

(ii)　[$_{PP}$ Addosso e_i]$_k$ non gli$_i$ è caduta t_k.

(iii)　[$_{VP}$ Incontrato e_i]$_k$ non l$_i$'ha t_k.
　　　　met　　　　　　　　(she) not him has

71. Forms like *li accanto/vicino*/etc. 'there near' might be taken at first sight to support the extractability of the PP through the Spec position. However, as Rizzi (1988) observes, they correspond in meaning not to a P+complement reading

('near there') but rather to 'there, near (it)', thus suggesting a different structure (perhaps an apposition).

If the antecedent government chain stops at Spec PP (see (i)), and binding is admitted, by analogy with Rizzi's (1990) analysis of subject gaps like (ii), then one would expect (i) (and (139a–b)) to be as marginal as (ii), which they are not:

(i) Gianni, a cui$_i$ non so perché siate andati [$_{PP}$ t'_i [incontro] t_i], …
  Gianni (to) whom I don't know why you went toward

(ii) *?Who$_i$ do you wonder whether we believe [$_{CP}$ t'_i [$_{IP}$ t_i can help us]]?

The passage through Spec and consequent successive cyclic Wh-Movement might be possible in the absence of weak islands, however. I also take the clitic case of (136b) to involve a government chain.

72. A notable difference between the two formulations would be represented by (141b) and (142b), which, in the latter formulation, are not distinguished from the simpler (140b) and (140c), respectively. Ways can be imagined to draw the relevant distinction, if indeed a distinction is to be drawn.

To my ear, in fact, structures of the form (ia) are often indistinguishable from the simpler (ib):

(i) a. wh$_i$ … [$_{CP}$ wh$_k$ … [$_{CP_{tensed}}$ … t_i …]] …
  b. wh$_i$ … [$_{CP_{tensed}}$ wh$_k$ … t_i …] …

See the virtually perfect (iia–b) and (142), with a pause after che cosa:

(ii) a. Laura, di cui$_i$ non so [$_{CP}$ se credere [$_{CP}$ che
  Laura with whom I don't know whether to believe that
  vi siate innamorati t_i]], …
  you fell in love

  b. Lucia, alla quale$_i$ mi chiedo [$_{CP}$ chi possa sostenere
  Lucia to whom I wonder who can claim
  [$_{CP}$ che va assegnato il primo premio t_i]], …
  that is to be assigned the first prize

Kayne (1981b, fn. 33) reports acceptable sentences comparable to (iia–b) in English.

73. Well-formed "double wh-island violations" are also reported by Engdahl (1980b) for Swedish, Italian, and Spanish, Obenauer (1984–85) for Spanish, and Dobrovie-Sorin (1990) for Romanian.

74. I owe this sentence to Maggie Browning. (144b) is from Frampton 1990.

75. The *Barriers* system could thus do away with the stipulation (which is problematic in any event, as we have seen) that multiple distinct crossings of a single barrier cumulate to yield an outcome similar to the crossing of more barriers simultaneously.

For the bounding system developed here, nothing special would have to be added either, given that no barriers for binding are expected with complement wh-questions.

76. Under the same cumulative interpretation, it would also incorrectly rule out extraction out of two weak (extraposition) islands:

(i) Gianni, al quale$_i$ [$_{VP}$ mi preoccupa [$_{CP}$ che vi possa [$_{VP}$ danneggiare
    Gianni to whom   it worries me   that it may harm you
    [$_{CP}$ PRO [$_{VP}$ mandare il mio messaggio t_i]]]]], ...
              to send my message

Each of the labeled CPs is non-L-marked (hence a barrier), so that movement of
al quale first from the embedded VP to the intermediate VP and then from the
intermediate VP to the highest VP crosses two barriers (cumulating the violations).

77. Recall that we intend long *Wh*-Movement of a non-NP (say, a PP), since
extraction of NPs is nonrepresentative. Extraction of a PP shows, in fact, that the
CP of (i)

(i) It is time [$_{CP}$ for John to visit Mary].

should not (contra Chomsky (1986b, 33)) be considered an adjunct. Compare (iia)
with (iib), which contains a bona fide adjunct:

(ii) a.   To whom is it time to write?
     b.   *To whom did you leave without writing?

I thank Ian Roberts for the relevant judgments.

Chapter 2

1. That CLLD should be analyzed as a separate construction from LD in Italian,
French, and Romanian was proposed in Cinque 1977, within a somewhat different
framework of assumptions. See also note 43 and corresponding text. For more
recent similar conclusions concerning Romanian and Spanish, see Dobrovie-Sorin
1987, 1990 and Dolci 1986, respectively.

2. For arguments that the resumptive clitic of CLLD cannot be identified with the
clitic of clitic doubling in a clitic-doubling language like Spanish, see Dolci 1986.

3. Forms like (2a) become marginally acceptable if the *wh*-phrase is more heavily
stressed and a phonological break separates it from what follows (the result being
an echo question). This does not affect the point made in the text, if, as suggested
by Cinque (1978b), Belletti (1979, 1980), and Belletti and Rizzi (1981), such forms
may be instances of questions (etc.) themselves parasitic on CLLD.

4. The only case of productive clitic doubling attested in colloquial Italian is that
of datives. But even that is severely limited. For reasons that are not understood,
clitic doubling of a dative is optimal only if it cooccurs with an object clitic. For
example:

(i)   *?Gli ho detto   una parolaccia a suo fratello.
         (I) to-him said a bad word   to his brother
(ii)   Gliel'ho detta   a suo fratello.
         (I) to-him-it said to his brother
(iii)   *Gli ho parlato   a suo fratello.
         (I) to-him spoke to his brother

The doubling of direct objects mentioned in the next note is only substandard.

5. Although counterexamples to Kayne's generalization have occasionally been
claimed to exist, Italian, in the substandard varieties that allow for clitic doubling

of direct objects, appears to obey it. So, for example, one finds (ia) and (ib), but only marginally (ic) or (id):

(i) a. %Seguimi   a me.
       follow-me to me
   b. %Ti seguo   a te.
       (I) you follow to you
   c. Seguimi   me.
       follow-me me
   d. Ti seguo   te.
       (I) you follow you

6. Further evidence against such an assimilation may derive from the following comparative observation. In an article discussing the interaction of weak crossover and clitic doubling, Aoun and Sportiche (1981) present evidence that the principle that (marginally) excludes weak crossover configurations becomes inoperative in clitic-doubling contexts (in Semitic). For example, in Lebanese Arabic a standard weak crossover case such as (i) (= Aoun and Sportiche's (9))

(i) *?emme   bthibb   kill   walad
    mother-*his* loves-she every boy
    'His mother loves every boy.'

becomes fully grammatical if the quantifier phrase is "doubled" by a clitic. See (ii) (= Aoun and Sportiche's (14)):

(ii) ?emme   bithibbe   la kill   walad
     mother-*his* loves-she-*him* to every boy

Though interesting in themselves, the implications of this observation for the proper treatment of weak crossover effects are not relevant here. What matters in this context is that the weak crossover effect found in the Italian sentence (iii)

(iii) *?Sua madre ama ogni bambino.
       his mother loves every boy

is apparently preserved in the corresponding CLLD form in spite of the presence of the clitic (see (iv)), thus suggesting a qualitative difference between the resumptive clitic in CLLD and the clitic of (clitic-doubling) constructions (in Semitic):

(iv) *?Ogni bambino, sua madre lo ama.
      every boy   his mother loves him

7. This account translates straightforwardly in Chomsky's (1986b) analysis of parasitic gaps, for which, in such cases as (5a), there is no real gap chain with which the parasitic gap chain can form a "composed chain."

8. Under Kayne's (1984, chap. 8) account of parasitic gaps, the inability of a (clitic) pronoun to license a parasitic gap follows from their being nonuniform (with respect to the empty/nonempty dimension) under Connectedness, quite apart from the pronoun's status as a base-generated element or the "spelling out" of a *wh*-trace (see especially section 8.3.1). If extended to (5a) and (8), however, such a uniformity requirement leaves the ability of the pronoun to license a parasitic gap in such Swedish cases as (8) unaccounted for.

9. A similar situation is apparently found in Vata (see Koopman 1984). The overt pronoun in the *wh*-constructions of this language would seem to exemplify what Sportiche (1983, chap. 3), following Zaenen, Engdahl, and Maling (1981), refers to as *syntactic resumptive pronouns*, as opposed to the *true* or *anaphoric resumptive pronouns* found (for example) in Spanish, Yiddish, and Hebrew (nonfree) relatives. What is relevant here is that the former differ from the latter in behaving like empty *wh*-traces. They are sensitive to island conditions, license parasitic gaps, and display weak crossover effects.

It is worth noting that CLLD does not fit into Sportiche's (1983, 117) typology of $\bar{\text{A}}$-/A-relations. Although it is immune to weak crossover effects and does not license parasitic gaps, it is sensitive to island conditions.

10. Such an incompatibility is presumably the consequence of general principles. Consider, for example, the configuration in (i):

(i) O (perator) [. . . cl(itic). . . *e*]   (where *cl* locally binds *e*, order irrelevant)

If *e* is locally bound by *cl*, possibly it does not qualify as a variable at LF, if the chain (*cl*, *e*) can qualify as a derivative variable at LF′ only. (On the difference between "being" and "being (derivately) interpreted as" a variable, see Kayne 1984, chap. 4, fn. 14 and corresponding text.) Then there will be a vacuous operator at LF.

This recalls Kayne's (1984, 222ff.) account of (ii),

(ii) *Qui amuse-t-il [*e* Marie]?
    who amuses-he   Marie

where, again, the possibility of taking (*il*, *e*) as a derivative variable bound by *qui* must not be capable of rescuing (ii).

Note that in both French and Italian, if a *wh*-quantified NP is substituted for the "bare" *wh*-quantifier, the form is substantially improved. For example:

(iii) a. (??)Quel homme n'aurait-il pas été séduit
       what man   neg-would-have-he not been seduced
       par un si joli argument? (Kayne 1984, chap. 4, (90))
       by a so pretty argument
    b. (??)Quale personaggio politico, lo conoscete così bene
       which political figure   him-(do-you) know so well
       da fidarvi di lui?
       that you will trust him

Later we will discuss some evidence that "bare" quantifiers differ systematically from quantified NPs in that the former but not the latter act as operators capable of identifying an EC as a variable (at S-Structure). If we assume that the former not only *can* be operators but *must* be (that is, must ($\bar{\text{A}}$-)bind an EC at LF), then (2a) and (ii) will be ruled out, as desired. (iiia–b) are then presumably parasitic on CLLD, being interpreted as a (derivative) operator-variable configuration only at LF′.

11. As mentioned in chapter 1, topicalization could more appropriately be termed *Focus Movement* in Italian, since its left-peripheral phrase obligatorily bears heavy stress, its pragmatic function being to contrast the "topicalized" constituent with some other constituent. I nonetheless retain the term *topicalization* here to emphasize its syntactic identity to the English construction (though the pragmatics of the

latter is indeed closer to that of CLLD in Italian; see Cinque 1983c). For the sake of clarity, I will continue to capitalize topicalized constituents.

12. The derivation indicated in figure 2.1 represents just one of a number of alternatives. The point is that whatever derivation is chosen, a different violation of Subjacency (or of the strict cycle) will ensue, as can easily be determined.

13. Presumably, the general ban against multiple foci in Italian (see Calabrese 1982, 1984).

14. This implies, among other things, that the "trace" of (non-NP) clitics cannot be an anaphor and cannot fall under the binding conditions. Thus, the strictly local relation between clitics and their "traces" should be ascribed to something other than Principle A of the binding theory. One possibility (suggested in Chomsky 1982, 87) is to assume, along lines proposed by Borer (1981), that the EC associated with a clitic must necessarily be *governed* by the clitic (hence its anaphorlike character).

That a (null) anaphor should be limited to a (null) NP category is tentatively suggested also by Kayne (1978, 160 and fns. 11 and 24).

15. That (22a–b) have the option of the latter derivation in addition to the successive cyclic derivation discussed above is indicated by the wider possibilities for subject extraction in Italian as compared to French, which has no Aux-to-Comp rule. For example, compare (i) and (ii):

(i) a. Eravamo convinti esser Gianna inadatta   a quel compito.
         we were convinced that Gianna was unsuitable for the task
     b. Gianna, che eravamo convinti   essere inadatta a quel compito, ...
         Gianna who we were convinced to be unsuitable for the task

(ii) a. *Nous étions convaincus être Gianna inapte pour la tâche.
     b. *Gianna, que nous étions convaincus être inapte pour la tâche, ...

16. A quantified NP in postverbal subject position of an unergative verb (in Burzio's (1981) sense) adjoined to VP or in adverb position admits no pronominalization form. Both the zero option and the *ne* option are excluded:

(i) a. (Di questi libri) *Credo che (ne) abbiano avuto successo solo due.
         (of these books) I think that (of-them) had success   only two
     b. (Di settimane) *A Milano, (ne) sono rimasto solo due.
         (of weeks)   in Milan (of-them) I stayed only two

For relevant discussion, see Belletti and Rizzi 1981, Rizzi 1982, chap. 4, and Longobardi 1987b.

17. In fact, even "short" *Wh*-Movement of a pronominalized quantified subject of an unaccusative V appears to require the *ne* option (abstracting away from the case mentioned in note 18), which suggests that *Wh*-Movement takes place obligatorily from the inverted position (even if, here, this is not motivated by the ECP). For discussion, see Rizzi 1982, chap. 4 and Longobardi 1987b, fn. 48.

18. Rizzi (1982, chap. 4, fn. 39) in fact points out that such obligatoriness holds with the ordinary neutral intonation, and that *ne* can be absent only with an intonation break after the Q. I take such cases to be instances of resumptive Agr, parallel to the case of the resumptive object clitic in (i):

(i) ??Quanti,   hai detto   che sono riusciti   a pubblicar*li*   entro dicembre?
     how many did you say that they managed to publish *them* by December

19. By contrast, speaker B's statement in (33) is ungrammatical without *ne* because the trace of *QUATTRO* cannot be found in the preverbal subject position (because that is not a properly head-governed position). Nor can it be locally bound by Agr, just as the EC associated with a topicalized object cannot be locally bound by a clitic. See (i) and note 10:

(i) *QUATTRO, credo che *le* abbiano smarrite.
     four (focus) I think that they have lost *them*

20. Concerning (40), see Chomsky 1981, 102, 330, and 228, fn. 56, Chomsky 1982, 47, Brody 1984, Kayne 1984, 222. The requirement that a variable be $\bar{\text{A}}$-bound *by an operator* is not always assumed. For instance, it is not in Chomsky's (1981, 330) definition (but see fn. 56, p. 228). It is suggested by Chomsky (1982, 47) and supported on various grounds by Kayne (1984, chap. 4), Taraldsen (1984), and other authors. The ensuing discussion, if correct, provides additional evidence for it. (40) differs minimally from the definition proposed by Kayne (1984, 222) in that it retains the notion of $\bar{\text{A}}$-binding (along with that of operator binding), which appears to play a role in preventing the EC in (i) and (ii) from (incorrectly) counting as a variable:

(i) *Hai convinto   chi di aver aiutato *e*?
     you have convinced who that you had helped

(ii) *Nessuno era sicuro che avremmo aiutato *e*.
      nobody was sure   that we would have helped

Such cases as (iii) suggest that the formulation in (40) is preferable to the formulation in (iv):

(iii) Who$_i$ did he say [t'_i [t_i was invited]]?

(iv) [$_{NP}$ *e*] in A-position, locally $\bar{\text{A}}$-bound by an operator.

In (iii) the variable is locally $\bar{\text{A}}$-bound and operator-bound, but it is not "locally $\bar{\text{A}}$-bound by an operator." If t'_i, the local $\bar{\text{A}}$-binder, counted as an operator, the variable would be bound by two distinct operators (*who$_i$* and *t'_i*). Null NPs in Spec CP, then, must *optionally* count as operators.

21. In this connection, the NP in the $\bar{\text{A}}$-position created by Heavy NP Shift and "Scrambling" in German and Dutch must count as an operator. I leave this question open.

22. This amounts to saying that [−pronominal, −anaphor] NP ECs cannot receive a free variable interpretation. See Chomsky 1982, Brody 1984. Apparently, only some designated pronominal elements can receive such an interpretation (for example, PRO and *si*, in Italian; see Manzini 1983, Cinque 1988).

23. Separate questions arise with respect to the proper analysis of the relation between the "normal" clitic-trace configuration and the "left-dislocated" phrase. Given that the dislocated phrase shows Connectivity even in the presence of a resumptive clitic, I take this to mean that it belongs to an $\bar{\text{A}}$-chain containing the EC and the clitic:

(i) [$_{PP}$ A se stessa]^k, credo   che Maria non ci^k pensi e^k.
     of herself   I believe that Maria does not there-think

In (i) the clitic must count as nonargumental. Evidence for this conclusion is possibly provided by the fact that *ci* in (i) does not trigger a Principle C violation, whereas it does in non-CLLD contexts. See (ii):

(ii) a. *Maria ci   pensa.
         Maria there thinks
         (with the meaning 'Maria thinks of herself')
     b. *Maria crede   che non ci pensiamo.
         Maria believes that we don't there think
         (with the meaning 'Maria believes that we don't think of her')

The fact that the resumptive element must be a *clitic* pronoun on the verb, rather than a tonic pronoun filling the A-position, is possibly a consequence of the need to reconstruct the CLLD phrase into the IP-internal position for Full Interpretation purposes.

24. Of course, base generation of a (null) operator in Spec CP is still possible in principle. But this is besides the point (even under free coindexing at S-Structure, as we will assume in chapter 3) if the presence of the operator is assumed to correlate strictly with a "topicalized" interpretation of the structure.

25. The pertinent reading is the one that has the usual CLLD contour and no focus associated with the left-peripheral NP. This reading should thus be distinguished from a second (irrelevantly possible) topicalization reading.

26. Possible evidence for the structure in (45a) is the fact that bare quantifiers are in general incompatible with specifiers and (nonappositive) modifiers. See for example (i)–(ii) and the extensive evidence for (45a) discussed by Kayne (1975, sec. 1.3):

(i) *Ho fatto un ultimo qualcosa prima di uscire.
     I did   one last something before going out

(ii) *Ho visto qualcosa   interessante.
     I saw   something interesting
     (Compare *Ho visto qualcosa di interessante.*)

27. Topicalization in English, which does not obviously appear to have a quantificational force (it is not necessarily a Focus Movement construction) raises a potential problem for this analysis, since it licenses (the movement of) a null operator.

We may assume that, in that case, positive evidence of its *Wh*-Movement nature (licensing of empty objects, and so on) suffices for a child to postulate the presence of an empty operator even in the absence of an overt quantificational force that would render that assumption necessary. If the primary data offer no positive evidence for the presence of a null operator, then in the absence of quantificational force the child would indeed postulate no operator.

As far as I can tell, the analysis sketched here would also be compatible with taking the topicalized phrase itself to be an operator moving to Spec CP, thus dispensing with the empty operator. The question hinges in part on the proper treatment of Reconstruction, which I cannot address here.

28. As is well known, quantifiers like *molti* 'many', *tutti* 'all', and *pochi* 'few', but not those like *alcuni/qualche* 'some' and *parecchi* 'several', can amalgamate with a negation (see Lasnik 1972 for discussion).

29. Alternatively, it is the post-Reconstruction level (where *per questa ragione* fills the position of the trace of *O*) that "feeds" the LF process of amalgamation.

30. Perhaps a residue of the Verb-second character of Old Italian (see Benincà 1986, Vanelli, Renzi, and Benincà 1985).

31. This construction (similar to English topicalization) also has no obvious quantificational force despite its involving an empty operator. See note 27.

32. To this class of (motivated) exceptions to our nonmovement analysis of CLLD is plausibly to be attributed the clitic left dislocation of constituents from a predicate containing a focused verb, which also require the same stringent discourse conditions (the dislocated phrase must have been mentioned in the immediately preceding discourse):

(i) a. In un modo strano, si E' comportato.
         in a strange manner he did behave
     b. Bella,   credo   che (lo) SIA.
         beautiful I believe that she is

For some reason, if the focused constituent is not contained in the predicate from which extraction takes place, these sentences become ungrammatical:

(ii) a. *In un modo strano, GIANNI dice   che vi siete comportati.
          in a strange manner Gianni (focus) says that you behaved
      b. *Bella,   CREDO   che (lo) sia.
          beautiful (I) believe (focus) that she is

33. I differ here from Cinque 1977 and an earlier version of this chapter, where I took such cases as (95a–b) and (96) to suggest that idiom chunks can be freely clitic left dislocated.

34. In the latter case either they are adjoined to VP, judging from the fact that they can be affected by VP-Preposing and Deletion, or they are dominated by some projection of I and hence lie outside VP. See Kuno 1975 and references cited there.

  Of the two IP-final positions, I will systematically disregard the position outside VP, which seems to differ neither in scope nor in meaning from the IP-initial position (see also note 35).

35. This does not mean that an adverbial changes meaning in all circumstances, according to whether it is in IP-initial or IP-final position. In such cases as (i), it does not:

(i) a. In Boston, there are many Italians.
     b. There are many Italians in Boston.

Interestingly, there is evidence that the adverbial is outside the VP in such cases, thus presumably having the same scope as the IP-initial variant (see Kuno 1975, 168–170).

36. This is also the conclusion reached by Geis (1986a, b).

37. Although *poiché* 'because' can appear both in IP-initial and IP-final position, there is evidence that in the latter case it can occupy only a position outside VP. This is suggested by the fact that, unlike *perché* 'because', it cannot be under the scope of negation, which usually affects VP elements (i), it cannot be fronted with the VP under VP-Preposing (ii), and it cannot be *Wh*-Moved (iii)—which, in fact, suggests that its base position is not properly head-governed (presumably because governed by C).

(i) Non la picchia $\left\{\begin{array}{l}\text{perché l'odia ma perché l'ama}\\ \text{*poiché l'odia ma poiché l'ama}\end{array}\right\}$.

he doesn't beat her because he hates her but because he loves her

(ii) Arrestato $\left\{\begin{array}{l}\text{perché}\\ \text{*poiché}\end{array}\right\}$ beve,   non è stato.

arrested   because he drinks he was not

(iii) E' $\left\{\begin{array}{l}\text{perché}\\ \text{*poiché}\end{array}\right\}$ l'ama   che la picchia.

it is   because he loves her that he beats her

38. See Longobardi 1983, 1988 for more careful discussion and relevant examples. The analysis of adjuncts developed here differs from Longobardi's only in admitting the *possibility* that adjuncts leave a trace in IP-final position. Note that the crossover argument just discussed shows that an adjunct must be able to move from an IP-initial position, not that it must always move from such a position. On the other hand, the scope facts discussed earlier show that an adjunct must be able to move from an IP-final (VP-adjoined) position as well.

39. Why it must (in other terms, why movement cannot take place from the IP-initial position) is not entirely clear. Perhaps *wh*-question formation, topicalization, clefting, and the like, and the limited instances of *Wh*-Movement in CLLD can only involve the phrase constituting the focus of the sentence, which is (in Italian) usually the rightmost constituent of the VP. Phrases outside VP usually cannot qualify as focus (recall the inability of the *poiché* phrase to be negated and *Wh*-Moved).

40. The contrast between the grammaticality of (85c) and the unacceptability of (108c) is particularly telling. It follows, under Relativized Minimality, only if the extraction site of the adverbial is, for (85c), outside, and, for (108c), inside the *wh*-island. Also see Longobardi 1983.

41. The special adverbial PP preposing case discussed by Rizzi (1990, chap. 3, app.)

(i) Per questa ragione$_i$, non immagino chi potrebbe essere licenziato t_i.

for this reason   I can't imagine who could be fired

should not be confused with the construction discussed here. Rizzi's case appears to be an instance of what I have called *Resumptive Preposing*, an ordinary *wh*-construction. And, in fact, the fronted PP retains the embedded VP-internal scope (unlike the Adverb Preposing cases discussed here).

If an operator is involved in Resumptive Preposing, as I have argued, then Relativized Minimality should, in Rizzi's spirit, be made sensitive to the type of operator (an Ā-specifier blocks an antecedent government relation only if it and the real Ā-antecedent involve the same kind of operator).

42. Contrary to what I concluded in Cinque 1977, mainly on the basis of the construction's sensitivity to islands and Connectivity, both of which properties I considered there as solid diagnostic criteria for (*Wh-*)Movement. The new conclusion, however, does not affect the evidence, discussed there and recalled above, for distinguishing between two "left dislocation" constructions in Italian and, more generally, in Romance. Napoli (1981, app.) has argued against the necessity of distinguishing two such constructions, but her arguments, where they do not misconstrue the facts, leave the main point unaffected, it seems to me.

Chapter 3

1. See Chomsky 1982, 30ff., which refines earlier analyses presented in Chomsky 1977, 1980a, b, 1981. We will return in section 3.3 to the nature of the abstract operator.

2. The contrast in (4) can be directly reduced to whatever principle accounts for the contrast in (i) (for discussion, see Fodor 1978, Pesetsky 1982),

(i) a. ?Who$_j$ didn't you know what$_i$ to say e_i to e_j?
   b. *What$_i$ didn't you know who$_j$ to say e_i to e_j?

if an abstract operator is postulated in the lower Spec CP of (4), which $\bar{\text{A}}$-binds the complement object, as shown in (ii):

(ii) a. Who$_j$ is that book$_i$ too boring [O_i [to send e_i to e_j]]?
    b. *What$_i$ is John$_j$ too boring [O_j [to send e_i to e_j]]?

On the other hand, no crossing effects are produced by the intersection of A-dependencies with $\bar{\text{A}}$-dependencies (Pesetsky 1982).

3. Under Kayne's (1984, chap. 9, 1985a) analysis of the dative construction, according to which the dative object is a left-branch PP (containing an empty preposition)—V [[P NP] NP]—the ungrammaticality of (5b) (and (6b)) follows straightforwardly from the Connectedness Condition (see especially Kayne 1984, chap. 9, fn. 19). It also follows from the ECP, as defined in chapter 1. For partially different analyses, see Czepluch 1982–83 and Barss and Lasnik 1986.

4. Note that the adjunct PP modifies the embedded, not the matrix, clause. Examples of this type are noted in Longobardi 1983.

5. Whether parasitic gaps and extraction from island gaps give rise to crossing effects is hard to ascertain, given the complexity and the marginality of the structures involved. However, the expectation is that they should—in which case the (b) examples in (i) and (ii) should be worse than the (a) examples:

(i) a. John$_i$, who$_i$ I don't know which present$_j$ they bought e_j without giving
      e_j to e_i, . . .
   b. An invitation$_j$ which$_j$ I don't know who$_i$ they invited e_i without giving
      e_j to e_i . . .

(ii) a. John$_i$, who$_i$ I don't know which present$_j$ they went away without giving
       e_j to e_i, . . .
    b. The present$_j$ which$_j$ I don't know who$_i$ they went away without giving
       e_j to e_i . . .

6. Unlike in Chomsky 1982, where they were regarded as [+pronominal] ECs at D-Structure and as [−pronominal, −anaphor] ECs at S-Structure "parasitically" Ā-bound by an independently moved operator. This analysis is rejected in Chomsky 1986b, essentially for its inability to express the island sensitivity of parasitic gaps.

7. Either from the independent requirement that a variable must be free in the domain of the head of its chain (including composed chains) or from a condition on the definition of A-chain (see Chomsky's (1986b) condition (147)).

8. For evidence in favor of the anti-c-command condition, see also Safir 1987, Koster 1987, 366ff., and Hornstein and Weinberg 1988. For a different view of the anti-c-command issue based on Case considerations, see Kiss 1985.

9. This is also noted by Koster (1984, 58ff.) and Aoun and Clark (1985, fn. 9). To make sure that one is dealing with real parasitic gap cases, some care must be taken in the choice of lexical items, since in many cases non-NP complements (as opposed to NP complements) are entirely optional. In such cases, presumably, the Projection Principle does not require that they be categorially present. A sentence such as (i), for example, contrasts with (15b) in that it is perfectly grammatical.

(i) A chi   hai scritto   senza dire   che saresti venuto?
    to whom did you write without saying that you would have come

But the acceptability contrast correlates rather clearly with the ability of *dire*, though not *rivolgersi*, to occur normally without a dative phrase:

(ii) a. Gli ho scritto senza dire   che sarei venuto.
         I wrote to him without saying that I would have come
     b. *Gli   ho sbattuto la porta in faccia   senza rivolgermi.
        to him I slammed the door in the face without addressing
        'I slammed the door in his face without addressing.'

If so, the grammaticality of (i) and the like is entirely irrelevant (they are not genuine parasitic gap cases).

Engdahl (1983, 17) claims that, in Swedish, parasitic gaps of categories other than NP are indeed possible. It is interesting, however, that all the examples she cites are of the subject type:

(iii) a. [PP Till himlen] är det inte säkert att alla,   som längtar [e],
         to heaven   it is not certain   that everyone who longs e
         Kommer [t].
         gets t
      b. [AP Fattig] vill ingen,   som nagonsin varit [e], bli [t] igen.
         poor   no one wants who has ever been   to become again

In Italian, too, examples of the subject type tend to sound better than those of the adjunct type, though they are not really acceptable. Perhaps, in the subject case, real movement from e can be involved. This recalls the phenomenon termed *Concorrenza del relativo* in the traditional grammar of Latin, also found in other languages: the apparent extraction of a relative phrase from an island. Of interest here is that the island must "immediately follow" the (apparently extracted) relative phrase (see Ernout and Thomas 1964, 333), the source of (iv), which suggests adjunction to the island rather than extraction. This is reminiscent of the properties of LF movement in cases of "inversely linked" quantifiers, as analyzed by May (1985, chap. 3). The Bavarian German example (v) is noted by Felix (1985), who discusses the phenomenon in relation to the similar parasitic gap case (vi), also peculiar to Bavarian German:

(iv) Magna vis (est) conscientiae,   quam qui neglegent, . . .
     great is the force of the conscience which those who will neglect
     se ipsi indicabunt. (Cic., *Cat.* 3, 27)
     will betray themselves

(v) Das ist die Frau   die wenn du *e* heiratest, bist du verrückt.
    this is the woman who if you marry   you are crazy

(vi) Das ist der Kerl den wenn ich *e* erwisch, erschlag ich *e*.
     this is the guy   who if I catch   I will beat up

10. On the QP nature of [*quanti*] in (15c), see Kayne 1979, app. Belletti and Rizzi (1981) and Rizzi (1982) assume the analysis [$_{NP}$[$_{QP}$ *quanti*] *t*], where *t* is the trace of *ne*. More recently, Luigi Rizzi (personal communication) has noted that the former, though not the latter, analysis may account for the ungrammaticality of (i) (without a pause after *quanti*), where a nonextraposed relative clause follows [*quanti*] in Spec CP:

(i) *Quanti   che ti piacevano ne hai visti?
    how many that you liked   have you seen of-them
    (Compare
    Quanti libri   che ti piacevano hai visto?
    how many books that you liked   have you seen)

11. Recall from chapter 1 that in Chomsky's (1986b) analysis, extractions (of complements) out of complex NPs of the N complement type are assumed to give rise to a weak Subjacency violation, with one barrier intervening, namely CP ("a barrier to movement (hence to government), though one that does not transmit barrierhood to NP" (sec. 7)). All of the examples considered there involve movement of NPs, however. If we attempt to extract non-NP complements, the violation becomes more severe (see (18b) and (ia–b)):

(i) a. *Carlo, di cui   abbiamo annunciato il piano di sbarazzarci, . . .
       Carlo of whom we announced   a plan   to get rid
    b. *Mario, con cui   abbiamo disapprovato l'idea   di parlare, . . .
       Mario with whom we disapproved   the idea of talking

This suggests that complex NPs of the N complement type are absolute islands (as argued in chapter 1) and that apparent extraction of NPs from them is in fact an instance of the resumptive pro strategy to be discussed below.

12. For the NP nature of such adjuncts, see Larson 1985.

13. In chapter 1 we observed that only referential NPs can enter into binding. The ungrammaticality of (20)–(21) suggests that in such cases even government is excluded because of the presence of a barrier (the adjunct PP). But under a *Wh*-Movement analysis of COD and parasitic gap constructions, nothing would seem to prevent a chain of antecedent government relations in (20), (21a), and (21c).

14. For parasitic gaps, this was noted by Taraldsen (1981). Also see Chomsky 1982, 53, from which (26a) is drawn. That the same property extends to gaps of apparent extraction from islands is noted by Pesetsky (1982). ((26b) is Pesetsky's example (vi), p. 581.) Example (26c) is noted by Schachter (1981), who points out the contrast between it and *??Mary is hard for me to believe John kissed.*

15. Once more, it is not clear why a successive cyclic derivation (that is, a chain of antecedent government relations) should be unavailable in COD and parasitic gap constructions.

The unacceptability of (26b) may instead (also) follow from Rizzi's (1990, chap. 3) analysis of similar extractions from *wh*-islands:

(i) *?Who$_i$ do you wonder whether we believe t_i can help us?

In that analysis, although binding is possible with [NP, IP], movement through the Spec CP (needed to enforce proper head government of the variable) ends up leaving an empty category that plays no role at LF (it is not part of a binding or government chain, it is not an operator, and so on) and thus fails to be licensed because of reasonable extensions of Chomsky's (1986a) Full Interpretation principle. See Chomsky 1988 and Rizzi 1990.

16. See Rizzi 1981, 1982, chap. 3 for a similar analysis of the corresponding phenomenon in Italian, and Chomsky 1981, 295ff., Pollock 1985, and Rizzi 1990 for further discussion.

17. Chomsky (1986b) derives the transparency of a single (versus double) sentential boundary (for specifier elements) by reformulating the notion of government. Note that the variable in subject position will be assigned Case if Case is assigned to indices, as suggested by Chomsky (1981, 296). Rizzi (1990) proposes that the variable in Spec IP is assigned Case by an abstract Agr in C.

18. Contrasts such as those between (34) and (37), and their relevance for a *Wh*-Movement analysis of these constructions, were noted by Richard Kayne in class lectures at the University of Venice in the spring of 1983.

19. A reviewer has suggested that for the French COD case the ungrammaticality of such forms as (i)

(i) *Cet homme$_i$ est facile [à PRO croire [PRO avoir vu e_i]].
     this man   is easy   to believe   to have seen

(whose analogue in Italian is also ungrammatical) weakens, or nullifies, the significance of the contrast between (34a) and (37a), since (34a) could be excluded independently by the ban against multiple embeddings apparently operative in COD constructions in Romance. This may be so for the COD case, though it is not entirely clear how the principle involved would distinguish between movement of the subject of a CP complement (34a) and movement of the subject of a small clause complement (37a), possibly CP too, if Kayne (lectures at the University of Venice, 1988) is correct.

In any event, the objection does not carry over to the parasitic gap case and the case of apparent extraction from islands. Compare the unacceptability of (32b) and (33b) with the relative acceptability of (ii) and (iii):

(ii) ?L'uomo$_i$ che apprezzavamo t_i pur senza ritenere   [di dover premiare e_i
the man who we appreciated without even thinking we had to reward
per quello che aveva fatto]...
for what he had done

(iii) ?L'unica personna$_i$ che siamo stati ricompensati per aver ritenuto
the only person   who we were rewarded   for having thought
[di non dover abbandonare e_i]...
we should not abandon

As with the case discussed in the previous section, under a *Wh*-Movement analysis of parasitic gap and COD constructions, it is not clear why a successive cyclic derivation should be unavailable.

20. The contrast between (45) and (i) appears to exclude an account based merely on complexity considerations:

(i) ?The book that we went to Scotland without hoping to be able to read after arriving there...

21. I assume that the feature content of an EC may not change in the course of the derivation (see Chomsky 1986b, sec. 5). If parasitic and extraction from island gaps (as well as COD gaps) are [+pronominal] at D-Structure (for thematic considerations), then they will have to remain [+pronominal] at S-Structure.

Another possibility is that the [+pronominal] EC moves to an Ā-position by S-Structure (thus acting as an empty operator). I discuss this possibility later, suggesting that it is unable to express, in a principled way, the systematic differences between the gap of the constructions in (1) and ordinary *wh*-traces. Quite apart from that, one may wonder how the [+pronominal] element would be identified in Spec CP, and interpreted at S-Structure and LF. I return to this point in section 3.4, concluding that [+pronominal] elements are possible in Spec CP only when the CP is governed directly by their antecedent:

(i) [The book [pro [that] [we know t]]...

This is yet another case, in addition to government by personal Agr in pro-drop languages and Ā-binding by an operator, in which the pronominal features of pro can be identified.

22. Contreras (1984) suggests that an object should be assumed to c-command an adjunct, thus leading to a violation of Principle C of the binding theory in such cases as (53). This appears doubtful, however. Comparable cases where the R-expression is in subject rather than object position sound relatively acceptable, especially if the VP of the adjunct clause is "heavy" (see Lakoff 1968, 11, from which (ia) is drawn):

(i) a. Mary hit him$_i$, before John$_i$ had a chance to get up.
    b. Lo$_i$ hanno estromesso, prima ancora che Gianni$_i$ potesse accorgersene.
       they turned him out   before Gianni could even realize it

Moreover, such VP-Preposing cases as (ii) indicate that adjuncts have at least the option of attaching outside VP (hence, presumably, outside the c-domain of objects):

(ii) ...and [fix it]$_i$ they did t_i without destroying anything.

Hornstein and Weinberg provide further evidence, based on their analysis of epithets, that object NPs do not (necessarily) c-command adjuncts (Weinberg and Hornstein 1986, fn. 7, Hornstein and Weinberg 1988, 149ff., Weinberg 1988). See also the discussions by Engdahl (1985) and Chomsky (1986b, sec. 10), based on observations by Luigi Rizzi.

The acceptability of such VP-Preposing cases as (iii)

(iii) ...and [convince him]$_i$ they did t_i that they were going to hire him.

indicates that even complement sentences have the option of attaching outside VP (possibly, after rightward adjunction). If so, the acceptability of (iv)

(iv) Who$_i$ did they convince t_i that they were going to hire e_i?

does not require postulating the presence of a null operator in order to prevent the real gap from c-commanding the parasitic gap. In principle, it should be possible to exchange the real with the parasitic gap in (iv). However, substituting an overt pronoun for the leftmost gap gives rise to much worse results:

(v) *Who$_i$ did they convince him that they were going to hire t_i?

This fact, which cannot be interpreted as a case of strong crossover, given (iii), may instead be attributed to weak crossover (Engdahl 1985). Under this view, the contrast between (iv) and (v) resembles that between (vi) and (vii):

(vi) ?Who$_i$ did [your interest in e_i] surprise t_i?
(vii) *Who$_i$ did [your interest in him] surprise t_i?

Browning (1987, sec. 3.2.3) reaches a similar conclusion.

23. I am assuming that such ungrammatical cases as (i), with the structure indicated (= (93) of Chomsky 1982, 70),

(i) *I wonder [O_i who$_i$[t_i filed the article without reading e_i]].

can be independently excluded even if operators base-generated in $\bar{\text{A}}$-position are indexed at S-Structure.

Although similar configurations may well arise at LF via LF Wh-Movement (see Aoun, Hornstein, and Sportiche 1981 and much later work), no S-Structure configurations such as (i) would be allowed if base-generated operators were only to be base-generated in the Spec CP: [O[C]]. In that case no landing site would be available to who moved to Spec CP in the syntax (for further discussion, see Chomsky 1982, 70ff.). Comparable LF configurations might instead involve adjunction to CP (see Pesetsky 1987).

24. Chomsky (1981, 185) defines a variable as an EC that is in A-position and is locally $\bar{\text{A}}$-bound. Chomsky (1982, 35) and Kayne (1984, 222) assume instead that the EC is in A-position and is locally operator bound (also see Chomsky 1981, 102). In Cinque 1986 I discuss evidence suggesting that both the notion of $\bar{\text{A}}$-binding and the notion of operator are involved in the definition of variable. Also see Taraldsen 1986, Chomsky 1986a, 184, and Dobrovie-Sorin 1990.

25. For example, they govern verbal agreement (*Which boy/boys do you think t is/are apt for this task?*) and enter into control (*Who did John convince t [PRO to wash himself]?*).

26. "At D-structure, we may have lexical or empty categories or the null category, lacking any features: the empty categories, by definition, have ϕ-features" (Chomsky 1981, 331).

27. That only variables should be taken as contextually defined (even adopting the "intrinsic" definition of ECs) is also argued by Safir (1984), who in addition reports the following relevant observation by a reviewer (fn. 22):

... the referential properties might be divided up into the three categories recognized by binding theory, namely, pronominals, anaphors, and referring expressions, the latter class including elements that have intrinsic reference. The reviewer believes that variables, being neither pronominals nor anaphors in some cases, are nonetheless elements that do not have intrinsic reference, and are therefore undefined, except by context (that is, they cannot have a [referring expression–KS] property).

28. For problems concerning the "contextual" or "functional" definition of ECs, see (among others) Safir 1982, 1984, Brody 1984, Chomsky 1986a, and Rizzi 1985.

29. The same assumption, within somewhat different analyses (see note 33), is made by Suñer (1982) and Obenauer (1984–85). This assumption is not immediately compatible with Rizzi's (1986) idea that pro is not formally licensed in English. Our analysis would lead us to hypothesize that English is unable to identify an object pro though it can formally license it, this being possibly a consequence of English not having clitics.

30. For reasons to be discussed shortly, I differ here from Stowell (1986), who takes the empty status of the operator to be the crucial factor responsible for some of the properties of these gaps and makes "the simplifying assumption that the relevant restrictions apply to all null operators."

For a different account of the limitation of parasitic gaps to NPs, see Frampton 1990.

31. See Chomsky 1982, 59. The base generation of operators in Spec CP accounts for such cases as *The man who they think that if Mary marries him, then everybody will be happy.* For the base generation of pro in A-positions, see Rizzi 1986.

For arguments in favor of S-Structure coindexing of base-generated phrases in the syntax of Palauan, see Georgopoulos 1985, chap. 4.

32. Unlike Chomsky (1982), I assume that the head of a (restrictive) relative clause, though possibly an Ā-position—especially if Vergnaud's (1974, 1985) raising analysis is correct—is unable to characterize an EC as a variable since it is not an operator. The fact that it cannot bind its own gap when it bears an index distinct from the phrase in Spec CP can be construed as supporting evidence; see Safir 1986 and example (i) (= Safir's (13c)):

(i) *The report$_i$[the author of which$_i$]$_j$ Mary married e_j without filing e_i] ...

Also, the idea that only operators in Ā-position (that is, inherent operators or null NPs in Spec CP) can characterize an EC as a variable was indirectly supported in chapter 2 by its ability to account for a number of subtle properties of the CLLD construction in Italian. For further discussion, see Kayne 1984, chap. 10, Cinque 1986, Taraldsen 1986, and Dobrovie-Sorin 1990.

33. It is crucial that only empty *NPs* have the option of being [+pronominal, −anaphor].

If we were to allow for the existence of empty non-NP pro-forms corresponding to overt non-NP pro-forms (such as empty variants of the pro-PP *ci* 'there' or *ne* 'of/from it' in Italian), then the explanation of the NP/non-NP asymmetry under extraction from (non-*wh*) islands would be lost (see (16)–(18)). I therefore differ here from Obenauer (1984–85), who makes the latter assumption. I also differ from Obenauer's position in not taking the pro hypothesis to provide an exhaustive alternative to the complement/adjunct asymmetry in extraction from *wh*-islands. Even assuming an empty variant for each overt pro-form (which I do not), the pro hypothesis apparently has nothing to say about such familiar contrasts as the one between (ia) and (ib), where neither the subcategorized PP nor the adjunct PP has a corresponding overt (or empty) pro-form:

(i) a.   To whom$_i$ did you wonder [what$_j$ to give $t_j t_i$]?
   b. *How$_i$ did John know [which problem$_j$ to solve $t_j t_i$]?

34. Richard Kayne (class lecture, University of Venice, spring 1983) and Koster (1984) both reached the same conclusion on independent grounds.

35. Which is in turn reminiscent of the output conditions occasionally suggested to hold of Heavy NP Shift, modulo, again, a different degree of strength. See for example Ross 1967 and Kayne 1985a.

36. I assume throughout that left-dislocated phrases are base-generated in Top (see Chomsky 1977), hence in $\bar{\text{A}}$-position. For the EC of (90) to qualify as a variable at S-Structure, it is crucial that indexing of phrases base-generated in $\bar{\text{A}}$-position be possible at S-Structure.

I leave aside here certain questions that arise concerning the θ-Criterion at D- and S-Structure in constructions like (90).

37. The idea that the bare quantifiers of (90) enter into an $\bar{\text{A}}$-chain with the EC that they bind is rendered plausible by the fact that they obligatorily "reconstruct" into the EC for the purposes of various grammatical phenomena. For discussion, see chapter 1.

38. Apparent extraction from island constructions and COD constructions give analogous results (as expected, if they do involve pro rather than a variable):

(i) a. *Qualcosa$_i$ se ne va via sempre   senza fare e_i.
     something he always goes away without doing
   b. *Qualcosa$_i$ è spesso difficile da fare e_i in tali circostanze.
     something is often difficult to do   in such circumstances

Note that in (ia) the relation between the quantifier and the EC can be unbounded:

(ii) Qualcosa, penso di poter fare e anch'io.
    something I think I can do too

(ib) could also be excluded by some requirement on the referentiality of subject NPs (see Guéron 1980).

39. Similar results obtain in parasitic gap and COD constructions. In (i) *quanti pazienti* cannot be in the scope of *ogni medico*,

(i) Quanti pazienti$_i$ hanno fatto entrare t_i
how many patients did they let in
perché ogni medico potesse visitare e_i?
so that each doctor could visit

nor can the quantified NP *molti pazienti* be in the scope of *ogni medico* in (ii), though it can in (iii):

(ii) Molti pazienti$_i$ sono difficili da presentare e_i ad ogni medico.
many patients are difficult to introduce   to each doctor

(iii) Ho presentato molti pazienti ad ogni medico.
I introduced   many patients to each doctor

Facts like these are hardly surprising. As a matter of fact, they do not bear on the choice between the *Wh*-Movement and the pro analyses of parasitic and COD gaps. See Oraviita and Taraldsen 1984, Haïk 1985, and Chomsky 1986b, sec. 10 for arguments that "Reconstruction" is in general impossible into parasitic gaps, and Chomsky 1981, sec. 5.4 for evidence supporting a similar conclusion for COD gaps. See also Barss 1986, chap. 4.

40. For discussion of other cases that apparently require analyzing an Ā-bound EC as pro rather than as a pure variable, see Nishigauchi and Roeper 1987, Cardinaletti 1989b, and Sirbu-Dumitrescu 1989, in preparation.

41. Bennis and Hoekstra (1984–85) and Koster (1984) make a similar proposal on independent grounds.

42. As noted earlier, a pure *Wh*-Movement analysis runs into similar problems. If it treats adjunct PPs as absolute islands, as in earlier versions of bounding theory, then it will account for the unacceptability of (125b), but it will be unable to account for the relative acceptability of (125a). If, on the other hand, it allows for an escape route out of adjunct PPs (for NPs), as Chomsky (1986b) suggests, then it will account for (125a) but will fail in the case of (125b).

43. This is noted by (among others) Ross (1967), Chomsky (1977, 1981, 314) for COD constructions, and Engdahl (1983) for parasitic gap constructions (also see Chomsky 1982, 52). The same restriction appears to hold for constructions of apparent extraction from islands, as in (ia) versus (ib),

(i) a. ?Il libro   che se ne andarono via dopo aver rubato e...
the book that they went away   after stealing
    b. *?Il libro   che se ne andarono via dopo che loro figlio aveva rubato e...
the book that they went away   after their son had stolen

and from *wh*-islands (Rizzi 1982, chap. 2, Chomsky 1981). Bordelois (1985) also notes that overt lexical subjects render a parasitic gap in their domain more marginal (for a similar observation concerning COD constructions, see Chomsky 1981, 314):

(ii) a. El poema que todos admiramos al leer...
the poem that we all admired   when reading
    b. *El poema que todos admiramos al leer el autor...
the poem that we all admired   when the author reading
(Compare: *El poema que todos admiramos al leerlo el autor...*)

This is apparently true of pied piping as well (see Nanni and Stillings 1978, from which (iiia) is drawn, Cinque 1981–82, and Ishihara 1984:

(iii) a.   The elegant parties, (*for us) to be admitted to one of which was a privilege, had usually been held at Delmonico's.

   b.   Paolo, per aver   (*?il figlio) invitato il quale, nessuno vorrà
         Paolo for having   the son invited whom   nobody will want
         andare alla festa, . . .
         to go to the party

I have no account for this restriction.

44. That such phrases as *whose book, which boy*, and *how tall* should be *wh*-phrases independently of (130b) is motivated in Kayne 1983. Note that (130b) could possibly be a special case of a more general principle of feature (upward) percolation such as (i):

(i) Some feature F of Y may percolate (upward) to X only if X is a g-projection of (the governor of) Y.

Prepositions are governors, though not "structural" governors in Italian-type languages (see Kayne 1984, chap. 3 and 8). Thus, as the contrast between (ia) and (ib) shows, they will start a g-projection in pied piping, though not in Ā-bound pro constructions where the EC needs a structural governor to license it:

(i) a.   Gianni, [aver scritto   [a [l quale]]] è stato un errore, . . .
         Gianni having written to whom   was a mistake

   b.   *Gianni, che abbiamo invitato *t* [senza scrivere [a [pro]]], . . .
         Gianni who we invited   without writing to

45. Certain cases of pied piping of an adjunct within a larger constituent appear to be possible:

(i) a.   Anna, partire senza la quale sarebbe un errore, . . .
         Anna to leave without whom would be an error

   b.   L'esame,   dormire durante il quale
         the examination sleeping during which
         può significare essere bocciati, . . .
         may mean failing it

   c.   I Rossi,   arrivare senza avvisare   i quali può essere scortese, . . .
         the Rossis to arrive without notifying whom may be unkind

However, the class is apparently quite limited and clearly definable. (ia–c) differ minimally from both (133b) and (131b)/(132b): from the latter, in that the adjunct is head-governed by a [+V] head; and from the former, in that the highest Spec CP of the pied-piped constituent is adjacent to the relative clause head.

   Adapting an idea of Longobardi's (forthcoming), I suggest that these contrasts become understandable if it is assumed that in (i) the adjunct actually moves at LF to a position adjacent to the relative clause head. Such movement is instead excluded in (133b)/(131)–(132). Consider some minimal contrasts:

(ii) a.   *Anna, invece di partire senza la quale faremo di tutto
          Anna instead of leaving without whom we'll try
          per convincerla, . . .
          to convince her

b. *L'esame,   pur senza aver dormito durante il quale
   the examination even without sleeping   during which
   siamo stati bocciati, . . .
   we have failed
c. *I Rossi,   prima di arrivare senza avvisare   i quali
   the Rossis before arriving   without notifying whom
   dovremmo pensarci due volte, . . .
   we should think it over

(ii) is ill formed compared to (i) presumably because the Spec CP to which the adjunct moves is not adjacent to the relative clause head (this presupposes that real LF *Wh*-Movement is substitution, not adjunction).

(iiia–b) (also see (131b)) are also expected to be ill formed in opposition to (i) if APs and NPs lack Comp and/or As and Ns are not structural governors for traces of *Wh*-Movement:

(iii) a. *Maria, nessuna partenza senza la quale è triste, . . .
        Maria no departure   without whom is sad
     b. *La sconfitta, le recriminazioni dopo la quale sono inutili, . . .
        the defeat   any recrimination after which   is useless

To sum up, the only apparent exception to pied piping an adjunct within a larger constituent is in cases where the adjunct is head-governed by a [+V] head and the matrix CP is adjacent to the relative clause head. The contrast with the other, impossible cases makes sense if we assume that the case in point has an option that the others do not: namely, actual movement of the adjunct at LF to the Spec of the matrix CP.

46. Given that the revised CC subsumes the (Sentential) Subject and Adjunct Conditions, it is thus far virtually identical to Huang's (1982) Condition on Extraction Domains (CED), though it differs from it, I assume, in holding uniformly of S-Structure and LF, without parametrization. I also take it not to be sufficient for genuine movement. There is a residue, which in Huang's system fell under Subjacency. See chapter 1 for discussion.

47. Stowell (1986), essentially following Rizzi (1982, chap. 2) and Chomsky (1981), relates the tense effect to the bounding nodes for Subjacency. (Also see Chomsky 1986b, sec. 7.) A Subjacency-based account for the tense effect in our constructions does not immediately carry over to the analogous effect found in pied piping (assuming the two effects to be related).

48. Haïk (1985) also proposes movement at LF of the parasitic pro.

49. The presence of the phrase *che ieri* 'but yesterday' under the scope of the negation is motivated by the necessity of preventing the adverbial itself [$_\alpha$ *senza*. . .] from being under the scope of negation, thus voiding the minimality effect induced by *non*. This is due to the fact that relatives (typically appositives) can be "parasitic" on CLLD, thus falling under the amalgamation case discussed in section 2.4. See (i), where the adverbial is necessarily under the scope of the negation:

(i) a. Senza salutare Gianni, credo che non siano partiti.
       without greeting Gianni I think that they did not leave

   b. Gianni, senza salutare il quale, credo che non siano partiti, ...
      Gianni without greeting whom I think that they did not leave

50. Less clear is the role of pied piping in COD constructions, where its application does not seem to be analogously called for. I leave this problem open.

   For a different account of the tense effect in parasitic gap constructions (and *wh*-islands), see Frampton 1990.

51. But see note 53. Contrasts of this type, although known for some time, were first discussed systematically by Chung and McCloskey (1983), within a different framework.

52. Note in fact that (1-) Subjacency is violated in both (147a) and (147b), repeated here as (i) and (ii), even assuming the VMH:

(i)   This is a paper$_i$ that we need to find [$_{NP}$ someone$_k$ [$_{CP}$[$_{IP}$ who$_k$ understands t_i]]].

(ii) *This is a paper$_i$ that we need to find [$_{NP}$ someone$_k$ [$_{CP}$ O_k that [$_{IP}$ we can intimidate t_k with t_i]]].

Movement of the operator binding t_i crosses at least two barriers (CP and NP, by inheritance) in both cases.

53. By contrast with (147b), however, Richard Kayne has noted certain cases of relativization on a nonsubject (respecting Pesetsky's Path Containment Condition) that do appear to be relatively well formed. See (i), for example, cited by Frampton (1990, fn. 21):

(i)   A wall$_i$ that [anything$_j$ you put t_j on e_i] would ruin t_t . . .

So it might be that such cases as (147b) are ill formed for independent reasons.

54. This implies that the computation of g-projections *can* take place before the LF movement of *who*.

55. If *Wh*-Movement of a subject in Italian is always from a postverbal position (Rizzi 1982, chap. 4), then it will never be vacuous. Nonetheless, essentially the same contrasts obtain. Compare (ia–c) with (147a–b)/(156), of which they are translations:

(i) a. ?Questo è un articolo$_i$ che dobbiamo trovare qualcuno che capisca t_i.
     b. *Questo è un articolo$_i$ che dobbiamo trovare qualcuno con cui spaventare t_i.
     c. *Questo è un articolo$_i$ che dobbiamo trovare qualcuno che siamo tutti d'accordo che capisce t_i.

I suggest that, although (ia) is ill formed with postverbal extraction, just like (ib–c), it is well formed with the non-*Wh*-Movement resumptive strategy open to pro-drop languages illustrated in (ii) (with irrelevant structure omitted) (on the resumptive strategy, see Taraldsen 1978, Rizzi 1982, Chomsky 1981):

(ii) ...[qualcuno$_i$ [$_{CP}$[ ] che$_i$ [$_{IP}$ pro$_i$ I$_i$ [capisca t]]]]

By Spec/Head and Head/Head agreement, CP bears the index of pro, which coincides with the index of the head NP. The resumptive strategy will not suffice to rescue (ic), where the g-projections of t_i will stop at the relative clause IP.

56. Even the compounding of two CNPs of the N-complement type gives rather
marginal results, despite the fact that g-projections can be formed exclusively via
selection by a head in this case. See (122b), repeated here:

(122) b.*Carlo$_i$, che ci siamo presentati [con la speranza di aumentare
        Carlo   who we turned up   with the hope   of increasing
        [le probabilità di salvare e_i]], ...
        the probabilities of saving

This might suggest the necessity of further tightening the notion of g-projection for
pied-piping purposes.

    This tightening is in fact independently supported. See the contrast between
(ia–b) and (ii), all of which are permitted by (130), even under the stricter formulation of g-projection discussed above:

(i)   a. Carlo, poter   dire   di aver tentato di superare il quale
         Carlo to be able to say to have tried   to surpass   whom
         non è certo un vanto, ...
         is certainly not something to boast
      b. Carlo, ogni discussione sulla correttezza   dei comportamenti del quale
         Carlo any discussion   on the correctness of the behavior   of whom
         sarebbe fuori luogo, ...
         would be irrelevant

(ii) *Carlo, la speranza di aumentare le probabilità   di salvare il quale
        Carlo the hope   of increasing the probabilities of saving whom
        è tenue, ...
        is flimsy

Despite the heaviness of all of these sentences there is a clear contrast between (i)
and (ii). One difference is that each intermediate maximal projection in (i) is selected
by the same category: $[+V, -N]$ for (ia), $[-V, +N]$ for (ib) (disregarding PPs).
In (ii), on the other hand, the selection is not uniform in terms of category
membership. The lowest is $[-V, +N]$, the middle one $[+V, -N]$, and the highest
again $[-V, +N]$.

    This might suggest a uniformity requirement on the government of intermediate
maximal projections, to the effect that each should be selected by the same
category. However, this suggestion appears to be contradicted by the relative
well-formedness of the following cases:

(iii) a. Gianni, l'idea   di dover emulare   il quale
         Gianni the idea of having to emulate whom
         non ci rendeva facile la vita, ...
         rendered our life difficult
      b. Carlo, ammettere la correttezza   dei comportamenti del quale
         Carlo to admit   the correctness of the behavior   of whom
         non era cosa facile, ...
         was not easy

What distinguishes (ii) and (iii) may be that in the latter the category of the selector
changes once, whereas in the former it changes twice, "reactivating" a previously
abandoned choice (which recalls the discussion in the text). I leave the question

open. Clearly, further reflection is needed before a conclusion on pied piping can be drawn from these facts with any confidence.

57. In Chomsky's (1982) functional definition of ECs, appeal to Principle C to account for strong crossover is rendered superfluous. See, however, Sportiche 1985 and the works cited in note 28.

58. The fact that (null) names must be A-free in the root sentence, not just in the domain of the operator binding them (unlike true variables), forces Stowell and Lasnik to claim that *tough* constructions, where this is clearly not the case, involve a kind of identity assertion similar to that found in equative structures like *That man is John Smith*, where the name is apparently also not A-free.

59. This requires a different treatment for the absence of weak crossover effects in topicalization and appositive relatives, which I regard as true movement constructions leaving a real variable (see section 3.4).

With respect to apparent extractions from islands, the relevant judgments seem delicate. Since such extractions are best in appositives in the first place, absence of weak crossover reduces in these cases to the independent absence of weak crossover in appositive relatives. In interrogatives, on the other hand, weak crossover effects should be detectable.

The contrast between (ia) and (ib) conforms to the expectation, although it is in part vitiated by the very marginal status of such extractions with interrogatives:

(i) a. ?Giorgio$_i$, che sono partito senza riuscire   a convincere suo$_i$ padre
        Giorgio who I left   without succeeding in convincing his father
        a lasciare partire e_i con me, . . .
        to let leave   with me
    b. *?Chi$_i$ sei partito   senza convincere   suo$_i$ padre
        who did you leave without convincing his father
        a lasciare partire e_i con te?
        to let leave   with you

60. Pesetsky reduces crossing effects to the violation of a general condition on paths in a tree, which is an elaboration of Kayne's (1983) Connectedness Condition. A proposal to extend (his version of) Pesetsky's condition on paths to all $\bar{A}$-bound elements (including base-generated and lexical ones) is also made by May (1985, chap. 5).

61. In (171)–(173) the variant with an overt pronominal is in fact the only one possible in Italian. This is arguably due to independent reasons, from which I abstract here (for discussion, see Cinque 1983b, 1990c). For some English speakers, the variant with a gap in (170)–(173) is slightly preferable to the one with an overt pronominal. I leave this question open here, noting that it might be related to the Avoid Pronoun Principle of Chomsky 1981. For a general discussion of these structures, also see Faraci 1974.

62. That the complement of such adjective qualifiers as *too* (and *enough*) need not be an open sentence was pointed out by H. Lasnik. (See Chomsky 1982, 32, which is the source of (176).)

63. But see Safir 1984, Epstein 1984, and Engdahl 1985, among others, for evidence against the Bijection Principle. Note also that the same contrast as that between

(183a) and (183b) is found in the subject position of tensed clauses in pro-drop languages, where the gap is pro (in fact necessarily pro, in (ia), if the conclusion in note 55 is correct):

(i) a. ??Un uomo$_i$ che quelli che dicevano   che *pro*$_i$ era disonesto
       a man   who those who used to say that   was dishonest
       in realtà non conoscevano t_i...
       in fact   did not know

   b. *Un uomo$_i$ che quelli che dicevano che *lui*$_i$ era disonesto in realtà non conoscevano t_i...

64. However, the variant of the pronominal without phonetic realization requires an empty operator at S-Structure to identify it, in the manner discussed above.

65. I assume that it is only when it is Ā-bound by an operator that such an EC becomes an argument (a variable).

66. Aoun and Clark (1985) object to this, citing cases like (ia–b),

(i) a. John wondered [which pictures of himself]$_i$ Mary liked e_i.

   b. [How proud of himself]$_i$ does [John think [Bill was e_i]]?

in which they claim *himself* can be bound to *Jonn*, suggesting that the governing category is the matrix CP, not the CP containing the trace. If the observation appears correct for (ia), it is however questionable for (ib). According to my informants, it is *Bill*, not *John*, that is the "antecedent" of *himself*, as becomes clear when a grammatically impossible "antecedent" is substituted for *Bill*:

(ii) *[How proud of himself]$_i$ does [John think [Mary was t_i]]?

A parallel conclusion can be drawn on the basis of reciprocals:

(iii) *[How proud of each other]$_i$ do [they think [Bill was t_i]]?

(See also Barss 1986, 1988.) Considering these data and those cited in the text, it is picture noun reflexivization that stands out as being special. Hence, it seems that no cogent argument can be built on the basis of (ia) against the conclusion discussed in the text.

67. A possible way to avoid this conclusion would consist in reserving obligatory Reconstruction for elements in Top while exempting from it elements in Spec CP. This is, however, dubious. It would imply that the VP of such forms as (188a) (which show obligatory Reconstruction) would necessarily have to be in Top (with an associated movement of an empty VP to Spec CP, as in Topicalization, to account for the *Wh*-Movement nature of the construction). The question would thus arise why an empty VP but no lexical VP should undergo direct movement to Spec CP.

68. This implies that the empty, or overt, phrase in the Spec CP of relative clauses cannot be an anaphor, contrary to what is suggested by Cinque 1981–82, Hendrick 1982, and Bouchard 1984. Their essential results can still be derived, though, following certain suggestions made by Kayne (1984, 183–184).

69. See Cinque 1981–82 for discussion of (193a–b) and Chomsky 1980a for discussion of (193c).

70. A reviewer has pointed out to me that the ill-formedness of such cases as (i)

(i) *I was looking for a man a picuture of whom to take.

may constitute a problem. Deletion of the *wh*-NP would violate recoverability, yet retention of the NP apparently leads to ungrammatically. In French and Italian, such cases are quite marginal too, though not entirely impossible (see Kayne 1976, Cinque 1981–82), which might suggest that a distinct factor is involved in (i).

71. Reasons against reducing the parasitic gap phenomenon to across-the-board phenomena are presented by Engdahl (1983) and Koster (1987, sec. 6.4) (also see Chomsky 1982, fn. 31). Nonetheless, Pesetsky (1982), Huybregts and Van Riemsdijk (1985), and Haïk (1985) attempt, in somewhat different ways, to relate the two phenomena.

72. The overt *wh*-phrase in (195b), where present, would have to be base-generated and treated somehow as "analogic" (see Chomsky 1982, 60).

73. Also see Browning 1987. I differ from Browning's analysis here in reserving $O_i = \text{pro}_i$ just for relative, cleft, and topicalized structures, and the like, for which I assume that movement (and $\bar{A}$-chain formation) is involved, unlike what happens in the constructions in (1).

References

Anderson, M. (1978). "NP-Preposing in Noun Phrases." In *Proceedings of the Eighth Annual Meeting, NELS*. GLSA, University of Massachusetts, Amherst.

Aoun, J. (1985). *A Grammar of Anaphora*. MIT Press, Cambridge, Mass.

Aoun, J. (1986). *Generalized Binding*. Foris, Dordrecht.

Aoun, J., and R. Clark (1985). "On Non-Overt Operators." In G. Gilligan et al., eds., *Studies in Syntax*. (Southern California Occasional Papers in Linguistics 10.) Department of Linguistics, University of Southern California.

Aoun, J., N. Hornstein, D. Lightfoot, and A. Weinberg (1987). "Two Types of Locality." *Linguistic Inquiry* 18, 537–577.

Aoun, J., N. Hornstein, and D. Sportiche (1981). "Some Aspects of Wide Scope Quantification." *Journal of Linguistic Research* 1, 69–95.

Aoun, J., and D. Sportiche (1981). "The Domain of Weak Cross-over Restrictions." In *MIT Working Papers in Linguistics* 3. Department of Linguistics and Philosophy, MIT.

Bach, E., and G. Horn (1976). "Remarks on 'Conditions on Transformations'." *Linguistic Inquiry* 7, 265–300.

Baltin, M. (1982). "A Landing Site Theory of Movement Rules." *Linguistic Inquiry* 13, 1–38.

Barbaud, P. (1976). "Constructions superlatives et structures apparentées." *Linguistic Analysis* 2, 125–174.

Barss, A. (1986). *Chains and Anaphoric Dependence*. Doctoral dissertation, MIT.

Barss, A. (1988). "Paths, Connectivity and Featureless Empty Categories." In Cardinaletti, Cinque, and Giusti 1988.

Barss, A., and H. Lasnik (1986). "A Note on Anaphora and Double Objects." *Linguistic Inquiry* 17, 347–354.

Bedzyk, F. (1987). "Successive Cyclic Wh-Movement in Bulgarian and Icelandic." Ms., Cornell University.

Belletti, A. (1979). "Sintagmi nominali quantificati e costruzioni dislocate a sinistra." *Annali della Scuola Normale Superiore di Pisa* 9(4), 1525–1568.

Belletti, A. (1980). "Italian Quantified NPs in LF." *Journal of Italian Linguistics* 5, 1–18.

Belletti, A. (1988). "Unaccusatives as Case Assigners." *Linguistic Inquiry* 19, 1–34.

Belletti, A., L. Brandi, and L. Rizzi, eds. (1981). *Theory of Markedness in Generative Grammar*. Scuola Normale Superiore, Pisa.

Belletti, A., and L. Rizzi (1981). "The Syntax of *ne*: Some Theoretical Implications." *The Linguistic Review* 1, 117–154.

Belletti, A., and L. Rizzi (1988). "Psych-Verbs and Th-theory." *Natural Language and Linguistic Theory* 6, 291–352.

Benincà, P. (1986). "Il lato sinistro della frase italiana." *Association of Teachers of Italian Journal* 47, 57–85.

Benincà, P. (1988). "L'ordine delle parole e le costruzioni marcate." In L. Renzi, ed. *Grande grammatica italiana di consultazione*. Il Mulino, Bologna.

Benincà, P., ed., (1989). *Dialect Variation and the Theory of Grammar*. Foris, Dordrecht.

Bennis, H. (1986). *Gaps and Dummies*. Foris, Dordrecht.

Bennis, H., and T. Hoekstra (1984–85). "Gaps and Parasitic Gaps." *The Linguistic Review* 4, 29–87.

Bennis, H., and T. Hoekstra (1985). "Parasitic Gaps in Dutch." In *Proceedings of the Fifteenth Annual Meeting, NELS*. GLSA, University of Massachusetts, Amherst.

Bordelois, I. (1985). "Parasitic Gaps: Extensions of Restructuring." Ms., University of Utrecht.

Borer, H. (1981). "On the definition of Variable." *Journal of Linguistic Research* 1(3), 7–40.

Borer, H. (1984a). *Parametric Syntax*. Foris, Dordrecht.

Borer, H. (1984b). "Restrictive Relatives in Modern Hebrew." *Natural Language and Linguistic Theory* 2, 219–260.

Bouchard, D. (1984). *On the Content of Empty Categories*. Foris, Dordrecht.

Bracco, C. (1980). "On the Island Character of Italian 'Quanto' Comparatives." *Journal of Italian Linguistics* 5, 19–46.

Brame, M. (1980). *"hope."* *Linguistic Analysis* 6, 247–259.

Brody, M. (1984). "On Contextual Definitions and the Role of Chains." *Linguistic Inquiry* 15, 355–380.

Browning, M. A. (1987). *Null Operator Constructions*. Doctoral dissertation, MIT.

Browning, M. A. (1989a). "Comments on 'Relativized Minimality'." Paper presented at the II Princeton Workshop on Comparative Grammar, Princeton University, April 1989.

Browning, M. A. (1989b). "ECP ≠ CED." *Linguistic Inquiry* 20, 481–491.

Burzio, L. (1981). *Intransitive Verbs and Italian Auxiliaries.* Doctoral dissertation, MIT.

Burzio, L. (1986). *Italian Syntax: A Government-Binding Approach.* Reidel, Dordrecht.

Calabrese, A. (1982). "Alcune ipotesi sulla struttura informazionale della frase in italiano e sul suo rapporto con la struttura fonologica." *Rivista di grammatica generativa* 7, 3–78.

Calabrese, A. (1984). "Multiple Questions and Focus in Italian." In W. de Geest and T. Putseys, eds., *Sentential Complementation.* Foris, Dordrecht.

Cardinaletti, A. (1987). "Aspetti sintattici della estraposizione della frase relativa." *Rivista di grammatica generativa* 12, 3–59.

Cardinaletti, A. (1989a). *Impersonal Constructions and Sentential Arguments in German.* Unipress, Padua.

Cardinaletti, A. (1989b). "Subject/Object Asymmetries in German Null-Topic Constructions and the Status of Spec C'." Ms., Università di Venezia.

Cardinaletti, A., G. Cinque, and G. Giusti, eds. (1988). *Constituent Structure: Papers from the XI GLOW Conference.* Foris, Dordrecht.

Cattell, R. (1976). "Constraints on Movement Rules." *Language* 52, 18–50.

Chomsky, N. (1965). *Aspects of the Theory of Syntax.* MIT Press, Cambridge, Mass.

Chomsky, N. (1976). "Conditions on Rules of Grammar." *Linguistic Analysis* 2, 303–351.

Chomsky, N. (1977). "On *Wh*-Movement." In P. Culicover, T. Wasow, and A. Akmajian, eds., *Formal Syntax.* Academic Press, New York.

Chomsky, N. (1980a). "On Binding." *Linguistic Inquiry* 11, 1–46.

Chomsky, N. (1980b). *Rules and Representations.* Basil Blackwell, Oxford.

Chomsky, N. (1981). *Lectures on Government and Binding.* Foris, Dordrecht.

Chomsky, N. (1982). *Some Concepts and Consequences of the Theory of Government and Binding.* MIT Press, Cambridge, Mass.

Chomsky, N. (1986a). *Knowledge of Language: Its Nature, Origin, and Use.* Praeger, New York.

Chomsky, N. (1986b). *Barriers.* MIT Press, Cambridge, Mass.

Chomsky, N. (1988). "Some Notes on Economy of Derivation and Representation." Ms., MIT.

Chomsky, N., and H. Lasnik (1977). "Filters and Control." *Linguistic Inquiry* 8, 425–504.

Chung, S., and J. McCloskey (1983). "On the Interpretation of Certain Island Facts in GPSG." *Linguistic Inquiry* 14, 704–713.

Cinque, G. (1977). "The Movement Nature of Left Dislocation." *Linguistic Inquiry* 8, 397–411.

Cinque, G. (1978a). "Towards a Unified Treatment of Island Constraints." In W. U. Dressler and W. Meid, eds., *Proceedings of the Twelfth International Congress of Linguists*. Innsbrücker Beiträge zur Sprachwissenschaft. (Also included in Cinque 1990b.)

Cinque, G. (1978b). "La sintassi dei pronomi relativi 'cui' e 'quale' nell'italiano contemporaneo." *Rivista di grammatica generativa* 3, 31–126.

Cinque, G. (1981). "On Keenan and Comrie's Primary Relativization Constraint." *Linguistic Inquiry* 12, 293–308.

Cinque, G. (1981–82). "On the Theory of Relative Clauses and Markedness." *The Linguistic Review* 1, 247–294.

Cinque, G. (1982). "Constructions with Left Peripheral Phrases, 'Connectedness,' Move α and ECP." Ms., Università di Venezia. (Also included in Cinque 1990b.)

Cinque, G. (1983a). "Island Effects, Subjacency, ECP/Connectedness and Reconstruction." Ms., Università di Venezia.

Cinque, G. (1983b). "Su una differenza tra l'italiano e l'inglese nelle costruzioni 'ad ellissi dell'oggetto'." *Rivista di grammatica generativa* 8, 127–151.

Cinque, G. (1983c). " 'Topic' Constructions in Some European Languages and 'Connectedness'." In K. Ehlich and H. van Riemsdijk, eds., *Connectedness in Sentence, Discourse and Text*. (Tilburg Studies in Language and Literature 4.) KUB, Tilburg.

Cinque, G. (1986). "Bare Quantifiers, Quantified NPs and the Notion of Operator at S-Structure." *Rivista di grammatica generativa* 11, 9–10. (Also included in Cinque 1990b.)

Cinque, G. (1988). "On *Si* Constructions and the Theory of *Arb*." *Linguistic Inquiry* 19, 521–581.

Cinque, G. (1989). " 'Long' Wh-movement and Referentiality." Paper presented at th II Princeton Workshop on Comparative Grammar, Princeton University, April 1989.

Cinque, G. (1990a). "Ergative Adjectives and the Lexicalist Hypothesis." *Natural Language and Linguistic Theory* 8, 1–39.

Cinque, G. (1990b). *Studies in Italian and Comparative Syntax*. Foris, Dordrecht.

Cinque, G. (1990c). "On a Difference between English and Italìan 'Complement Object Deletion' Constructions." Forthcoming in J. Mascaró and M. Nespor, eds., *Grammar in Progress: GLOW Essays for Henk van Riemsdijk*. Foris, Dordrecht.

Comorovski, I. (1985). "Discourse-Linked WH-Phrases." Paper presented at the Annual Meeting of the LSA, Seattle, Wash.

Comorovski, I. (1989). "Discourse-Linking and the WH-Island Constraint." In *Proceedings of the Nineteenth Annual Meeting, NELS*. GLSA, University of Massachusetts, Amherst.

Condon, S. (1982). "More Syntax and Semantics of Purpose Clauses." In *Texas Linguistic Forum* 21. Department of Linguistics, University of Texas, Austin.

Contreras, H. (1984). "A Note on Parasitic Gaps." *Linguistic Inquiry* 15, 698–701.

Czepluch, H. (1982–83). "Case Theory and the Dative Construction." *The Linguistic Review* 2, 1–38.

De Vincenzi, M. (1989). *Syntactic Parsing Strategies in a Null Subject Language*. Doctoral dissertation, University of Massachusetts, Amherst.

Dobrovie-Sorin, C. (1987). *Chaînes thématiques en roumain*. Thèse de Doctorat d'Etat, Université de Paris VII.

Dobrovie-Sorin, C. (1990). "Clitic Doubling, WH-Movement, and Quantification in Romanian." *Linguistic Inquiry* 21, 351–397.

Dolci, R. (1986). *Algunas construcciones con anteposición de constituyentes oracionales en español: Su determinación y analysis sintáctico*. Tesi di Laurea, Università di Venezia.

Emonds, J. (1970). *Root and Structure-Preserving Transformations*. Doctoral dissertation, MIT.

Engdahl, E. (1980a). *The Syntax and Semantics of Questions in Swedish*. Doctoral dissertation, University of Massachusetts, Amherst.

Engdahl, E. (1980b). "Wh-Constructions in Swedish and the Relevance of Subjacency." In *Proceedings of the Tenth Annual Meeting, NELS*. GLSA, University of Massachusetts, Amherst.

Engdahl, E. (1983). "Parasitic Gaps." *Linguistics and Philosophy* 6, 5–34.

Engdahl, E. (1985). "Parasitic Gaps, Resumptive Pronouns and Subject Extractions." *Linguistics* 23, 3–44.

Epstein, S. D. (1984). "A Note on Functional Determination and Strong Crossover." *The Linguistic Review* 3, 299–305.

Ernout, A., and F. Thomas (1964). *Syntaxe latine*. Klincksiek, Paris.

Faraci, R. (1974). *Aspects of the Grammar of Infinitives and For-Phrases*. Doctoral dissertation, MIT.

Felix, S. W. (1985). "Parasitic Gaps in German." In *Groninger Arbeiten zur Germanistischen Linguistik* 22, 1–46. (Also in W. Abraham, ed. (1985). *Erklärende Syntax des Deutschen*. Gunter Narr, Tübingen.)

Fillmore, C. (1965). *Indirect Object Constructions in English and the Ordering of Transformations*. Mouton, The Hague.

Fodor, J. D. (1978). "Parsing Strategies and Constraints on Transformations." *Linguistic Inquiry* 9, 427–473.

Fodor, J. D., and I. A. Sag (1982). "Referential and Quantificational Indefinites." *Linguistics and Philosophy* 5, 355–398.

Frampton, J. (1990). "Parasitic Gaps and the Theory of *Wh*-Chains." *Linguistic Inquiry* 21, 49–77.

Geis, M. (1986a). "On the Superiority of Monostratal to Multistratal Accounts of Adverb Preposing." *ESCOL* 2, 67–79.

Geis, M. (1986b). "Pragmatic Determinants of Adverb Preposing." In *Papers from the Parasession on Pragmatics and Grammatical Theory at the 22nd Regional Meeting of the Chicago Linguistic Society*. Chicago Linguistic Society, Chicago, Ill.

George, L. (1980). *Analogical Generalizations of Natural Language Syntax*. Doctoral dissertation, MIT.

Georgopoulos, C. P. (1985). *The Syntax of Variable Binding in Paluan*. Doctoral dissertation, UCSD.

Giorgi, A., and G. Longobardi (1990). *The Syntax of Noun Phrases*. Cambridge University Press, Cambridge.

Giusti, G. (1989). "*Zu*-Infinitivals and the Structure of IP in German." Ms., Università di Venezia.

Grimshaw, J. (1986). "Subjacency and the S/S′ Parameter." *Linguistic Inquiry* 17, 364–369.

Grimshaw, J. (1990). *Argument Structure*. MIT Press, Cambridge, Mass.

Groos, A., and H. van Riemsdijk (1981). "Matching Effects in Free Relatives: A Parameter of Core Grammar." In Belletti, Brandi, and Rizzi 1981.

Gruppo di Padova (1974). "L'ordine dei sintagmi nella frase." In M. Medici and A. Sangregorio, eds., *Fenomeni morfologici e sintattici nell'italiano contemporaneo, vol. 1*. Bulzoni, Roma.

Guéron, J. (1979). "Relations de coréférence dans la phrase et dans le discours." *Langue française* 44, 42–79.

Guéron, J. (1980). "On the Syntax and Semantics of PP Extraposition." *Linguistic Inquiry* 11, 637–678.

Guéron, J. (1984). "Topicalization Structures and Constraints on Coreference." *Lingua* 63, 139–174.

Guéron, J., H.-G. Obenauer, and J.-Y. Pollock, eds. (1985). *Grammatical Representation*. Foris, Dordrecht.

Gundel, J. (1975). "Left Dislocation and the Role of Topic-Comment Structure in Linguistic Theory." In *Working Papers in Linguistics* 18. Ohio State University.

Haaften, T. van, R. Smits, and J. Vat (1983). "Left Dislocation, Connectedness and Reconstruction." In K. Ehlich and H. van Riemsdijk, eds., *Connectedness in Sentence, Discourse and Text*. KUB, Tilburg.

Haider, H. (1986). "Affect α: A Reply to Lasnik and Saito, 'On the Nature of Proper Government'." *Linguistic Inquiry* 17, 113–126.

Haider, H., and M., Prinzhorn, eds. (1986). *Verb Second Phenomena in Germanic Languages*. Foris, Dordrecht.

Haïk, I. (1984). "Indirect Binding." *Linguistic Inquiry* 15, 185–223.

Haïk, I. (1985). *The Syntax of Operators*. Doctoral dissertation, MIT.

Hantson, A. (1980). "*For, With* and *Without* as Non-finite Clause Introducers." Linguistic Agency, University of Trier.

Hendrick, R. (1982). "Construing Relative Pronouns." *Linguistic Analysis* 9, 205–224.

Higginbotham, J. (1980a). "Anaphora and GB: Some Preliminary Remarks." In *Proceedings of the Tenth Annual Meeting, NELS*. GLSA, University of Massachusetts, Amherst.

Higginbotham, J. (1980b). "Pronouns and Bound Variables." *Linguistic Inquiry* 11, 679–708.

Higginbotham, J. (1983). "Logical Form, Binding, and Nominals." *Linguistic Inquiry* 14, 395–420.

Hirschbühler, P., and M.-L. Rivero (1983). "Non-matching Concealed Questions in Catalan and Spanish and the Projection Principle." *The Linguistic Review* 2, 331–363.

Hoekstra, T. (1984). *Transitivity*. Foris, Dordrecht.

Hornstein, N., and A. Weinberg (1988). "Logical Form. Its Existence and Its Properties." In Cardinaletti, Cinque, and Giusti (1988).

Huang, C.-T. J. (1982). *Logical Relations in Chinese and the Theory of Grammar*. Doctoral dissertation, MIT.

Huybregts, R. and H. van Riemsdijk (1985). "Parasitic Gaps and ATB." In *Proceedings of the Fifteenth Annual Meeting, NELS*. GLSA, University of Massachusetts, Amherst.

Ishihara, R. (1984). "Clausal Pied Piping: A Problem for GB." *Natural Language and Linguistic Theory* 2, 397–418.

Jaeggli, O. (1982). "*Topics in Romance Syntax*. Foris, Dordrecht.

Johnson, K. (1985). *A Case for Movement*. Doctoral dissertation, MIT.

Kaufman, E. S. (1974). "Navajo Spatial Enclitics: A Case for Unbounded Rightward Movement." *Linguistic Inquiry* 5, 507–533.

Kayne, R. (1975). *French Syntax*. MIT Press, Cambridge, Mass.

Kayne, R. (1976). "French Relative 'que'." In F. Hensey and M. Luján, eds., *Current Studies in Romance Linguistics*. Georgetown University Press, Washington, D.C.

Kayne, R. (1978). "Le condizioni sul legamento, il Collocamento dei clitici e lo Spostamento a sinistra dei quantificatori." *Rivista di grammatica generativa* 3, 147–171.

Kayne, R. (1979). "ECP Extensions." Ms., Université de Paris VIII. (Published as Kayne 1981b without the appendix.)

Kayne, R. (1980). "Extensions of Binding and Case-Marking." *Linguistic Inquiry* 11, 75–96.

Kayne, R. (1981a). "Two Notes on the NIC." In Belletti, Brandi, and Rizzi 1981. (Also included in Kayne 1984.)

Kayne, R. (1981b). "ECP Extensions." *Linguistic Inquiry* 12, 93–133. (Also included in Kayne 1984.)

Kayne, R. (1981c). "On Certain Differences between French and English." *Linguistic Inquiry* 12, 349–371.

Kayne, R. (1983). "Connectedness." *Linguistic Inquiry* 14, 223–249. (Also included in Kayne 1984.)

Kayne, R. (1984). *Connectedness and Binary Branching*. Foris, Dordrecht.

Kayne, R. (1985a). "Principles of Particle Constructions." In Guéron, Obenauer, and Pollock 1985.

Kayne, R. (1985b). "L'accord du participe passé en français et en italien." *Modèles linguistiques* 7, 73–89.

Kayne, R. (1989a). "Facets of Romance Past Participle Agreement." In Benincà 1989.

Kayne, R. (1989b). "Null Subjects and Clitic Climbing." In O. Jaeggli and K. Safir, eds., *The Null Subject Parameter*. Kluwer, Dordrecht.

Kenstowicz, M. (1987). "The Phonology and Syntax of Wh-Expressions in Tangale." *Phonology Yearbook* 4, 229–241.

Kiparsky, P., and C. Kiparsky (1970). "Fact." In M. Bierwisch and K. Heidolph, eds., *Progress in Linguistics*. Mouton, The Hague.

Kiss, É. K. (1985). "Parasitic Chains." *The Linguistic Review* 5, 41–74.

Klima, E. (1964). "Negation in English." In J. A. Fodor and J. J. Katz, eds., *The Structure of Language*. Prentice-Hall, Englewood Cliffs, N.J.

Koopman, H. (1984). *The Syntax of Verbs*. Foris, Dordrecht.

Koopman, H., and D. Sportiche (1982). "Variables and the Bijection Principle." *The Linguistic Review* 2, 139–160.

Koopman, H., and D. Sportiche (1985). "Theta-Theory and Extraction." *GLOW Newsletter 14*. Paper presented at the 1985 GLOW Colloquium in Brussels.

Koopman, H., and D. Sportiche (1986a). "Covert Categories and Theta-Theory." Ms., UCLA.

Koopman, H., and D. Sportiche (1986b). "A Note on Long Extraction in Vata and the ECP." *Natural Language and Linguistic Theory* 4, 357–374.

Koopman, H., and D. Sportiche (1988). "Subjects." Ms., UCLA.

Koster, J. (1978). *Locality Principles in Syntax*. Foris, Dordrecht.

Koster, J. (1984). "Global Harmony." Ms., University of Tilburg.

Koster, J. (1987). *Domains and Dynasties: The Radical Autonomy of Syntax*. Foris, Dordrecht.

Koster, J. (1989). "Left-Right Asymmetries in the Dutch Complementizer System." In D. Jaspers, W. Klooster, Y. Putseys, and P. Seuren, eds., *Sentential Complementation and the Lexicon: Studies in Honour of Wim de Geest*. Foris, Dordrecht.

Koster, J., and R. May (1982). "On the Constituency of Infinitives." *Language* 58, 117–143.

Kuno, S. (1975). "Conditions on Verb Phrase Deletion." *Foundations of Language* 13, 161–175

Lakoff, G. (1968). "Pronouns and Reference." Indiana University Linguistics Club, Indiana University, Bloomington.

Larson, R. (1985). "Bare-NP Adverbs." *Linguistic Inquiry* 16, 585–621.

Lasnik, H. (1972). *Analyses of Negation in English*. Doctoral dissertation, MIT.

Lasnik, H., and R. Fiengo (1974). "Complement Object Deletion." *Linguistic Inquiry* 5, 535–571.

Lasnik, H., and M. Saito (1984). "On the Nature of Proper Government." *Linguistic Inquiry* 15, 235–289.

Longobardi, G. (1983). "*Connectedness*, complementi circostanziali e soggiacenza." *Rivista di grammatica generativa* 5⟨1980⟩, 141–185.

Longobardi, G. (1985a). "Connectedness and Island Constraints." In Guéron, Obenauer, and Pollock 1985.

Longobardi, G. (1985b). "Connectedness, Scope, and C-Command." *Linguistic Inquiry* 16, 163–192.

Longobardi, G. (1985c). "The Theoretical Status of the Adjunct Condition." Ms., Scuola Normale Superiore, Pisa. (Published in Longobardi (1988.)

Longobardi, G. (1986). "L'estrazione dalle 'isole' e lo *scope* dei sintagmi quantificati." In Lichem, Mara, and Knaller, eds., *Parallela 2: Aspetti della sintassi dell'italiano contemporaneo*. Gunter Narr, Tübingen.

Longobardi, G. (1987a). "The Proper Treatment of ECP." Paper presented at the II Syntax Roundtable, Vienna, September 1987.

Longobardi, G. (1987b). "Extraction from NP and the Proper Notion of Head Government." Published as chapter 2 of Giorgi and Longobardi 1990.

Longobardi, G. (1988). *Symmetry Principles in Syntax*. Unipress, Padua.

Longobardi, G. (forthcoming). *Movement, Scope and Island Constraints*.

Lonzi, L. (1988). 'Tipi di gerundio." *Rivista di grammatica generativa* 13, 59–80.

McCloskey, J. (1989). "Resumptive Pronouns, Ā-Binding and Levels of Representation in Irish." To appear in R. Hendrick, ed., *The Syntax of the Modern Celtic Languages*. Academic Press, San Diego.

Maling, J. (1978). "An Asymmetry with Respect to *Wh*-Islands." *Linguistic Inquiry* 9, 75–89.

Manzini, R. (1980). "Sulla struttura di un tipo di frasi infinitivali italiane." *Studi Mediolatini e Volgari* 27, 125–137.

Manzini, R. (1983). *Restructuring and Reanalysis*. Doctoral dissertation, MIT.

Manzini, R. (1988). "Constituent Structure and Locality." In Cardinaletti, Cinque, and Giusti 1988.

May, R. (1985). *Logical Form: Its Structure and Derivation*. MIT Press, Cambridge, Mass.

May, R. (1988). "Bound Variable Anaphora." In R. M. Kempson, ed., *Mental Representations*. Cambridge University Press, Cambridge.

Montalbetti, M. (1983). "Pronouns and Binding Theory." Ms., MIT.

Montalbetti, M. (1984). *After Binding*. Doctoral dissertation, MIT.

Moro, A. (1988). "Per una teoria unificata delle frasi copulari." *Rivista di grammatica generativa* 13, 81–110.

Nanni, D., and J. Stillings (1978). "Three Remarks on Pied Piping." *Linguistic Inquiry* 9, 310–318.

Napoli, D. J. (1981). "Subject Pronouns: The Pronominal System of Italian vs. French." In *Papers from the 17th Regional Meeting of the Chicago Linguistic Society*. University of Chicago.

Nishigauchi, T., and T. Roeper (1987). "Deductive Parameters and the Growth of Empty Categories." In T. Roeper and E. Williams, eds., *Parameter Setting*. Reidel, Dordrecht.

Obenauer, H.-G. (1984–85). "On the Identification of Empty Categories." *The Linguistic Review* 4, 153–202.

Oehrle, R. (1976). *The Grammatical Status of the English Dative Alternation*. Doctoral dissertation, MIT.

Oraviita, I., and T. Taraldsen (1984). "Case Marking and Parasitic Gaps in Finnish." *Nordlyd* 8, 53–71.

Pesetsky, D. (1982). *Paths and Categories*. Doctoral dissertation, MIT.

Pesetsky, D. (1987). "*Wh*-in-situ: Movement and Unselective Binding." In E. Reuland and A. ter Meulen, eds., *The Representation of (In)definiteness*. MIT Press, Cambridge, Mass.

Pollock, J.-Y. (1985). "On Case and the Syntax of Infinitives in French." In Guéron, Obenauer, and Pollock 1985.

Pollock, J.-Y. (1986). "Sur la syntaxe de 'en' et le paramètre du sujet nul." In D. Couquaux and M. Ronat, eds., *La Grammaire modulaire*. Editions de Minuit, Paris.

Pollock, J.-Y. (1988). "Extraction from NP in French and English: A Case Study in Comparative Syntax." Ms., Université de Haute Bretagne, Rennes II.

Pollock, J.-Y. (1989). "Verb Movement, Universal Grammar, and the Structure of IP." *Linguistic Inquiry* 20, 365–424.

Postal, P. (1971). *Crossover Phenomena*. Holt, Rinehart and Winston, New York.

Reinhart, T. (1983). "Coreference and Bound Anaphora: A Restatement of the Anaphora Question." *Linguistics and Philosophy* 6, 47–88.

Reuland, E. (1983). "Governing -*ing*." *Linguistic Inquiry* 14, 101–136.

Riemsdijk, H. van (1978). *A Case Study in Syntactic Markedness* Foris, Dordrecht.

Riemsdijk, H. van, and E. Williams (1981). "NP-Structure." *The Linguistic Review* 1, 171–217.

Rizzi, L. (1981). "Nominative Marking in Italian Infinitives." In F. Heny, ed., *Binding and Filtering*. Croom Helm, London.

Rizzi, L. (1982) *Issues in Italian Syntax*. Foris, Dordrecht.

Rizzi, L. (1985). "Conditions de bonne formation sur les chaînes." *Modèles linguistiques* 7, 119–157.

Rizzi, L. (1986). "Null Objects in Italian and the Theory of *pro*." *Linguistic Inquiry* 17, 501–557.

Rizzi, L. (1988). "Il sintagma preposizionale." In L. Renzi, ed., *Grande grammatica italiana di consultazione*. Il Mulino, Bologna.

Rizzi, L. (1990). *Relativized Minimality*. MIT Press, Cambridge, Mass.

Roberts, I. (1989). "Some Notes on VP-fronting and Head-government." Ms., Université de Genève.

Ross, J. (1967). *Constraints on Variables in Syntax*. Doctoral dissertation, MIT.

Ross, J. R. (1984). "Inner Islands." *Proceedings of the 10th Annual Meeting, BLS*. Berkeley Linguistics Society, Berkeley, Calif.

Ross, J. R. (1986). *Infinite Syntax*. Norwood, N.J.: Ablex. (Published version of Ross 1967.)

Rudin, C. (1986). *Aspects of Bulgarian Syntax: Complementizers and WH Constructions*. Slavica, Columbus, Ohio.

Safir, K. (1982). *Syntactic Chains and the Definiteness Effect*. Doctoral dissertation, MIT.

Safir, K. (1984). "Multiple Variable Binding." *Linguistic Inquiry* 15, 603–638.

Safir, K. (1986). "Relative Clauses in a Theory of Binding and Levels." *Linguistic Inquiry* 17, 663–689.

Safir, K. (1987). "The Anti-C-Command Condition on Parasitic Gaps." *Linguistic Inquiry* 18, 678–683.

Saito, M. (1985). *Some Asymmetries in Japanese and Their Theoretical Implications*. Doctoral dissertation, MIT.

Satyanarayana, P., and K. V. Subbarao (1973). "Are Rightward Movement Rules Upward Bounded?" *Studies in the Linguistic Sciences* 3, 182–192.

Schachter, R. (1981). "Lovely to Look At." *Linguistic Analysis* 8, 431–448.

Scorretti, M. (forthcoming). Doctoral dissertation, University of Amsterdam.

Sells, P. (1984). *Syntax and Semantics of Resumptive Pronouns*. Doctoral dissertation, University of Massachusetts, Amherst.

Sirbu-Dumitrescu, D. (1989). "Un modelo de analysis sintactico de las preguntas eco en español y rumano." Paper presented at the XIX International Congress of Romance Linguistics and Philology. Santiago de Compostela.

Sirbu-Dumitrescu, D. (in preparation). *The Grammar of Echo Questions: Syntax, Semantics and Pragmatics*. Doctoral dissertation, University of Southern California.

Sportiche, D. (1983). *Structural Invariance and Symmetry in Syntax*. Doctoral dissertation, MIT.

Sportiche, D. (1985). "Remarks on Crossover." *Linguistic Inquiry* 16, 460–469.

Sportiche, D. (1988). "Conditions on Silent Categories." Ms., UCLA.

Steriade, D. (1980). "Clitic Doubling in the Romanian *Wh*-Constructions and the Analysis of Topicalization." In *Papers from the 16th Regional Meeting of the Chicago Linguistic Society*. University of Chicago.

Stowell, T. (1981). *Origins of Phrase Structure*. Doctoral dissertation, MIT.

Stowell, T. (1985). "Licensing Conditions on Null Operators." Ms., UCLA.

Stowell, T. (1986). "Null Antecedents and Proper Government." In *Proceedings of the Sixteenth Annual Meeting, NELS*. GLSA, University of Massachusetts, Amherst.

Stowell, T. (1989). "Weak and Strong Crossover." Paper presented at the III Syntax Roundtable, Vienna, October 1989.

Stowell, T., and H. Lasnik (1987). "Weakest Crossover." Ms., UCLA and University of Connecticut.

Suñer, M. (1982). "Big PRO and Little pro." Ms., Cornell University.

Tappe, T. (1981). "Wer glaubst du hat recht? Einige Bemerkungen zur COMP-COMP-Bewegung im Deutschen." In M. Kohrt and J. Lenerz, eds., Sprache: Formen und Strukturen. Niemcyer, Tübingen.

Taraldsen, T. (1981). "The Theoretical Interpretation of a Class of Marked Extractions." In Belletti, Brandi, and Rizzi 1981.

Taraldsen, T. (1984). "On the Complementarity of Bounding and Binding." GLOW Newsletter 12, 71–73.

Taraldsen, T. (1986). "On Verb Second and the Functional Content of Syntactic Categories." In Haider and Prinzhorn 1986.

Vanelli, L., L. Renzi, and P. Benincà (1985). "Typologie des pronoms sujets dans les langues romanes." In Actes du XVIIème Congrès International de Linguistique et Philologie Romanes. Publications de l'Université de Provence, III.

Vergnaud, J.-R. (1974). French Relative Clauses. Doctoral dissertation, MIT.

Vergnaud, J.-R. (1985). Dépendances et niveaux de représentation en syntaxe. Benjamins, Amsterdam.

Wanner, D. (1981). "Surface Complementizer Deletion: Italian che–∅." Journal of Italian Linguistics 6(1), 47–82.

Weinberg, A. (1988). Locality Principles in Syntax and Parsing. Doctoral dissertation, MIT.

Weinberg, A., and N. Hornstein (1986). "On the Necessity of LF." Ms., University of Maryland.

Williams, E. (1986). "A Reassignment of the Functions of LF." Linguistic Inquiry 17, 265–299.

Zaenen, A., E. Engdahl, and J. Maling (1981). "Resumptive Pronouns Can Be Syntactically Bound." Linguistic Inquiry 12, 679–682.

Zanuttini, R. (1988). "Two Strategies for Negation: Evidence from Romance." In Proceedings of the 5th Annual Meeting, ESCOL.

Zanuttini, R. (forthcoming). " Two Types of Negative Markers." In Proceedings of the Twentieth Annual Meeting, NELS. GLSA, University of Massachusetts, Amherst.

Index